COMMENTARY ON GENESIS
(VOLUME II)

COMMENTARY ON GENESIS
(VOLUME II)

MARTIN LUTHER, JOHN NICHOLAS LENKER

ISBN: 978-93-5614-374-6

Published: -

© 2022
LECTOR HOUSE LLP

LECTOR HOUSE LLP
E-MAIL: lectorpublishing@gmail.com

COMMENTARY ON GENESIS (VOLUME II)

LUTHER ON SIN AND THE FLOOD

TRANSLATED AND EDITED IN COMPLETE FORM

BY

JOHN NICHOLAS LENKER, D.D.

TRANSLATOR OF LUTHER'S WORKS INTO ENGLISH;
AUTHOR OF "LUTHERANS IN ALL LANDS"

VOL. II

SECOND THOUSAND

DEDICATION.

*To all interested in studying the Christian
Missionary problems of "the last times"
of the modern world, this
volume is dedicated.*

FOREWORD.

The first volumes of the "American Luther" we selected for publication were his best commentaries, then eight volumes of his Gospel and Epistle sermons and one volume of his best catechetical writings. These rich evangelical works introduced us to the real Luther, not the polemical, but the Gospel Luther. They contain the leaven of the faith, life and spirit of Protestantism. We now return to his spiritual commentaries on the Bible which are the foundation of all his writings. The more one reads Luther the greater he becomes as a student of the One Book.

CONTENTS OF THIS VOLUME.

This, the second volume of Luther's great commentary on Genesis, appears now in English for the first time.

It covers chapters four to nine inclusive of Genesis. The subjects discussed are: Cain's murder, his punishment, Cain's sons, Seth and his sons, the wickedness of the old world, the ark, Noah's obedience, the universal destruction, the salvation of Noah's family, his sacrifice, his blessing, the rainbow covenant, Noah's fall, Ham cursed and Shem and Japheth blessed. These great themes are discussed by Moses and Luther. They have vital relations to problems pertaining to the end of the modern world. Our hope and prayer are that God may use this volume to make the book of Genesis and the whole Old Testament a greater spiritual blessing to the Church and that it may serve the servants of God in these latter days in calling people to repentance, faith and prayer like Noah and Luther did.

In his "Dear Genesis" Luther proved that the free Evangelical religion he taught was not new, but as old as the first book of the Bible, and that it does not consist in outward forms, organizations and pomp, but in true faith in Christ in our hearts and lives. Genesis contains the only historic records accessible of the first 2364 years of the 4004 years before Christ. It is worthy of study in our day as it was in the days of the Reformation.

ACKNOWLEDGMENTS.

Luther advised no one should translate alone and he practiced what he taught. We have followed his rule and example. Pastor C. B. Gohdes of Baltimore translated chapter six and President Schaller of Milwaukee Theological Seminary, chapters five, seven, eight and nine.

Inaccuracies may be due to the revision and editing, and not to the translators, for every good translation must be fluent and idiomatic, to secure which is the most difficult task. Pastor Gohdes also rendered valuable help in the final revision of parts. The translation of the analyses is by the undersigned.

The few last pages of the first edition of volume one we revised and reprint in this volume in order to make the pages of each volume of our edition to correspond with the German and Latin volumes of the Erlangen edition. The paragraphs are numbered and the analyses given according to the old Walch edition.

CONTENTS

Page

LUTHER AND WORLD-EVANGELIZATION.

In translating Luther into practical English in practical America, and in this age that is growing more and more practical, we need to be reminded that this work is for practical use and purposes. Luther was radical along Bible lines in applying the truth personally and to the world.

It is a year since the last volume of the "American Luther" appeared. The delay was caused by an effort to raise the work to a higher standard and by the publication of a book on "The True Place of Germans and Scandinavians in the Evangelization of the World", not a revision of, but a new companion volume to "Lutherans In All Lands" that appeared seventeen years ago. By comparing these two books one has the best evidence of the marvelous progress of God's Kingdom in recent years, and the growing world-significance of Luther's evangelistic writings. Evangelization at home and abroad is the popular religious theme today in the German fatherland and in the whole Protestant world. The word "world" is becoming so common its full meaning is not appreciated. When world-evangelization is discussed, it is too often from the standpoint of the nation discussing it. Each nation is so active in its own work that it fails to appreciate what others are doing. For example how little the world missionary conferences in English lands have to say of the German and Scandinavian missions and the Reformed Churches of the Lutheran work. Hence the fruits of Luther's evangelical writings are underestimated by the English people. It is opportune to translate not only Luther but also the best fruits of those writings in various languages during the past 400 years, especially since the memorable date of 1917 is soon to be celebrated by universal Protestantism. Luther in all languages and Lutherans in all lands go together. We ought to consider most carefully the great Reformer in his relation to the modern world and modern world-evangelization. The known world in his day was not so large. He had, however, a clear view of it all in his writings, which is due to his faithful study of the Scriptures. The Bible gave him a knowledge of the world, including all lands and all times. His commentary of eleven volumes on Genesis illustrates this. The first volume on Genesis treats of the first part of the ancient world; the second volume, the one before us, treats of the second part and end of the old world. This Luther would have us apply to the last times of the modern world.

LUTHER EDUCATIONAL AND DEVOTIONAL.

Here, as everywhere in his catechisms, sermons and commentaries, Luther is unique among religious authors in that he is both educational and devotional, appealing equally to head and heart. He is "religiously helpful and intellectually profitable," covering every phase of religious, moral and social conditions, and touching every interest of humanity. "His words went to the mark like bullets and left marks like bullets." Being beyond criticism they have a unique place to fill in the literature and libraries of the world.

Although the cry, "Read Luther!" has been raised here in the new world the multitudes of the English people are not rushing for his writings, as the Germans did when they first appeared in the old world, under conditions similar to what they are in America at present. If asked what made the German people what they are, the answer is, these writings, so universally circulated and read. If the Anglo-Saxons appreciated their educational and devotional value the 35,000 copies circulated the last seven years would easily, as a professor suggested, be increased to a hundred thousand copies.

NATIONS HELPING NATIONS.

The world-consciousness is growing, so is the national consciousness. Both are characteristic of our times. Perhaps never did the national spirit develop as in recent years. The great powers, instead of dividing China, witness the national spirit growing everywhere—in Japan, China, India, Africa, South America, Norway, Sweden, as well as in Germany, England, Russia and the United States. This is a good sign, for the world-family is composed of nations, and each nation has at least one talent not to be crushed, but with which to serve all the others. One serves the world when he serves his nation. Luther's words, "I live for my countrymen", illustrates this. It is not the nations that have the largest armies and navies that are the greatest blessing to the world, but the nations that work out the best Christian civilization for the world to imitate and send over the earth the best farmers to show other nations and tribes how to cultivate the earth, the best teachers, preachers and authors to train the people, the best medical skill to relieve human suffering, the best mechanics and servants, the greatest philanthropists, the best Christians. In educational, industrial, medical and charitable mission work the nations dominated by Luther's writings stand high. Nations, like individuals, are the greatest which serve others best; not the nations which have the most territory, but nations which do the greatest service for the whole human family. The students missionary movement develops men, and the laymen's missionary movement raises money. Both are needed, but men must be trained to do their work in the best way and the money be used to bring the best results. Hence nations should help and study one another most carefully with this in view. Luther and his writings in the evangelization of Europe ought not to be overlooked in the evangelization of other continents. By helping abroad the home does not suffer. Among American Lutherans the Norwegians prove this, for they have done the most for the heathen and have the best home mission work.

TRANSITION AND TRANSLATION
OR TRANSITION AND REVOLUTION.

While we are translating Luther for all Anglo-Saxons, we do not overlook the fact that Luther's disciples, Germans and Scandinavians, are themselves being translated, or are in a state of transition. The translation of a people and of their literature or spirit clearly presents a double problem, both sides of which demand at once the most careful work. The translation of both the people and their literature should run parallel and in the same, and not in an opposite, direction. Germans and Scandinavians have always, and do still, make the fatal blunder of translating from English into their own languages, instead of from their languages into English. They thus cross one another's path never to meet again. Their children and grandchildren, however, find it easier to translate into English, their mother tongue; but, alas, they have little interest in doing it. They make the mistake in thinking their old thoughts and classics are not needed in the new language. Their motto seems to be, "new literature for the new language", when to the English public, if not to themselves, the old writings would be the newest. It is marvelous how wide-awake preachers are mislead.

BEST LITERATURE IS TRANSLATIONS.

People who are prejudiced against translations, forget that the Bible and our best literature are translations of the classics of the world's leading languages. Translations should be welcomed by a people who themselves are in a state of translation, especially if the translations are from their mother tongue into the language they are learning. What endless friction and confusion would be avoided, if people and their life and literature were translated at the same time. As we have said, a transition of a people without a translation of their literature is no transition, but a revolution. To this various church bodies witness. During the transition of language the best literature for the children to read is the translations of the classics of the language of the parents. There may be better literature, but not for these particular children, if the unity of the family life is to be perpetuated. Hence it becomes a vital concern that both children and parents understand that the best literature for them is such translations. But where are the German or Scandinavian teachers and preachers who are enthusing over putting this thought deep into the family life of their congregations.

A LESSON FROM LUTHER AND WESLEY IN AMERICA.

What unwisdom even to attempt to build up the Lutheran Christian life in free, aggressive Protestant Anglo-Saxon civilization without Luther's writings in good Anglo-Saxon! Muhlenberg (b. 1711; d. 1787) and Wesley (b. 1703; d. 1791) came to America about the same time. Wesley returned home in 1738 after a stay of two years in the south. Muhlenberg spent his ministerial life of 45 years (1742-1787) in America, in the Keystone state, in and near Philadelphia, the metropolis of the new world. When the two Palatinate Germans from Limerick County, Ireland, Philip Embury and Barbara Heck, a lay-preacher and a godly woman, held the first Methodist service in America, in 1766, in New York City, the Lutheran faith had been planted here by the Dutch since 1657 in the same city, by the Swedes on the Delaware since 1639, (Torkillus), by the Germans since 1708 (Kocherthal); Muhlenberg had arrived in Philadelphia in 1742, built churches the following year in Philadelphia and "The Trappe", and organized the Synod of Pennsylvania among its 60,000 Lutherans in 1748. All these Lutherans to some extent learned, preached and confirmed in English. Muhlenberg was naturalized in 1754 as a subject of Great Britain. This and his stay in England gave an Anglican turn to his German pietism. When we became a free people in 1776, the Methodists had only 20 preachers and 3418 members in America and less than 76,000 followers in Europe from which to receive immigrant members, while the Lutherans were strong here and in Europe. Today American Methodists report 60,737 churches, and the Lutherans 13,533. Why did Wesley's followers become the dominating religious force in America? Not because Wesley and his writings were greater than Luther and his writings. Methodists did not bear Wesley's name, but they did have his spirit and writings. Even to the present day every Methodist preacher must pass an examination in Wesley's writings before ordination. Where were Luther's spirit and writings among his early American followers?

Language is no more a barrier to Luther's spirit than to Wesley's. Methodism forged its way from English into German, Norwegian, Danish and Swedish and among Indians, Mexicans and Negros. People, regardless of language, color or condition, could not help but learn what real spiritual Methodism is. It was preached and sung in such simple, plain Anglo-Saxon, and in good translations, that it could not be misunderstood nor misrepresented. Wesley's simple evangelical message was abroad in the land in the hearts of the people. But the evangelical voice of Luther, the prince of translators, was hardly heard and even today the English world has no clear popular view of what spiritual Evangelical Lutheranism is. Often when they speak of it, they seem to think it is the opposite of what it is. Germans, Scandinavians and all know the spiritual side of Methodism, but the English world does not know the spiritual side of Lutheranism, and it never will until Luther's spiritual writings are translated into readable English and circulated broadcast over the land, and the hearts of the people come into direct and close touch with the heart of the great Reformer himself.

The English world knows the statistics, the numerical strength of Lutherans. That needs no apology. But what does need a defense among Americans is the spirituality of the Lutherans. That is developed by the translations into the plainest vernacular of God's Word and Luther's evangelical sermons and commentaries. These are the best literature for young Germans and Scandinavians. Although translations, and not perfect, they are the best for them. The Bible first; Luther's spiritual writings second, not first nor third. Have not Lutherans in America been following the disciples of Luther instead of Luther; while Methodists have followed Wesley and not Wesley's disciples. The Dutch, Swedish and German Lutherans in the east, all learned English. We say it was a transition, but was it not a revolution? Their history stands forth as beacon lights of warning to the polyglot Lutherans migrating to the ends of earth and learning all languages. They will no more keep up their faith with one language than the English nation will keep up their trade by refusing to learn other languages. Strange it is that nations can learn and use other languages in one line and not in another—the English in church work and not in trade; the Germans in trade, but not in church work.

It is said there are 30 million people in the United States with some German blood in their veins. Two thirds of these, or 20 millions, may be said to have some Lutheran mixture in their makeup, but only one and a half million of these 20 millions are communicant members of English and German Lutheran churches. What people in America can show a worse religious record? Yet the tenders of the sheep and lambs are afraid to feed them in the only way they can be fed. Verily whatever you sow, that shall you also reap. Lift up your eyes, behold the harvest! Can you not discern the signs of the times?

It is no wonder that the United States Census of 1890, the latest reliable statistics on the subject, gave the number of Lutheran communicants using only English in this English land at 198,907; General Synod 143,764; United Synod South 37,457; General Council 14,297; Ohio Synod 287; Missouri Synod 1,192 — after 150 years of work. Our good German and Scandinavian parents, in the light of these figures, need not fear losing many members to purely English churches. "Reading Luther" in German, Swedish, Norwegian and English will bring better results to old and young than if read only in one language. The Church of the Reformation is not one-tongued, but many-tongued.

ENGLISH LUTHER IN
GERMAN AND SCANDINAVIAN CHURCHES.

April 12th, 1910, became a memorable date in the North-west by the introduction of the Scandinavian languages into all the high schools of Minneapolis. German and Scandinavian taxpayers are gradually becoming more interested in having their children learn the language of their mothers in the public schools. This will prove to be a great blessing to children and home, society and state. The Church however will blunder, if she thinks there will now be no need of circulating English literature in German and Scandinavian congregations. Translating Luther and teaching German and Scandinavian are two ways of doing the same thing, for language is not an end, but a means to an end. Many young people are being confirmed in English and they often attend services in foreign languages. Many know more of the language than of the matter preached. When weak in the language they understand better what is preached if they are familiar with the thought. The reason many do not appreciate a sermon with the Luther ring is because they are familiar with neither the language nor the thought. Hence the need of our young people becoming familiar with Luther's sermons and commentaries in English. One understands better in a strange language what he is familiar with. This familiar knowledge would help to bridge the chasm between Lutheran parents and children. Ask parents and they will tell about the "Old Luther Readers," in their native land and tongue. All admit that if the young people are not interested to read Luther in English, they will never read him. All who do will the better understand sermons in German and Scandinavian. The universal reading of the English Luther, on the part of the young people, will therefore help, and not harm, the German and Scandinavian congregations. Luther's teachings thoroughly understood in a living way will bind the young to their Christian convictions, as much as the knowledge of a language binds them to that language. The passive interest therefore, on the part of German and Scandinavian pastors and congregations in circulating the English Luther, as far as their young people are concerned, should give way to active interest, for the sake of their own work in the future. It is important to learn your mother's language. You may do that and forget her faith—Better retain the faith than the language.

J. N. Lenker.

The Fiftieth Day (Pentecost), 1910.
Minneapolis, Minn.

COMMENTARY ON GENESIS.

CHAPTER IV.

IV. CAIN MURDERS HIS BROTHER; CALLED TO ACCOUNT.
A. HOW CAIN MURDERED HIS BROTHER.

1. What moved Cain to commit murder.
2. Cain's hypocritical actions in concealing his anger that he might the more easily commit the murder.
* Cain the picture of all hypocrites.
* The attitude of hypocrites to their neighbors. Also, how we are to view the efforts of the pope and bishops in behalf of peace and unity.
* Against what people we should most guard.
3. How Cain listened to no warning in his thoughts of murder.
* Complaint of the world's attitude to good admonition.
* The ways of the hypocrite. Also, why falsehood wears a friendly aspect.
4. Whether Cain's passion to murder Abel was noticeable.
5. Cain took no notice of Abel's sighing and praying.
* The origin of man's cruel and tyrannical nature.

B. HOW CAIN WAS CALLED TO ACCOUNT, AND HIS BEHAVIOR.

1. Who questioned Cain, and his defiant actions.
2. Cain accused himself most when he tried to clear himself.
* Liars speak against themselves, as is proved by examples.
3. Cain's vindication more foolish than that of the first parents in paradise.
* St. Martin will absolve the devil if he repents.
* Whoever excuses his sin follows the example of Satan and makes his case worse.
4. How Cain heaps sin upon sin.
5. Cain despairs and is in a worse state than our first parents after their fall.
6. How Cain placed himself in a position where nothing could help him.
7. Gently accused, and yet defiant.

8. Cain has not the least reverence for God or his father.

  * This is a picture of all hypocrites.

9. How his defense ends.

  * How man ought to act when his conscience accuses him of sin.

  * The hypocrite's actions when his conscience is awakened, and what he is to do.

10. In Cain's defense wickedness and folly are mingled.

  * How God reveals hypocrites.

  * Moses says much in few words.

  * Whether Abel and our first parents anticipated Cain's murder.

  * Without a thought of what might restrain him, Cain commits the deed.

  * The picture of the sacrifice of Iphigenia applied to Moses' description of Cain's murder.

  * Cain's is no ordinary murder, and how he differs from other murderers.

  * The hypocrite's hatred is different from other hatred, and is found among the Jews and the Papists.

  * Cain the father of all murderers.

  * How the first parents felt over this whole affair.

      a. Their grief was so great that they could not have endured without special divine comfort.

      b. Their severe trial in view of the first sin.

      c. Very likely because of this murder they refrained so long from bearing children.

        * Whether the first parents had at the time more children than Cain and Abel.

  * Why Cain slew Abel, and how he did it.

11. The time and occasion when Cain was called to account.

12. Adam with the authority of God calls Cain to account.

IV. HOW CAIN MURDERED HIS BROTHER AND WAS REQUIRED TO GIVE AN ACCOUNT, AND HOW HE CONDUCTED HIMSELF.

A. How Cain Murdered His Brother.

V. 8a. *And Cain told (talked with) Abel his brother.*

107. Our translation adds that Cain said: "Let us go out doors." But this is one of the comments of the rabbins, whose relative claim to credit I have fully shown on a previous occasion. Lyra, following the invention of Eben Ezra, relates that Cain told his brother how severely he had been rebuked of the Lord. But who

would believe statements for which there is no authority in the Scriptures? We hold therefore to an explanation which has the warrant of the Scriptures, namely that Cain, finding himself rejected of God, indulged his anger, and added to his former sins contempt of his parents and of the Word, thinking within himself: "The promised seed of the woman belongs to me as the first-born. But my brother, Abel, that contemptible, good-for-nothing fellow, is evidently preferred to me by divine authority, manifest in the fire consuming his sacrifice. What shall I do, therefore? I will dissemble my wrath until an opportunity of taking vengeance shall occur."

108. Therefore the words, "Cain told Abel his brother," I understand to mean that Cain, dissembling his anger, conducted himself toward Abel as a brother, and spoke to him and conversed with him, as if he bore with good nature the sentence pronounced upon him by God. In this manner also Saul simulated an attitude of kindness toward David. "I know well," said Saul, "that thou shalt surely be king," 1 Sam 24, 20; and yet he was all the while planning to prevent this by killing David. Just so Cain now conversed with Abel his brother, and said: I see that thou art chosen of the Lord; I envy thee not this divine blessing, etc. This is just the manner of hypocrites. They pretend friendship until an opportunity of doing the harm they intend presents itself.

109. That such is the true sense of the passage, all the circumstances clearly show. For if Adam and Eve could have gathered the least suspicion of the intended murder, think you not that they would either have restrained Cain or removed Abel, and placed the latter out of danger? But as Cain had altered his countenance and his deportment toward his brother, and had talked with him in a brotherly manner, they thought all was safe, and the son bowed to and acquiesced in the admonition of his father. The appearance deceived Abel also, who, if he had feared anything like murder from his brother, would doubtless have fled from him, as Jacob fled from Esau when he feared his brother's wrath. What, therefore, could possibly have come into the mind of Jerome when he believed the rabbins, who say Cain was expostulating with his brother?

110. Accordingly, Cain is the image and picture of all hypocrites and murderers, who kill under the show of godliness. Cain, possessed by Satan, hides his wrath, waiting the opportunity to slay his brother Abel; meanwhile he converses with him, as a brother beloved, that he might the sooner lay his hands upon him unawares.

111. This passage, therefore, is intended for our instruction in the ways of murderers and hypocrites. Still Cain talks in a brotherly manner with his brother, and, on the other hand, Abel still trusts Cain as a brother should trust a brother; and thus he is murdered, and the pious parents meanwhile are deceived.

Just so the pope and the bishops of our day talk and confer much concerning the peace and concord of the Church. But he is most assuredly deceived who does not understand that the exact opposite is planned. For true is that word of the Psalm, "The workers of iniquity speak peace with their neighbors, but mischief is in their hearts," Ps 28, 3. For it is the nature of hypocrites that they are good in appearance, speak kindly to you, pretend to be humble, patient and charitable, give alms, etc.; and yet, all the while they plan slaughter in their hearts.

112. Let us learn, then, to know a Cain and especially to beware when he speaks kindly, and as brother to brother. For it is in this way that our adversaries, the bishops and the pope, talk with us in our day, while they pretend a desire for concord, and seek to bring about doctrinal harmony. In reality, if an opportunity of seizing us and executing their rage upon us should present itself, you would soon hear them speak in a very different tone. Truly, "there is death in the pot," 2 Kings 4, 40; and under the best and sweetest words there lies concealed a deadly poison.

V. 8b. *And it came to pass, when they were in the field, that Cain rose up against Abel his brother, and slew him.*

113. Here you see the deceptive character of those alluring words. Cain had been admonished by his father with divine authority to guard against sin in the future, and to expect pardon for that of the past. But Cain despises the twofold admonition, and indulges his sin, as all the wicked do. For true is the saying of Solomon, "When the wicked cometh, there cometh also contempt, and with ignominy cometh reproach," Prov 18, 3.

114. Our ministry at the present day deserves no blame. We teach, we exhort, we entreat, we rebuke, we turn ourselves every way, that we may recall the multitude from security to the fear of God. But the world, like an untamed beast, still goes on and follows not the Word, but its own lusts, which it tries to smooth over by a show of uprightness. The prophets and the apostles stand before us as examples, and our own experience is instructive, also. Our adversaries, so often warned and convicted, know they are doing wrong, and yet they do not lay aside their murderous hate.

115. Learn, then, what a hypocrite is; namely, one who lays claim to the worship of God and to charity, and yet, at the same time, destroys the worship of God and slaughters his brother. And all this semblance of good-will is only intended to bring about better opportunities of doing harm. For, if Abel had foreseen the implacable wrath and the truly diabolical anger, he would have saved himself by flight. But as Cain betrayed no such anger, uttered a friendly greeting and manifested his usual courtesy, Abel perished before he felt any fear.

116. There is no doubt that Abel, when he saw his brother rising up against him, entreated and implored him not to pollute himself with this awful sin. However, a mind beset by Satan pays no regard to entreaties, nor heeds uplifted hands, but as a father's admonition had been disregarded, so now the brother is spurned as he pleads upon his knees.

117. Light is cast here upon the bondage to Satan by which our nature, entangled in sins, is oppressed. Hence Paul's expression, "children of wrath," Eph 2, 3, and the declaration that such are taken captive by Satan unto his will, 2 Tim 2, 26. For when we are mere men; that is, when we apprehend not the blessed seed by faith, we are all like Cain, and nothing is wanting but an opportunity. For nature, destitute of the Holy Spirit, is impelled by that same evil spirit which impelled

wicked Cain. If, however, there were in any one those ample powers, or that free will, by which a man might defend himself against the assaults of Satan, these gifts would most assuredly have existed in Cain, to whom belonged the birthright and the promise of the blessed seed. But in that very same condition are all men! Unless nature be helped by the Spirit of God, it cannot maintain itself. Why, then, do we absurdly boast of free-will? Now follows another remarkable passage.

B. How Cain Had to Give an Account, and His Conduct.

V. 9. *And Jehovah said unto Cain, Where is Abel thy brother? And he said, I know not: Am I my brother's keeper?*

118. Good God! into what depth of sin does our miserable nature fall when driven onward by the devil. Murder had been committed on a brother, and perhaps murdered Abel lay for days unburied. Thereupon, as Cain returned to his parents at the accustomed time, and Abel returned not with him, the anxious parents asked him: Cain, thou art here, but where is Abel? Thou hast returned home, but Abel has not returned. The flock is without their shepherd. Tell us therefore, where thy brother is. Upon this, Cain, becoming abusive, makes answer to his parents, by no means with due reverence, "I know not: Am I my brother's keeper?"

119. But it happened to Cain as to all the wicked, that by excusing himself he accused himself, according to the words of Christ, "Out of thine own mouth will I judge thee, thou wicked servant," Luke 19, 22. Also the heathen had a striking proverb among them, "A liar ought to have a good memory." Such was the judgment of heathen men, though they knew nothing of the judgment of God and of conscience, and had nothing to guide their judgment but their experience in civil affairs. And true it is that liars run much risk of being discovered and unmasked. Hence the Germans have the proverb, "A lie is a very fruitful thing." For one lie begets seven other lies, which become necessary to uphold the first lie. And yet it is impossible, after all, to prevent conscience from arousing and betraying itself at times, if not in words, then in gestures. This is proved by numberless examples. I will cite only one example here:

120. In Thuringia there is a small town in the district of Orla, called Neustadt. In this town a harlot had murdered her infant, to which she had secretly given birth, and had thrown it, after the murder, into a neighboring fishpond. Accidentally the little piece of linen in which she had wrapped the infant, brought the horrid deed to light. The case was brought before the magistrate; and as the simple men of the place knew no better means of investigating the crime, they called all the young women of the town into the town hall and closely examined them, one by one. The face and the testimony of each one of these proclaimed her innocent. But when they came to her who was the real perpetrator of the deed, she did not wait for questions to be put to her, but immediately declared aloud that she was not the guilty person. The contrast she presented to the others in making such haste to defend herself, confirmed the suspicion of the magistrates. At once she was seized by the constables and put to death.

Indeed, instances are innumerable and of daily occurrence which show that people, in their eagerness to defend themselves, accuse themselves. Sin may, indeed, lie asleep, but that word which we have just heard, is true. It lies at the door.

121. Just so in the present case. Cain thinks he has made an effectual excuse for himself by saying that he is not his brother's keeper. But does he not confess by the very word "brother" which he takes upon his lips that he ought to be his keeper? Is not that equal to accusing himself, and will not the fact that Abel is nowhere in evidence arouse the suspicion in the minds of his parents that he has been murdered? Just so also Adam excuses himself in paradise, and lays all the blame on Eve. But this excuse of Cain is far more stupid; for while he excuses his sin he doubles it, whereas the frank confession of sin finds mercy and appeases wrath.

122. It is recorded in the history of St. Martin, that when he absolved certain notorious sinners, he was rebuked by Satan for doing so. St. Martin is said to have replied, "Why, I would absolve even thee, if thou wouldst say from thy heart, I repent of having sinned against the Son of God, and I pray for pardon." But the devil never does this. For he persists in committing sin and defending the same.

123. All liars and hypocrites imitate Cain their father, by either denying their sin or excusing it. Hence they cannot find pardon for their sins. And we see the same in domestic life. By the defense of wrong-doing, anger is increased. For whenever the wife, or the children, or the servants, have done wrong, and deny or excuse their wrong-doing, the father of the family is the more moved to wrath; whereas, on the other hand, confession secures pardon or a lighter punishment. But it is the nature of hypocrites to excuse and palliate their sin or to deny it altogether and under the show of religion, to slay the innocent.

124. But here let us survey the order in which sins follow each other and increase. First of all Cain sins by presumption and unbelief when, priding himself on the privilege of his birthright, he takes it for granted that he shall be accepted of God on the ground of his own merit. Upon this pride and self-glorification immediately follow envy and hatred of his brother, whom he sees preferred to himself by an unmistakable sign from heaven. Upon this envy and hatred follow hypocrisy and lying. Though he designs to murder his brother, he accosts him in a friendly manner and thereby throws him off his guard. Hypocrisy is followed by murder. Murder is followed by the excusing of his sin. And the last stage is despair, which is the fall from heaven to hell.

125. Although Adam and Eve in paradise did not deny their sin, yet their confession was lukewarm, and the sin was shifted from the one to the other. Adam laid it on Eve, and Eve on the serpent. But Cain went even farther, for he not only did not confess the murder he had committed, but disclaimed responsibility for his brother. And did not this at once prove his mind to be hostile against his brother? Therefore, though Adam and Eve made only a half-hearted confession, they had some claim to pardon, and in consequence were punished with less severity. But Cain, because he resolutely denied his sin, was rejected, and fell into despair.

And the same judgment awaits all the sons of Cain, popes, cardinals, and bishops, who, although they plan murder against us day and night, say likewise, "I know not: Am I my brother's keeper?"

126. There was a common proverb of old, "What is it to the Romans that the Greeks die?" So we think that our dangers and calamities only belong to ourselves. But how does this principle agree with the commandment of God? For his will is that we should all live together, and be to each other as brethren. Cain, therefore, by this very saying of his, heavily accuses himself when he makes the excuse that the custody of his brother was no affair of his. Whereas, if he had said to his father, "Alas, I have slain Abel, my brother. I repent of the deed I have done. Return upon me what punishment thou wilt," there might have been room for a remedy; but as he denied his sin, and, contrary to the will of God, disclaimed responsibility for his brother altogether, there was no place left for mercy or favor.

127. Moreover, Moses took special pains in the preparation of this account, that it might serve as a witness against all hypocrites, and as a chronicle containing a graphic description of their character and of the ire to which they are aroused by Satan against God, his Word and his Church. It was not enough for this murderer that he had killed his brother, contrary to the command of God, but he added the further sin that he became filled with indignation and rage when God inquired of him concerning his brother. I say, "when God inquired of him," because, although it was Adam who spoke these words to his son Cain, yet he spoke them by the authority of God and by the Holy Spirit. In view of so great a sin, was it not quite gentle to inquire, "Where is Abel thy brother?" And yet, to this word, which contained nothing severe, the hypocrite and murderer is ferocious and proud enough to reply, "I know not." And he is indignant that he should be called to an account concerning the matter at all. For the reply of Cain is the language of one who resists and hates God.

128. But to this sin Cain adds one still worse. Justly under indictment for murder, he presently becomes the accuser of God, and expostulates with him: "Am I my brother's keeper?" He prefaces his reply with no such expression of reverence or honor as is due both to God and to his father. He did not say, "Lord, I know not." He did not say, "My Father, didst thou make me the keeper of my brother?" Such expressions as these would have indicated a feeling of reverence toward God or toward his parent. But he answers with pride as if he himself were the Lord, and plainly manifests that he felt indignation at being called to account by him who had the perfect right to do so.

129. This is a true picture of all hypocrites. Living in manifest sins, they grow insolent and proud, aiming all the while to appear righteous. They will not yield even to God himself and his Word when upbraided by them. Nay, they set themselves against God, contend with him, and excuse their sin. Thus David says, that God is judged of men, but that at length he clears and justifies himself, and prevails, Ps 51, 4. Such is the insolence of the hypocrites Moses has here endeavored to paint.

130. But what success has Cain with his attempt? This, that his powerful effort to excuse himself becomes a forcible self-accusation. Christ says, "Out of thine own mouth will I judge thee, thou wicked servant," Lk 19, 22. Now, this servant wished to appear without guilt, saying: "I knew thee that thou art a hard man, reaping where thou didst not sow; and I was afraid, and hid thy talent," Mt 25,

24-25. Could he have brought a stronger accusation against himself, in view of the fact that Christ immediately turns his words against him? Thereby Christ evidences the wisdom of the Holy Spirit.

131. Such illustrations help us to learn not to contend with God. On the contrary when you feel in your conscience that you are guilty, take heed with all your soul that you strive neither with God nor with men by defending or excusing your sin. Rather do this: When you see God point his spear at you, flee not from him; but, on the contrary, flee to him with a humble confession of your sin, and with prayer for his pardon. Then God will draw back his spear and spare you. But when, by the denial and excuse of your sin, you flee farther and farther from him, God will pursue you at close range with still greater determination, and bring you to bay. Nothing, therefore, is better or safer than to come with the confession of guilt. Thus it comes to pass that God's victory becomes our victory through him.

132. But Cain and hypocrites in general do not this. God points his spear at them, but they never humble themselves before him nor pray to him for pardon. Nay, they rather point their spear at God, just as Cain did on this occasion. Cain does not say, "Lord, I confess I have killed my brother; forgive me." On the contrary, though being the accused, he himself accuses God by replying, "Am I my brother's keeper?" And what did he effect with his pride? His reply was certainly equal to the confession that he cared naught for the divine law, which says, "Thou shalt love thy neighbor as thyself," Lev 19, 18. And again, "Do not unto another that which you would not have another do unto you," Mt 7, 12. This law was not first written in the Decalog; it was inscribed in the minds of all men. Cain acts directly against this law, and shows that he not only cares nothing for it, but absolutely despises it.

133. In this manner, Cain represents a man who is not merely wicked, but who occupies such a height of wickedness as to combine hypocrisy with bloodshed, and yet is so eager to maintain the appearance of sanctity that he rather accuses God than concedes the justice of the accusation against himself. And this is what all hypocrites do. They blaspheme God and crucify his Son, and yet wish to appear righteous. For after their sins of murder, blasphemy and the like their whole aim is to seek means whereby to excuse and palliate the same. But the result always is that they betray themselves and are condemned out of their own mouths.

134. While Cain makes an effort to clear himself, he exhibits the foulest stains. He thinks he made a most plausible excuse when he said, "Am I my brother's keeper?" But this very excuse becomes his most shameful accusation. The maxim of Hilary, that wickedness and stupidity always go hand in hand, finds unvarying application. If Cain had been as wise as he was wicked, he would have excused himself in quite a different manner. Now, under the operation of the divine rule that wickedness and stupidity are running mates, he becomes his own accuser. The same principle operates in favor of the truth, and makes her defense against all adversaries easy. Just as Cain betrayed by word and mien his indifference and hate toward his brother, so all adversaries of the truth betray their wickedness, the one in this way, the other in that.

135. Facts of importance and apt for instruction are, therefore, here set before us. And their general import is that God does not permit hypocrites to remain hidden for any length of time, but compels them to betray themselves just when they make shrewd efforts to hide their hypocrisy and crime.

136. Moses does not exhibit in his narrative the verbose diction characteristic of pagan literature, where we often find one and the same argument embellished and polished by a variety of colors. We find by experience that no human power of description can do justice to inward emotions. In consequence, verbosity, as a rule, comes short of expressing emotion. Moses employs the opposite method, and clothes a great variety of arguments in scant phraseology.

137. Above the historian used the expression, "when they were in the field." Thereby Moses indicates that the murderer Cain had watched his opportunity to attack his brother when both were alone. All the circumstances plainly show that Abel was not idle at the time; for he was in the field, where he had to do the things his father committed to him. From Moses' statement we may infer that Abel's parents felt absolutely no fear of danger. For, although at the outset they had feared that the wrath of Cain would eventually break out into still greater sin, Cain, by his gentleness and pretended affection, prevented all suspicion of evil on the part of his parents. For had there been the least trace of apprehension, they certainly would not have permitted Abel to go from their presence alone. They would have sent his sisters with him as companions; for he no doubt had some. Or his parents themselves would have prevented by their presence and authority the perpetration of so great a crime. As already stated, also the mind of Abel was perfectly free from suspicion. For, had he suspected the least evil at the hand of his brother, he would doubtless have sought safety by flight. But after he had heard that Cain bore the judgment of God with composure, and did not envy the brother his honor, he pursued his work in the field with a feeling of security.

138. What orator could do justice to the scene which Moses depicts in one word: "Cain rose up against his brother?" Many descriptions of cruelty are to be found on every hand, but could any be painted as more atrocious and execrable than is the case here? "He rose up against his brother," Moses writes. It is as if he had said, Cain rose up against Abel, the only brother he had, with whom he had been brought up and with whom he had lived to that day. But not only the relationship Cain utterly forgot; he forgot their common parents also. The greatness of the grief he would cause his parents by such a grave crime, never entered his mind. He did not think that Abel was a brother, from whom he had never received any offense whatever. For Cain knew that the honor of having offered the more acceptable sacrifice, proceeded not from any desire or ambition in Abel, but from God himself. Nor did Cain consider that he, who had hitherto stood in the highest favor with his parents, would lose that favor altogether and would fall under their deepest displeasure as a result of his crime.

139. It is recorded in history of an artist who painted the scene of Iphigenia's sacrifice, that when he had given to the countenance of each of the spectators present its appropriate expression of grief and pain, he found himself unable to portray the vastness of the father's grief, who was present also, and hence painted his

head draped.

140. Such is the method, I think, Moses employs in this passage, when he uses the verb *yakam*, "Rose up against." What tragical pictures would the eloquence of a Cicero or a Livy have drawn in an attempt to portray, through the medium of their oratory, the wrath of the one brother, and the dread, the cries, the prayers, the tears, the uplifted hands, and all the horrors of the other! But not even in that way can justice be done to the subject. Moses, therefore, pursues the right course, when he portrays, by a mere outline, things too great for utterance. Such brevity tends to enlist the reader's undivided attention to a subject which the vain adornment of many words disfigures and mars, like paint applied to natural beauty.

141. This is true also of the additional statement, "He slew him." Occasionally we see men start a quarrel and commit murder for a trivial cause, but no such ordinary murder is described here. Murderers of this kind immediately afterward are filled with distress; they grieve for the deeds they have done and acknowledge them to be delusions of the devil by which he blinded their minds. Cain felt no distress; he expressed no grief, but denied the deed he had done.

142. This satanic and insatiable hatred in hypocrites is described by Christ in the words, "When they kill you, they will think that they do God service," Jn 16, 2. So the priests and the kings filled Jerusalem with the blood of the prophets and gloried in what they did as a great achievement; for they considered this as proof of their zeal for the Law and the house of God.

143. And the fury of popes and bishops in our day is just the same. They are not satisfied with having excommunicated us again and again, and with having shed our blood, but they wish to blot out our memory from the land of the living, according to the description in the Psalm, "Rase it, rase it, even to the foundation thereof," Ps 137, 7. Such hatred is not human but satanic. For all human hatred becomes mellow in time; at all events, it will cease after it has avenged our injury and gratified its passion. But the hatred of these Pharisees assumes constantly larger dimensions, especially since it is smoothed over by a show of piety.

144. Cain, therefore, is the father of all those murderers who slaughter the saints, and whose wrath knows no end so long as there remains one of them, as is proved in the case of Christ himself. As for Cain, there is no doubt of his having hoped that by putting Abel to death he should keep the honor of his birthright. Thus, the ungodly always think that their cruelty will profit them in some way. But when they find that their hope is vain they fall into despair.

145. Now, when the fact of this shameful murder was made known to the parents, what do we think must have been the sad scenes resulting? What lamentations? What sighs and groans? But I dwell not on these things; they are for the man with the gifts of eloquence and imagination to describe. It was certainly a marvel that both parents were not struck lifeless with grief. The calamity was rendered the greater by the fact that their first-born, who had aroused so large hopes concerning himself, was the perpetrator of this horrible murder.

146. If, therefore, Adam and Eve had not been helped from above, they could never have been equal to this disaster in their home; for there is nothing like it in

all the world. Adam and Eve were without that consolation which we may have in sudden and unexpected calamities, namely, that like evils have befallen others and have not come upon us alone. Our first parents had only two sons, though I believe that they had daughters also; and therefore they lacked such instances of grief in the human family as we have before our eyes.

147. Who can doubt, moreover, that Satan by this new species of temptation increased greatly the grief of our first parents? They no doubt thought, Behold, this is all our sin. We, in paradise, wished to become like God; but by our sin we have become like the devil. This is the case also with our son. We loved only this son, and made everything of him! Our other son, Abel, was righteous before us, above this son; but of his righteousness we made nothing! This elder son we hoped would be he who should crush the serpent's head; but behold, he himself is crushed by the serpent! Nay, he himself has become like the serpent, for he is now a murderer. And whence is this? Is it not because he was born of us, and because we, through our sin, are what we are? Therefore it is to our flesh; therefore it is to our sin, that this calamity must be traced.

148. It is very probable, accordingly, and the events of the series of years which followed strengthen this probability, that the sorrowing parents, shaken to the core by their calamity, abstained for a long time from connubial intercourse. For it appears that when Cain committed this murder he was about thirty years of age. During this period some daughters were born unto Adam. In view of the subsequent statements, verse 17, that "Cain knew his wife," he no doubt married a sister. Moreover, since Cain himself says in verse 14, "It shall come to pass that everyone that findeth me shall slay me", and as it is further said in verse 15, "The Lord set a mark upon Cain, lest any finding him should kill him" — it appears most probable from all these circumstances that Adam had many children besides Cain and Abel, but these two only are mentioned, on account of their important and memorable history, and because these two were their first and most remarkable children. It is my full belief that the marriage of our first parents was most fruitful during the first thirty years of their union. Somewhere Calmana and Dibora are mentioned as daughters of Adam, but I know not whether the authors are worthy of credence. Inasmuch, therefore, as the birth of Seth is recorded as having taken place a long time after this murder, it seems to me very probable that the parents, distressed beyond measure at this monstrous crime in the bosom of their family, refrained for a long time from procreation. While Moses does not touch upon all these things, he intimates enough to arouse in the reader a desire to dwell upon the noteworthy events which the absence of detailed information permits us to survey only from a distance.

149. But I return to the text before us. Cain is an evil and wicked man, and yet, in the eyes of his parents, he is a divine possession and gift. Abel, on the contrary, is in the eyes of his parents nothing; but in the eyes of God he is truly a righteous man; an appellation with which also Christ honors him when he calls him "righteous Abel"! Mt 23, 35. This divine judgment concerning Abel, Cain could not endure, and, therefore, he thought that by murder not only the hatred against his brother could be satisfied, but also his birthright be retained. But he was far from

thinking that was sin; as the first-born he thought he had exercised his right. He killed Abel, not with a sword, as I think, but with a club or a stone, for I hold that there were as yet no iron weapons.

150. After the murder, Cain remained unconcerned, for he thought the deed could be concealed by hiding the body, which he buried, or perhaps cast into a river, thinking that thus it would surely remain undiscovered by his parents.

When Abel, however, had been from home a longer time than had been his habit, the Holy Spirit prompted Adam to inquire of Cain concerning Abel, saying, "Where is Abel thy brother?" The above-mentioned utterance of Adam, "If not, sin lieth at the door," was a prophecy which now began to come true. Cain thought he had laid his sin to rest, and all would thus remain hidden. And true it was that his sin did lie at rest, but it lay at rest "at the door." And who opens the door? None other than the Lord himself! He arouses the sleeping sin! He brings the hidden sin to light!

151. The same thing must come to pass with all sinners. For, unless by repentance you first come to God, and yourself confess your sin to God, God will surely come to you, to disclose your sin. For God cannot endure that any one should deny his sin. To this fact the psalmist testifies: "When I kept silence, my bones wasted away through my roaring all the day long. For day and night thy hand was heavy upon me; my moisture was changed as with the drouth of summer." Ps 32, 3-4. For, although sin has its sleep and its security, yet that sleep is "at the door"; it cannot long last, and the sin cannot remain hidden.

152. When Moses introduces Jehovah as speaking, I understand him to mean, as above, that it was Adam who spoke by the Holy Spirit in the place of God, whom he represented in his relation as father. The expression of the Holy Spirit, therefore, is intended to set forth the high authority of parents; when children dutifully hear and obey these, they hear and obey God. And I believe Adam knew by the revelation of the Holy Spirit that Abel had been slain by his brother; for his words intimate the commission of murder at a time when Cain still dissembled as to what he had done.

V. CAIN PUNISHED FOR HIS MURDER.

A. CAIN'S PUNISHMENT IN GENERAL.

1. By whom and how he is punished.
2. Why he was not put to death.
* The double grief of the first parents.
* What was Adam's church and altar.
3. How Cain was excommunicated.
* God's inquiry about Abel's blood.
   a. How unbelievers refer to it.
   b. How a theologian should use it.
   c. It is a great and important matter.

* How Abel's death is to be viewed.

d. Why God does not inquire after the blood of beasts.

e. Whether this inquiry was from God direct or made through Adam.

f. How Cain felt upon this inquiry.

* The result of sin to murderers and other sinners.

* An evil conscience the result of evil-doing.

g. How to understand the statement that Abel's blood crieth to heaven.

* How God's children are to comfort themselves when the world oppresses them and seemingly God refuses to help.

h. This inquiry is a sign of God's care for Abel.

* The blood of many Evangelical martyrs cry to the Papists.

* How God opportunely judges the afflictions of believers.

* Why God's vengeance does not immediately follow.

i. The time this inquiry occurred.

* God indeed has regard for the sufferings and tears of his children.

* How sinners can meet the judgments of God.

4. The miserable life Cain must have led after his punishment.

B. CAIN'S PUNISHMENT IN DETAIL.

1. The Church suffered.

a. How Cain's punishment and curse differed from Adam's.

b. Why Cain's person was cursed.

* The more Cain desired honor, the less he received.

* The beginning of both churches, the true and the false.

* Cain's whole posterity perished in sin.

c. How his curse and punishment were lightened.

* Whether any of Cain's posterity were saved, and holy.

* The way the heathen had part in the promise.

* The way Cain withheld his children from the true Church.

2. The Home suffered.

a. How this curse affected the earth.

b. Why Adam used such severe words in this curse.

c. How it caused the earth to be less fruitful.

* The difference between "Arez" and "Adama".

3. The State suffered.

* What "No" and "Nod" mean, and how they differ.

* Cain's sin punished in three ways and in each the sin was mitigated.

  * Cain a fugitive and a wanderer.

   a. This refers chiefly to the true Church, as is illustrated by many examples of the saints.

   b. It refers less to the false.

   c. Many take offense at this.

V. HOW CAIN WAS PUNISHED FOR HIS MURDER.

A. Cain's Punishment in General.

153. If Eve overheard these words, what think you must have been the state of her mind! Her grief must have been beyond all description. But the calamity was brought home to Adam with even greater force. As he was the father, it fell to him to rebuke his son and to excommunicate him for his sin. Since, according to the ninth chapter, the law concerning the death-penalty for murderers was not promulgated until afterward when the patriarchs beheld murder becoming alarmingly frequent, Adam did not put Cain to death, but safeguarded his life in obedience to the prompting and direction of the Holy Spirit; still, it is a fact not to be gainsaid that the punishment ordained for him and all his posterity was anything but light. For in addition to that curse upon his body he suffered excommunication from his family, separation from the sight of his parents and from the society of his brothers and sisters, who remained with their parents, or in the fellowship of the Church.

154. Now, Adam could not have done all this, nor could Eve have heard it without indescribable anguish. For a father is a father, and a son is a son. Gladly would Adam have spared his son and retained him at home, as we now sometimes see murderers become reconciled to the brothers of their victims. But in this case no place was left for reconciliation. Cain is bidden at once to be a fugitive upon the face of the earth. The pain of the parents was doubled in consequence. They see one of their sons slain, and the other excommunicated by the judgment of God and cut off forever from the fellowship of his brethren.

155. Moreover, when we here speak of excommunication from the Church, it stands to reason that not our houses of worship, built in magnificent style and ample proportions out of hewn stone, are meant. The sanctuary, or church, of Adam was a certain tree, or a certain little hill under the open heaven, where they assembled to hear the Word of God and to offer their sacrifices, for which purpose they had erected altars. And when they offered their sacrifices and heard the Word, God was present, as we see from the experience of Abel.

Also elsewhere in the sacred story, mention is made of such altars under the open heaven, and of sacrifices made upon them. And, if we should come together at this day under the open sky to bend our knees, to preach, to give thanks, and to bless each other, a custom would be inaugurated altogether beneficial.

156. It was from a temple of this kind and from such a church, not a conspicuous and magnificent church at a particular place, that Cain was cast out. He was thus doubly punished; first, by a corporal penalty, because the earth was accursed to him, and secondly, by a spiritual penalty, because by excommunication, he was

cast out from the temple and the church of God as from another paradise.

157. Lawyers also have drawn upon this passage, and quite properly brought out the fact that Jehovah first investigated the matter and then passed sentence. Their application is, that no one should be pronounced guilty until his case has been tried; until he has been called to the bar, proved guilty and convicted. This, according to a previous statement, was also done with Adam: "The Lord God called unto Adam, and said unto him. Where art thou?" Gen 3, 9. And further on: "I will go down now, and see whether they have done altogether according to the cry of it, which is come unto me; and if not, I will know," Gen 11, 5; 18, 21.

158. However, dismissing the matter in its bearings upon public life, let us view its more attractive theological features. The element of doctrine and of hope is found in the fact that Jehovah inquires concerning the dead Abel. Clearly there is pointed out to us here the truth of the resurrection of the dead. God declared himself to be the God of Abel, although now dead, and he inquired for the dead, for Abel. Upon this passage we may establish the incontrovertible principle that, if there were no one to care for us after this life, Abel would not have been inquired for after he was slain. But God inquires after Abel, even when he had been taken from this life; he has no desire to forget him; he retains the remembrance of him; he asks: "Where is he?" God, therefore, we see, is the God of the dead. My meaning is that even the dead, as we here see, still live in the memory of God, and have a God who cares for them, and saves them in another life beyond and different from this corporal life in which saints suffer affliction.

159. This passage, therefore, is most worthy of our attention. We see that God cared for Abel, even when dead; and that on account of the dead Abel, he excommunicated Cain, and visited him, the living, with destruction in spite of his being the first-born. A towering fact this, that Abel, though dead, was living and canonized in another life more effectually and truly than those whom the pope ever canonized! The death of Abel was indeed horrible; he did not suffer death without excruciating torment nor without many tears. Yet it was a blessed death, for now he lives a more blessed life than he did before. This bodily life of ours is lived in sin, and is ever in danger of death. But that other life is eternal and perfectly free from trials and troubles, both of the body and of the soul.

160. No! God inquires not after the sheep and the oxen that are slain, but he does inquire after the men who are slain. Accordingly men possess the hope of a resurrection. They have a God who brings them back from the death of the body unto eternal life, a God who inquires after their blood as a most precious thing. The Psalmist says: "Precious in the sight of Jehovah is the death of his saints," Ps 116, 15.

161. This is the glory of the human race, obtained for it by the seed of the woman which bruised the serpent's head. The case of Abel is the first instance of such promise made to Adam and Eve, and God showed by the same that the serpent did not harm Abel, although it caused his murder. This was indeed an instance of the serpent's "bruising the heel" of the woman's seed. But in the very attempt to bite, its own head was crushed. For God, in answer to Abel's faith in the promised

seed, required the blood of the dead, and proved himself thereby to be his God still. This is all proved by what follows.

V. 10. *And he said, What hast thou done? The voice of thy brother's blood crieth unto me from the ground.*

162. Cain's sin hath hitherto lain at the door. And the preceding circumstances plainly show how hard he struggled to keep his sin asleep. For being interrogated by his father concerning his brother Abel and his whereabouts, he disclaimed knowledge of the matter, thus adding to murder lying. This answer of Cain is sufficient evidence that the above words were spoken by Adam in his own person, and not by God in his divine Majesty. For Cain believed that the deed was hidden from his father, as he was a mere man, while he could not have thought this of the divine Majesty. Therefore, had God spoken to him in his own person, he would have returned a different answer. But, as he thought himself dealing with a human being only, Cain denied his deed altogether, saying: "I know not. How numerous are the perils by which a man may perish. He may have been destroyed by wild beasts; he may have been drowned in some river; or he may have lost his life by some other death."

163. Thus Cain thought that his father would think of any other cause of death than the perpetration of murder. But Cain could not deceive the Holy Spirit in Adam. Adam therefore, as God's representative, arraigns him with the words, "What hast thou done?" As if he had said "Why dost thou persist in denying the deed; be assured thou canst not deceive God, who hath revealed to me all. Thou thinkest the blood of thy brother is hidden by the earth. But it is not so absorbed and concealed thereby as to prevent the blood crying aloud unto God." That meant to awaken the sin lying at the door, and to drag it forth.

164. The text before us, then, provides much consolation against the enemies and murderers of the Church; for it teaches us that our afflictions and sufferings and the shedding of our blood fill heaven and earth with their cries. I believe, therefore, that Cain was so overwhelmed and confounded by these words of his father that, as if thunderstruck, he knew not what to say or what to do. No doubt his thoughts were, "If my father Adam knows about the murder which I have committed, how can I any longer doubt that it is known unto God, unto the angels, and unto heaven and earth? Whither can I flee? Which way can I turn, wretched man that I am?"

165. Such is the state of murderers to this day. They are so harassed with the stings of conscience, after the crime of murder has been committed, that they are always in a state of alarm. It seems to them that heaven and earth have put on a changed aspect toward them, and they know not whither to flee. A case in point is Orestes pursued by the furies, as described by the poets. A horrible thing is the cry of spilled blood and an evil conscience.

166. The same is true of all other atrocious sins. Those who commit them, experience the same distresses of mind when remorse lays hold of them. The whole creation seems changed toward them, and even when they speak to persons with whom they have been familiar, and when they hear the answers they make, the

very sound of their voice appears to them altogether changed and their countenances seem to wear an altered aspect. Whichever way they turn their eyes, all things are clothed, as it were, in gloom and horror. So grim and fierce a monster is a guilty conscience! And, unless such sinners are succored from above, they must put an end to their existence because of their anguish and intolerable pain.

167. Again Moses' customary conciseness is in evidence, which, however, is more effective than an excess of words. In the first place, he personifies a lifeless object when he attributes to blood a voice filling with its cries heaven and the earth. How can that voice be small or weak which, rising from earth, is heard by God in heaven? Abel, therefore, who when alive was patient under injuries and gentle and placid of spirit, now, when dead and buried in the earth, can not brook the wrong inflicted. He who before dared not murmur against his brother, now fairly shrieks, and so completely enlists God in his cause that he descends from heaven, to charge the murderer with his crime. Moses, accordingly, here uses the more pregnant term. He does not say, "The voice of thy brother's blood speaketh unto me from the ground," but, "The voice of thy brother's blood crieth unto me." It is a cry like the shout of heralds when they raise their voices to assemble men together.

168. These things are written, as I have observed, to convince us that our God is merciful, that he loves his saints, takes them into his special care, and demands an account for them; while, on the other hand, he is angry with the murderers of his saints, hates them and designs their punishment. Of this consolation we stand in decided need. When oppressed by our enemies and murderers, we are apt to conclude that our God has forgotten and lost interest in us. We think that if God cared for us, he would not permit such things to come upon us. Likewise, Abel might have reasoned: God surely cares nothing for me; for if he did, he would not suffer me thus to be murdered by my brother.

169. But only look at what follows! Does not God safeguard the interests of Abel better than he could possibly have done himself? How could Abel have inflicted on his brother such vengeance as God does, now that Abel is dead? How could he, if alive, execute such judgment on his brother as God here executes? Now the blood of Abel cries aloud, who, while alive, was of a most retiring disposition. Now Abel accuses his brother before God of being a murderer; when alive he would bear all the injuries of his brother in silence. For who was it that disclosed the murder committed by Cain? Was it not, as the text here tells us, the blood of Abel, fairly deafening with its constant cries the ears of God and men?

170. These things, I say, are all full of consolation; especially for us who now suffer persecution from the popes and wicked princes on account of our doctrine. They have practiced against us the utmost cruelty and have vented their rage against godly men, not in Germany only, but also in other parts of Europe. And all this sin is disregarded by the papacy, as if it were nothing but a joke. Nay, the Papists really consider it to be a service toward God, Jn 16, 2. All this sin, therefore, as yet "lieth at the door." But it shall become manifest in due time. The blood of Leonard Kaiser, which was shed in Bavaria, is not silent. Nor is the blood of Henry of Zutphen, which was shed in Dietmar; nor that of our brother Anthony, of En-

gland, who was cruelly and without a hearing slain by his English countrymen. I could mention a thousand others who, although their names are not so prominent, were yet fellow-sufferers with confessors and martyrs. The blood of all these, I say, will not be silent; in due time it will cause God to descend from heaven and execute such judgment in the earth as the enemies of the Gospel will not be able to bear.

171. Let us not think, therefore, that God does not heed the shedding of our blood! Let us not imagine for a moment that God does not regard our afflictions! No! he collects all our tears, and puts them into his bottle, Ps 56, 8. The cry of the blood of all the godly penetrates the clouds and the heavens to the very throne of God, and entreats him to avenge the blood of the righteous, Ps 79, 10.

172. As these things are written for our consolation, so are they written for the terror of our adversaries. For what think you can be more horrible for our tyrants to hear than that the blood of the slain continually cries aloud and accuses them before God? God is indeed long-suffering, especially now toward the end of the world; and therefore sin lies the longer "at the door," and vengeance does not immediately follow. But it is surely true that God is most grievously offended with all this sin, and that he will never suffer it to pass unpunished.

173. Such judgment of God on Cain, however, I do not believe to have been executed on the first day, but some time afterward. For it is God's nature to be long-suffering, inasmuch as he waits for the sinner to turn. But he does not, on that account, fail to punish him. For he is the righteous judge both of the living and of the dead, as we confess in our Christian Faith. Such judgment God exercised in the very beginning of the world with reference to these two brothers. He judged and condemned the living murderer, and justified murdered Abel. He excommunicated Cain and drove him into such agonies of soul that the space of the whole creation seemed too narrow to contain him. From the moment Cain saw that God would be the avenger of his brother's blood, he felt nowhere safe. To Abel, on the other hand, God gave for enjoyment the full width of earth and heaven.

174. Why, then, should we ever doubt that God ponders and numbers in his heart the afflictions of his people, and that he measures our tears and inscribes them on adamantine tablets? And this inscription the enemies of the Church shall never be able to erase by any device whatever except by repentance. Manasseh was a terrible tyrant and a most inhuman persecutor of the godly. And his banishment and captivity would never have sufficed to blot out these sins. But when he acknowledged his sin and repented in truth, then the Lord showed him mercy.

So Paul had, and so the pope and the bishops have now, only one way left them: to acknowledge their sin and to supplicate the forgiveness of God. If they will not do this, God in his wrath will surely require at their hands the blood of the godly. Let no one doubt this!

175. Abel is dead, but Cain is still alive. But, good God, what a wretched life is that which he lives! He might wish never to have been born, as he hears that he is excommunicated and must look for death and retribution at any moment. And in due time this will be the lot of our adversaries and of the oppressors of the Church.

B. Cain's Punishment In Detail.

V. 11. *And now cursed art thou from the ground, which hath opened its mouth to receive thy brother's blood from thy hand;*

176. We have heard, so far, of the disclosure of Cain's sin through the voice of Abel's blood, of his conviction by Adam his father, and of the decision rendered with reference to the two brothers, namely, that the one should be canonized, or declared a saint—the first fruits, as it were, of the blessed seed; but that the other, the first-born, should be condemned and excommunicated, as shall presently be shown. Now Moses mentions the penalties to be visited upon such fratricide.

177. First of all, we should mark as particularly worthy of note the discrimination exercised by the Holy Spirit. Previously, when the penalty for his sin was inflicted upon Adam, a curse was placed not upon the person of Adam, but only upon the earth; and even this curse was not absolute but qualified. The expression is this: "Cursed is the ground for thy sake"; and in the eighth chapter of the Romans, verse twenty, we read: "The creature was made subject to vanity, not willingly." The fact is, that the earth, inasmuch as it bore guilty man, became involved in the curse as his instrument, just as also the sword, gold, and other objects, are cursed for the reason that men make them the instruments of their sin. With fine reasoning the Holy Spirit discriminates between the earth and Adam. He diverts the curse to the earth, but saves the person.

178. But in this instance the Holy Spirit speaks of Cain. He curses the person of Cain. And why is this? Is it because the sin of Cain, as a murderer, was greater than the sin of Adam and Eve? Not so. But because Adam was the root from whose flesh and loins Christ, that blessed seed, should be born. It is this seed, therefore, that was spared. For the sake of this seed, the fruit of the loins of Adam, the curse is transferred from the person of Adam to the earth. Thus, Adam bears the curse of the earth, but his person is not cursed; from his posterity Christ was to be born.

179. Cain, however, since he fell by his sin, must suffer the curse being inflicted upon his person. He hears it said to him, "Cursed art thou," that we might understand he was cut off from the glory of the promised seed, and condemned never to have in his posterity that seed through which the blessing should come. Thus Cain was cast out from the stupendous glory of the promised seed. Abel was slain; therefore there could be no posterity from him. But Adam was ordained to serve God by further procreation. In Adam alone, therefore, after Cain's rejection, the hope of the blessed seed rested until Seth was born unto him.

180. The words spoken to Cain, "Cursed art thou," are few, but nevertheless entitled to a great deal of attention, in that they are equal to the declaration: Thou art not the one from whom the blessed seed is hoped for. With this word Cain stands cast out and cut off like a branch from the root, unable longer to hope for the distinction around which he had circled. It is a fact, that Cain craved the distinction of passing on the blessing; but the more closely he encircled it the more elusive it became. Such is the lot of all evildoers: their failure is commensurate with their efforts to succeed.

181. From this occurrence originate the two churches which are at war with

each other: the one of Adam and the righteous, which has the hope and promise of the blessed seed; the other of Cain, which has forfeited this hope and promise through sin, without ever being able to regain it. For in the flood Cain's whole posterity became extinct, so that there has been no prophet, no saint, no prince of the true Church who could trace his lineage back to Cain. All that was denied Cain and withdrawn from him, when he was told: "Cursed art thou."

182. We find added, however, the words, "from the ground." These words qualify the fearful wrath. For, if God had said, "from the heavens," he would have deprived his posterity forever of the hope of salvation. As it is, the words, "from the ground," convey, indeed, the menacing decision that the promise of the seed has been forfeited, but the possibility is left that descendants of Cain as individuals, prompted by the Holy Spirit, may join themselves to Adam and find salvation.

This, in after ages, really came to pass. While it is true the promise of the blessed seed was a distinction confined to the Jews, according to the statement in Psalm 147, 20: "He hath not dealt so with any nation," the Gentiles, nevertheless, retained the privilege of beggars, so to speak. It was in this manner that the Gentiles, through divine mercy, obtained the same blessing the Jews possessed on the ground of the divine faithfulness and promise.

183. In like manner, all rule in the Church was absolutely denied also to the Moabites and Amorites; and yet many private individuals among them embraced the religion of the Jews. Thus, every right in the Church was taken away from Cain and his posterity absolutely, yet permission was left them to beg, as it were, for grace. That was not taken from them. Cain, because of his sin, was cast out from the right of sitting at the family table of Adam. But the right was left him to gather up, doglike, the crumbs that fell from his father's table, Mt 15, 26-27. This is signified by the Hebrew expression *min haadama*, "From the ground."

184. I make these observations because there is a great probability that many of the posterity of Cain joined themselves to the holy patriarchs. But their privileges were not those of an obligatory service toward them on the part of the Church, but mere toleration of them as individuals who had lost the promise that the blessed seed was to spring from their flesh and blood. To forfeit the promise was no trifle; still, even that curse was so mitigated as to secure for them the privilege of beggars, so that heaven was not absolutely denied them, provided they allied themselves with the true Church.

185. But this is what Cain, no doubt, strove to hinder in various ways. He set up new forms of worship and invented numerous ceremonies, that thereby he might also appear to be the Church. Those, however, who departed from him and joined the true Church, were saved, although they were compelled to surrender the distinction that Christ was to be born from their flesh and blood. But let us now return to the text.

186. Moses here uses a very striking personification. He represents the earth as a dreaded beast when he speaks of her as having opened her mouth and swallowed the innocent blood of Abel. But why does he treat the earth so ruthlessly since all this was done without her will? Yes, being a creature of God which is good, did not

all transpire in opposition to her will and in spite of her struggle against it, according to Paul's teaching: "The earth was made subject to vanity, not willingly," Rom 8, 20. My reply is: The object was to impress Adam and all his posterity, so that they might live in the fear of God and beware of murder. The words of Adam have this import "Behold the earth hath opened her mouth and swallowed the blood of thy brother; but she ought to have swallowed thee, the murderer. The earth is indeed a good creature, and is good to the good and godly; but to the wicked she is full of pitfalls." It is for the purpose of inspiring murderers with fear and dread that these terrifying words were spoken. Nor is there any doubt that Cain, after hearing the words from an angry father, was overwhelmed with terror and confusion, not knowing whither to turn. The expression, "which hath opened its mouth to receive thy brother's blood from thy hand," is, indeed, terrifying, but it portrays the turpitude of the fratricidal deed better than any picture.

V. 12a. *When thou tillest the ground, it shall not henceforth yield unto thee its strength.*

187. The Lord said above to Adam, "Thorns also and thistles shall it bring forth to thee." But the words spoken to Cain are different. As if he had said, "Thou hast watered and fertilized the earth, not with healthful and quickening rain, but with thy brother's blood. Therefore the earth shall be to thee less productive than to others. For the blood thou hast shed shall hinder the strength and the fruitfulness of the earth." This material curse is the second part of the punishment. The earth, although alike cultivated by Adam and Cain, should be more fruitful to Adam than to Cain and yield its return to the former for his labors. But to the labors of Cain it should not yield such returns, though by nature desirous to give in proportion to its fruitfulness and strength, because it was hindered by the blood spilled by Cain.

188. Here we must offer a remark of a grammatical nature. In the present passage Moses terms the earth *haadama.* In the passage following, "A fugitive and a wanderer shalt thou be in the earth" he uses the term *arez.* Now *adama* signifies, according to grammatical interpreters, that part of the earth which is cultivated, where trees grow and other fruits of the earth adapted for food. But *arez* signifies the whole earth, whether cultivated or uncultivated. This curse, therefore, properly has reference to the part of the earth cultivated for food. And the curse implies that where one ear of wheat brings forth three hundred grains for Adam, it should bring forth scarcely ten grains for Cain the murderer; and this for the purpose that Cain might behold on every side God's hatred and punishment of the shedding of blood.

V. 12b. *A fugitive and a wanderer (vagabond) shalt thou be in the earth.*

189. This is a third punishment resting on murderers to our day. For, unless they find reconciliation, they have nowhere a fixed abode or a secure dwelling-place.

We find here, in the original, two words, *No Vanod,* signifying vagabond and fugitive. The distinction I make between them is, that *No* designates the uncertainty of one's dwelling-place. An illustration is furnished by the Jews, who have no established habitation, but fear every hour lest they be compelled to wander forth.

Nod, on the other hand, signifies the uncertainty of finding the dwelling-place sought; with the uncertainty of a present permanent dwelling-place there is linked the uncertainty of a goal to strive for when the present uncertain dwelling-place must be abandoned. Thus, the punishment contains two features, the insecurity of the present dwelling-place and a lack of knowledge whither to turn when thrust forth from the insecure abode of the present. In this sense the term is used in Psalm 109, 10: "Let his children be continually *vagabonds*." That means, Nowhere shall they find a certain abode; if they are in Greece this year, they shall migrate to Italy the next, and so from place to place.

190. Just such is evidently the miserable state of the Jews at the present day. They can fix their dwelling-place nowhere permanently. And to such evil God adds this other in the case of Cain, that when he should be driven from one place of abode he should not know where to turn, and thus should live suspended, as it were, between heaven and earth, not knowing where to abide nor where to look for a permanent place of refuge.

191. In this manner the sin of Cain was visited with a threefold punishment. In the first place he was deprived of all spiritual or churchly glory; for the promise that the blessed seed was to be born from his posterity, was taken from him. In the second place, the earth was cursed, which is a punishment affecting his home life. The third punishment affects his relations to the community, in that he must be a vagabond without a fixed abode anywhere.

192. Notwithstanding, an open door of return into the Church is left, but without a covenant. For, as has been explained, in the event that any one of Cain's posterity should ally himself with the true Church and the holy fathers, he was saved. Thus the Home is left, but without a blessing; and the State is left so that he may found a city and dwell there, but for how long, is uncertain. Without exaggeration, therefore, he may be likened to a beggar in Church, Home and State.

193. This punishment is mitigated by the prohibition to slay him forthwith after the commission of the murderous deed, a law providing for the punishment of murderers which was reserved for a later day. Cain was saved that he might be an example for others, to teach them to fear God and to beware of murder. So much about the sin, arraignment, and punishment of Cain.

194. But there are some who reply that, the godly, likewise sometimes endure these same curses, while the wicked, on the contrary, are free from them. Thus, Paul says that he also "wandered about and had no certain dwelling-place," 1 Cor 4, 11. Such is even our condition to-day, who are teachers in the churches. We have no certain dwelling-place; either we are driven into banishment or we expect banishment any hour. Such was the lot also of Christ, the apostles, the prophets, and the patriarchs.

195. Concerning Jacob the Scriptures say "The elder shall serve the younger," Gen 25, 23. But does not Jacob become a servant when we see him, from fear of his brother, haste away into exile? Does he not, on his return home, supplicate his brother and fall on his knees before him? Is not Isaac also seen to be a most miserable beggar? Gen 6, 1-35. Abraham, his father, goes into exile among the

Gentiles and possesses not in all the world a place to set his foot, as Stephen says, Acts 7, 1-5. On the other hand, Ishmael was a king, and had the princes of the land of Midian as his offspring before Israel entered into the land of promise, Gen 25, 16. Thus, as we shall see a little later, Cain first built the city of Enoch, and, furthermore, became the ancestor of shepherds, workers in metals, and musicians. All this appears to prove that it is a mistake to attribute to Cain and his posterity a curse. The curse seems to rest with weight upon the true Church, while the wicked appear to thrive and flourish.

196. These things are often a stumbling-block, not to the world only, but even to the saints, as the Psalms in many places testify. And the prophets, also, are frequently found to grow indignant, as does Jeremiah, when they see the wicked possess freedom as it were from the evils of life, while they are oppressed and afflicted in various ways. Men may therefore inquire, Where is the curse of the wicked? Where is the blessing of the godly? Is not the converse the truth? Cain is a vagabond and settled nowhere; and yet Cain is the first man that builds a city and has a certain place to dwell in. But we will answer this argument more fully hereafter. We will now proceed with the text of Moses.

VI. CAIN'S CONDUCT WHEN PUNISHED.

1. How he despaired. "My punishment is greater" etc.
    a. These words have greatly perplexed interpreters.
    b. The way Augustine explains them.
    c. The explanation of the rabbins.
    * How the rabbins pervert the Scriptures and whence their false comments.
    d. Why the rabbins' interpretation cannot be accepted.
    e. The true understanding of these words.
    * The punishment troubles Cain more than his sin.
    f. What makes these words difficult.
    * The right understanding of the words "Minso" and "Avon".
    * Grammarians cannot get at the right meaning of the Scriptures.
    * How we should proceed in interpreting Scripture.
2. How Cain viewed his political punishment.
3. How he viewed his ecclesiastical punishment.
    * Why Cain was excommunicated by Adam.
    * In what sense Cain was a fugitive and a wanderer.
    * Adam received his punishment in a better way.
    * The meaning of being a fugitive and a wanderer. How the same is found among the papists.
    * The grace of God was guaranteed to Seth and his posterity.

   * Why no temptation can harm believers.

4. Cain's fear that in turn he would be slain.

   * God shows Cain a double favor in his punishment. Why he does this.

   * Whether any of Cain's posterity, under the Old Testament, were saved.

5. Whether Cain prayed that he might die, as Augustine, Lyra and others relate.

   * The fables of the rabbins cause Luther double work and why he occasionally cites them.

   * Whether God changed his judgment upon Cain.

   * Why God still showed Cain incidental grace.

   * The fables of the Jews concerning Cain's death and Lamech's punishment.

   * It is foolish to dispute concerning the sevenfold vengeance to be visited upon the one who slew Cain.

   * The divine promises.

      a. They are twofold, of the law and of grace.

      b. The promise Adam received.

      c. Whether God gave Cain one of these promises.

      d. The kind of promises well organized police stations have.

      e. The promises the Church has.

      f. Cain's promise is temporal, incidental and incomplete.

      * Was Cain murdered.

6. How Cain had cause to fear, even though there were no people on the earth except Adam and Eve and his sisters.

   * The sign that is put upon Cain.

      a. Can anything definite be said of it. What the fathers thought of it.

      b. Why this sign was placed upon him.

      c. How he had to carry it his whole life.

      d. How the sign was a confirmation and a promise of the law.

7. Of Cain's departure, and his excommunication from the presence of Jehovah.

      a. The first parents in obedience to God made Cain an outcast.

      b. How the first parents overcame their parental affections in expelling Cain.

      * What should urge men to flee from their false security.

      c. His expulsion must have pierced Cain to the heart.

      * What is the presence of Jehovah.

      d. How he went from the presence of Jehovah, to be without that presence.

      e. It was a sad departure, both for Cain and his parents.

 f. Whither he resorted.

 * What meaning of "in the land of Nod".

 * Of Paradise.

  (1) The deluge very likely destroyed paradise.

  (2) Where was paradise.

 * Of the Deluge.

  (1) The deluge destroyed paradise.

  * Cain lived where Babylon was built later.

  (2) The deluge gave the earth an entirely different form.

VI. CAIN'S CONDUCT UPON BEING PUNISHED.

V. 13. *And Cain said unto Jehovah, My punishment (iniquity) is greater than I can bear (than can be remitted).*

197. Here Moses seems to have fixed a cross for the grammarians and the rabbins; for they crucify this passage in various ways. Lyra recites the opinions of some who see in this passage an affirmation, considering it to mean that in his despair Cain claimed his sin to be greater than could be pardoned. This is our rendering. Augustine likewise retained this view of the passage, for he says, "Thou liest, Cain; for the mercy of God is greater than the misery of all the sinners."

198. The rabbins, however, expound the passage as a denial in the form of a question, as if he had said, "Is my iniquity greater than can be remitted?" But if this rendering be the true one, Cain not only does not acknowledge his sin, but excuses it and, in addition, insults God for laying upon him a punishment greater than he deserves. In this way the rabbins almost everywhere corrupt the sense of the Scriptures. Consequently I begin to hate them, and I admonish all who read them, to do so with careful discrimination. Although they did possess the knowledge of some things by tradition from the fathers, they corrupted them in various ways; and therefore they often deceived by those corruptions even Jerome himself. Nor did the poets of old so fill the world with their fables as the wicked Jews did the Scriptures with their absurd opinions. A great task, therefore, is incumbent upon us in endeavoring to keep the text free from their comments.

199. The occasion for all this error is the fact that some men are competent to deal only with grammatical questions, but not with the subject matter itself; that is, they are not theologians at the same time. The inevitable result is mistakes and the crucifixion of themselves as well as of the Scriptures. For how can any one explain what he does not understand? Now the subject matter in the present passage is that Cain is accused in his own conscience. And no one, not only no wicked man, but not even the devil himself, can endure this judgment; as James witnesses, "The devils also believe and tremble before God," Jas 2, 19. Peter also says, "Whereas angels which are greater in power and might cannot endure that judgment which the Lord will exercise upon blasphemers," 2 Pet 2, 11. So also Manasseh in his prayer, verses 4 and 5, confesses that all men tremble before the face of the Lord's

anger.

200. All this is sufficient evidence that Cain, when arraigned by God, did not have courage to withstand and to argue with him. For God is an almighty adversary; the first assault he makes is upon the heart itself when he takes the conscience into his grasp. Of this the rabbins know nothing, nor can they understand it; in consequence they speak of this arraignment as if it took place before men, where the truth is either denied or facts are smoothed over. This is impossible when God arraigns men; as Christ says in Matthew 12, 37, "By thy words thou shalt be justified and by thy words thou shalt be condemned."

201. Cain thus acknowledges his sin, although it is not so much the sin he grieves over as the penalty inflicted. The statement, then, is to be understood in the affirmative, and it reveals the horrors of despair.

A further proof of Cain's despair is, that he does not utter one word of reverence. He never mentions the name of God or of his father. His conscience is so confused and so overwhelmed with terror and despair that he is not able to think of any hope of pardon. The Epistle to the Hebrews gives the same description of Esau when it states that he "for one mess of meat, sold his own birthright. For ye know that even when he afterward desired to inherit the blessing, he was rejected; for he found no place for change of mind, though he sought it diligently with tears," Heb 12, 16-17. Thus in the present instance, Cain feels his punishment, but he grieves more for his punishment than for his sin. And all persons, when in despair, do the same.

202. The two original words of this passage, *minneso* and *avon*, are a pair of crosses for grammarians. Jerome translates this clause, "My iniquity is greater than can be pardoned." Sanctes, the grammarian of Pagnum, a man of no mean erudition and evidently a diligent scholar, renders the passage, "My punishment is greater than I can bear." But by such a rendering we shall make a martyr of Cain and a sinner of Abel. Concerning the word *nasa*, I have before observed that when it is applied to sin it signifies, to lift sin up, or off, or on high; that is, to take it out of the way. Similarly the figure has found currency among us: the remission of sins, or to remit sin. In the Thirty-second Psalm, verse one, we find the expression, *Aschre Nesu Pascha*. This, literally translated, would make: Being blessed through the removal of crime, or sin. We make it: Blessed is he whose transgression is forgiven, or taken away. The same is found in Isaiah 33, 24, The people that dwell therein shall be *Nesu Avon*, that means, relieved from sin—shall be the people whose sin is forgiven.

203. The other original term, *avoni*, grammarians derive from the verb *anah*, which signifies "to be afflicted," as in Zechariah 9, 9: "Behold thy king cometh unto thee lowly (or afflicted)." Our translation renders it "meek." Likewise in Psalms 132, 1: "Jehovah, remember for David all his affliction." From the same root is derived the expression, "low estate," or "lowliness," used by the Virgin Mary in her song, Lk 1, 48. This fact induces Sanctes to render it "punishment."

But here *avoni* signifies "iniquity" or "sin," as it does also in many other passages of the Holy Scriptures, which appears more plainly from the verb "remit," which stands connected with it.

204. Hence it is that grammarians, who are nothing but such and know nothing of the divine things, find their crosses in all such passages, and crucify, not only the Scriptures, but themselves and their hearers as well. In the interpretation of the Holy Scriptures, the sense is first to be determined; and when that appears in all respects consistent with itself, then the grammatical features are to receive attention. The rabbins, however, take the opposite course, and hence it grieves me that divines and the holy fathers so frequently follow them.

V. 14. *Behold, thou hast driven me out this day from the face of the ground; and from thy face shall I be hid; and I shall be a fugitive and a wanderer in the earth; and it will come to pass, that whosoever findeth me will slay me.*

205. From these words it appears that the sentence on Cain was pronounced through the mouth of Adam. Cain acknowledges that he is driven first from Home and State, and then also from the Church. Of the difference between the words *adamah* and *erez* we spoke above. We showed that *erez* signifies the earth generally, while the word *adamah* means the cultivated part of the earth. The meaning therefore is: I am now compelled to flee from thy presence and from that part of the earth which I have cultivated. The whole world indeed lies before me, but I must be a fugitive and a vagabond upon the earth; that is, I shall have no certain dwelling place. In the same way fugitive murderers among us are punished with exile. These words, accordingly, cast additional light upon the utterance of Adam, "Cursed art thou from the ground." They refer to Cain's banishment. This part of Cain's punishment therefore is a civil punishment, and by it he is shut out from civic association.

206. But that which Cain next adds, "From thy face shall I be hid," is an ecclesiastical punishment and true excommunication. For, as the priesthood and the kingdom rested with Adam, and Cain on account of his sin was excommunicated from Adam, he was thereby also deprived of the glory both of priesthood and kingdom. But why Adam adopted this punishment is explained by the words, "When thou tillest the ground, it shall not henceforth yield unto thee its strength;" as if he had said, Thou art cursed and thy labors are cursed also. Therefore if thou shalt remain with us upon earth it cannot be but that both thyself and we likewise must perish with hunger. For thou hast stained the earth with thy brother's blood, and wherever thou art, thou must bear about the blood of thy brother, and even the earth itself shall exact her penalties.

207. A similar sentence we find pronounced in 1 Kings 2, 29-33, where Solomon gives commandment to Benaiah, son of Jehoiada, saying, "Fall upon Joab, that thou mayest take away the blood, which Joab shed without cause, from me and from my father's house. And Jehovah will return his blood upon his own head. But unto David, and unto his seed, and unto his house, and unto his throne, shall there be peace for ever from Jehovah." As much as to say, If Joab suffer not this punishment of his unjust murder, the whole kingdom must suffer that punishment and be shaken by wars. The meaning of Adam then, in this passage is, If thou shalt remain on the earth with us, God will bring punishment upon us for thy

sake, in that the earth shall not yield us her fruit.

208. But now let us reply to the question raised above. It was said to Cain, "A fugitive and wanderer shalt thou be in the earth." And yet, Cain was the first man who builds a city, and his posterity so increased from that time that they debauched and oppressed the Church of God, and so utterly overthrew it as not to leave more than eight persons of the posterity of Seth. All of the remainder of mankind, which perished in the flood, had followed Cain, as the text plainly declares when it affirms that the sons of God, when they came unto the daughters of men, begat giants and mighty men, which were of old, men of renown, Gen 6, 4. Therefore, since Cain had so great a posterity, and he built the first city, how can it be true, men ask, that he was a fugitive and wanderer upon earth?

209. We will reply in accordance with what is written. The illustrations from the New Testament above mentioned, Paul, the apostles, Christ, and the prophets, assuredly belong to quite a different category. When Adam here says to Cain, "A fugitive and a wanderer shalt thou be in the earth," he speaks these words to him to send him away, without further precept. He does not say to him, "Go to the east;" he does not say, "Go to the south;" he does not mention any place to which he should go. He gives him no command what to do; but simply casts him out. Whither he goes and what he does, is no concern of his. He adds no promise of protection, he does not say: God shall take care of thee; God shall protect thee. On the contrary; as the whole sky is free to the bird, which is at liberty to fly whither it pleases, but is without a place where it may be secure from the attacks of other birds, so Adam turns Cain away. The latter feels this. Hence his rejoinder: "It shall come to pass that every one that findeth me, shall slay me."

210. The condition of Adam was different and better. Adam had sinned, and by his sin he had sunk into death. But when he was driven out of paradise, God assigned him a particular task—that he should till the earth in a particular place. God also clothed him with a covering of skins. This, as we said, was a sign that God would take care of him and protect him. And, last but not least, a glorious promise was made to the woman concerning the seed which should bruise the serpent's head. Nothing like this was left to Cain. He was sent away absolutely without assignment of any particular place or task. No command was given him nor was any promise made him. He was like a bird aimlessly roving beneath the wide heavens. This is what it means to be a vagabond and wanderer.

211. Unsettled and aimless, likewise, are all who lack God's Word and command, wherein person and place receive adequate direction. Such were we under the papacy. Worship, works, exercises—all these were present; but all these existed and found acceptance without a divine command. A trying condition was that and Cainlike—to be deprived of the Word; not to know what to believe, what to hope, what to suffer, but to undertake and to perform everything at haphazard. What monk is there who could affirm that he did anything right? Everything was man's tradition and man's teaching, without the Word. Amid these we wandered, being driven to and fro, and like Cain, uncertain what verdict God would pass, whether we should merit love or hate. Such was, in those days, our instruction.

Unsettled and aimless like this was Cain's whole posterity. They had neither promise nor command from God, and lacked all definite guidance for life and for death. Hence, if any of them came to the knowledge of Christ, and allied themselves with the true Church, it was not by reason of a promise but through sheer compassion.

212. Seth, however, who was born subsequently, had, together with his posterity, a definite promise, a definite abode and a definite mode of worship; on the other hand, Cain was aimless. He founded a city, it is true, but he did not know how long he should dwell in it, not having a divine promise. Whatever we possess without a promise is of uncertain duration; at any amount Satan may disturb it or take it. However, when we go into the fray equipped with God's command and promise, the devil fights in vain; God's command insures strength and safety. Therefore, although Cain was lord of the whole world and possessed all the treasures of the world, still, lacking the promise of God's help and the protection of his angels, and having nothing to lean upon but man's counsels, he was in every respect aimless and unsettled. This he himself admits when he further says:

V. 14b. *And it shall come to pass that every one that findeth me shall slay me.*

213. This result was quite to be expected. Having neither God nor his father to look to for succor, having forfeited his rights both as priest and as ruler, he saw the possibility before him that any one found him, might slay him, for he was outlawed, body and soul. Notwithstanding, God conferred upon the nefarious murderer a twofold blessing. He had forfeited Church and dominion, but life and progeny were left. God promised him to protect his existence, and also gave him a wife. Two blessings these by no means to be despised; and when he heard the first part of his sentence pronounced by his father, they were more than he had a right even to hope for. They were valuable for the additional reason that opportunity and time for repentance were granted, though, in the absence of a clear promise, there was neither covenant nor commission. In the same manner, we found our way under the papacy to uncovenanted mercy (*fortuita gratia*), if I may use this expression, for no promise was previously given that the truth was to be revealed in our lifetime, and the Antichrist to become manifest. The reason to which these blessings are attributable, is consideration for the elect. It is quite credible that many of Cain's offspring were saved, namely, those who joined the true Church. Likewise, at a later day, provision was made among the Jews for proselytes and Gentiles.

214. While a stern law existed according to which the Moabites and Ammonites were not admitted to the religious services, Ammonites and Moabites were saved, such as came to the kings of Judah to serve under them. Also Ruth, the mother and ancestress of our Saviour, was a Moabite. This is what I call uncovenanted mercy, no previous promise having rendered it certain.

215. Also Naaman, and the king of Nineveh, and Nebuchadnezzar, and Evilmerodach, and others from among the Gentiles, were saved by such uncovenanted mercy; for, unlike the Jews, they had no promise of Christ. In the same way, bodily safety is vouchsafed to Cain, and a wife with offspring, for the sake of the elect to

be saved by uncovenanted mercy. For, although what we said of the Moabites is true of all his posterity, that it was to live under a curse, it is true, notwithstanding, that some of the patriarchs took their wives from the same.

V. 15a. *And Jehovah said unto him, Therefore whosoever slayeth Cain, vengeance shall be taken on him sevenfold.*

216. Jerome, in his Epistle to Damascus, contends that Cain had begged of the Lord that he might be slain, an opinion into which he rushes full sail, as it were, entertaining no doubt whatever concerning its truth. Lyra follows Jerome, and resolutely affirms that the context requires this interpretation. But this error of theirs should be laid at the door of the rabbins from whom they received it. The true sense of the passage is rather that everyone was prohibited from killing Cain. Judgment is pronounced here by God, and when he spares Cain's life and in addition permits him afterward to marry, it is done to stay its execution.

217. Moreover, how is it likely that an ungodly person asks death at the very time when God exercises judgment? Death is the very punishment of sin; therefore he flees and dreads death as the greatest part of his penalty. Away, therefore, with such vagaries of the rabbins! With these also Lyra's suggestion may safely be classed that the text ought to be divided and made to mean, Whoever shall kill Cain, shall surely meet with severe punishment. And when it is further stated, He shall be punished sevenfold, they would explain it as meaning that in the seventh degree—in the seventh generation—the punishment is to be inflicted.

218. Such vagaries are worthy of the rabbins after having cast away the light of the New Testament. However, they impose a double labor upon us, inasmuch as we are compelled to defend the text and to clear it of such corruptions, and to correct their absurd comments. If I quote them occasionally, it is to avoid the suspicion of proudly despising them, or of failing to read, and to give sufficient consideration to, their writings. While we read them intelligently, we do so with critical discrimination, and we do not permit them to obscure Christ, and to corrupt the Word of God.

219. The Lord, accordingly, does not in this passage at all alter the sentence upon Cain whereby he had been doomed to a curse on earth, but merely vouchsafes to him this uncovenanted mercy for the sake of the elect that are to be saved from that curse as from a mass of dregs. That is the reason he said Cain should not be killed, as he feared.

There is, then, no necessity for doing violence to this text as Rabbi Solomon does, who, after the words "whosoever slayeth Cain," puts a stop; making it to be a hiatus or (ellipsis), as we find in that noted line in Virgil (Aeneas, 135)—

Quos ego—sed motos praestat componere fluctus.
Whom I—but now, be calm, ye boist'rous waves.

And then the expression, "shall be punished sevenfold," the rabbi refers to Cain himself, who was punished in his seventh generation. For Cain begat Enoch, and Enoch begat Irad, and Irad begat Mehujael, and Mehujael begat Methusael, and Methusael begat Lamech.

220. And the Jews' absurd comment upon that passage (verse 23, below), is that Lamech, when he was old, and his eyes dim, was taken by his son Tubal-Cain into a wood to hunt wild beasts, and that, when there shooting at a wild beast, Lamech accidently shot Cain, who in his wanderings had concealed himself in the wood. Such interpretations are only fables, unworthy a place or notice in our schools. Moreover, they militate against the very truth of the text. For if Cain was really designed of God to be killed in the seventh generation, and if that time was thus fixed for his death, he was not "a fugitive and a vagabond upon earth."

221. We condemn, therefore, this interpretation of Rabbi Solomon, on the ground of critical discrimination, because it militates directly against that sentence which God had before pronounced; and God is not man, that he should change his mind, 1 Kings 15, 29-30. This rule should be strictly observed in all interpretation of the Holy Scripture, that the rendering of one passage must not subsequently conflict with that of another. And when the rabbins, moreover, say that the deluge was the particular punishment of Lamech's sin in thus killing Cain, Lyra refutes them. He very truly affirms that the deluge was the common punishment of the whole world of wicked men. We leave, therefore, all these Jewish absurdities and hold fast the true meaning of the text before us, that, when Cain feared lest he should be slain by any one who should find him, the Lord prevented him from being thus slain, and denounced on such murderer a punishment sevenfold greater than that of Cain.

222. And, though Lyra argues and inquires how it could be that he who should slay Cain could deserve a sevenfold greater vengeance than Cain deserved, who slew his own brother, of what profit is it to us to inquire into the counsel of God in such matters as these, especially when it is certain that God permitted his mercy to stray to Cain in the form of promises and blessings under the Law, if I may so express myself, thus securing his safety.

223. There are two kinds of promises, or a twofold promise, as we have often explained. There are the legal promises, if I may so call them, which depend, as it were, upon our own works, such as the following: "If ye be willing and obedient, ye shall eat the good of the land," Is 1, 19. Again, I am God, showing mercy unto thousands of them that love me and keep my commandments, Ex 20, 6. And also above, in this case of Cain, "If thou doest well, shall not thy countenance be lifted up?" Gen 4, 7. And these legal promises have for the most part their corresponding threats attached to them.

But the other kind of promises are promises of grace, and with them no threats are joined. Such are the following: "Jehovah thy God will raise up unto thee a prophet from the midst of thee, of thy brethren, like unto me; unto him ye shall hearken," Deut 18, 15. Again, "I will put my law in their inward parts, in their heart will I write it; and I will be their God, and they shall be my people," Jer 31, 33. And again, "I will put enmity between thee and the woman," Gen 3, 15. Now, these promises depend not in any way upon our works, but absolutely and only upon the goodness and grace of God, because he was pleased to make those promises and to do what he thus promised. Just in the same way we have the promise of Baptism, of the Lord's Supper, and of the Keys, etc., in which God sets before us his good will and his mercy and his works.

224. Now, God gave no promise of the latter kind to Cain. He only said to him, Whosoever shall slay thee shall be punished sevenfold. But Adam had such a promise of grace made to him. And Cain, because he was the first-born, ought to have received that promise as an inheritance from his parents. That promise was the large and blessed promise of eternal glory, because by it the seed was promised which should bruise the serpent's head, and this without any work or merit of man. For that promise had no condition attached to it, such as, If thou shalt offer thy sacrifices, if thou shalt do good, etc.

225. If, therefore, you compare this promise of grace with the words God spake to Cain, the latter are as a mere crust held out to a beggar. For even Cain's life is not promised him absolutely. Nothing more is said than a threat pronounced against those who should slay him. God does not say positively, No man shall slay thee. He does not say, I will so overrule all others that no one shall slay thee. Had the words been thus spoken, Cain might have returned into the presence of God and of his parents. But a command only is given to men that they slay not Cain. If, therefore, the words spoken to Cain be at all considered as a promise, it is that kind of promise which, as we have before said, depends on the works and will of man. And yet, even such promise is by no means to be despised, for these legal promises often embrace most important things.

226. Thus, Augustine observes that God gave to the Romans their empire on account of their noble virtues. And in the same manner we find, even to this day, that the blessings of those nations which keep from murder, adultery, theft, etc., are greater than those of other nations in which these evils prevail. And yet, even governments which, as far as mere reason can succeed, are especially well established, possess nothing beyond these temporal promises.

227. The Church, however, possesses the promises of grace, even the eternal promises. And although Cain was left utterly destitute of these promises, yet it was a great favor that the temporal mercies were left him: that he was not immediately killed, that a wife was given him, that children were born unto him, that he built a city, that he cultivated the earth, that he fed his cattle and had possessions, and that he was not utterly ejected from the society and fellowship of men. For God could not only have deprived Cain of all these blessings, but he could have added pestilence, epilepsy, apoplexy, the stone, the gout, and any other disease. And yet there are men disposed curiously to argue in what manner God could possibly have multiplied the curse of Cain sevenfold on himself or on any other.

As God above deprives Cain of all the divine blessings, both spiritual—or those pertaining to the Church—and civil, so here he mitigates that sentence by commanding that no one shall slay Cain. But God does not promise at the same time that all men shall surely obey his command. Therefore Cain, even possessing this promise in reference to his body, is still a fugitive and a wanderer. And it might be that if he continued in his wickedness, he was liable to be slain at any moment; whereas, if he did well, he might live a long time. But nothing is promised him with certainty, for although these corporal or legal promises are great and important, yet they are positively uncertain and uncovenanted.

228. Whether, therefore, Cain was killed or not, I cannot with any certainty say, for the Scriptures afford no plain information upon that point. This one thing, however, evidently can be proved from the present text, that Cain had no certain promise of the preservation of his life; but God left him to a life of uncertainty, doubt and restless wandering, and did no more than protect the life of Cain by a command and a threat which might restrain the wicked from killing him, on account of the certain awful punishment which would follow such destruction of the murderer. But a promise that he should not be murdered was withheld. We know, moreover, what is the nature of the law, or a legal command, and that there are always very few who obey it. Therefore, although it is not recorded at what time, in what place, or by whom, Cain was slain, yet it is most probable that he was killed. The Scriptures however make no mention of it, even as they are quite silent also concerning the number of the years of Cain, and say nothing about the day of his birth or the day of his death. He perished, together with his whole generation; to use a popular proverb, "without cross, candle, or God." A few only of his generation are excepted, who were saved by the uncovenanted mercy of God.

229. The question is here usually asked, To what persons could the words of Cain possibly apply, when he says, "Everyone that findeth me shall slay me," when it is evident that besides Adam and Eve and their few daughters, no human beings were in existence. I would at once reply that they bear witness to the fact that we see the wicked "flee when no man pursueth," as the Scriptures say; for they imagine to themselves various perils where none really exist. Just so we see it to be the case with murderers at the present day, who are filled with fears where all is safe, who can remain quiet nowhere, and who imagine death to be present everywhere.

230. However, when it follows in the command of God, "Yea, verily, whosoever slayeth Cain shall be punished sevenfold," these words cannot be referred exclusively to the fears of Cain, for Cain had sisters, and perhaps he greatly dreaded that sister whom he had married, lest she should take vengeance on him for the murder of her brother. Moreover, Cain had perhaps a vague apprehension of a long life, and he saw that many more sons might be born of Adam. He feared, therefore, the whole posterity to Adam. And it greatly increased these fears that God had left him nothing more than his stray mercy. I do not think that Cain feared the beasts at all, or dreaded being slain by them; for what had the sevenfold vengeance threatened upon murderers to do with beasts?

V. 15b. *And Jehovah appointed a sign for (set a mark upon) Cain, lest any finding him should smite him (slay him).*

231. What this mark was is not to be found in the Holy Scriptures. Therefore commentators have entertained various opinions. Nearly all, however, have come to this one conclusion — they have inferred that there was apparent in Cain a great tremor of his head and of all his limbs. They suppose that, as a physical cause of his trembling, God had changed, or disarranged, or mutilated some particular organ in his body, but left the body whole as it was first created, merely adding a visible

outward mark, such as the trembling. This conjecture of the fathers contains much probability, but it cannot be proved by any testimony of the Scriptures. The mark might have been of another kind. For instance, we observe in nearly all murderers an immediate change in the eyes. The eyes wear an appearance of sullen ferocity, and lose that softness and innocence peculiar to them by nature.

232. But whatever this mark was, it was certainly a most horrible punishment; for Cain was compelled to bear it during his whole life as God's penalty for the awful murder which he had committed. Rendered conspicuous by this degrading mark, hateful and abominable in the eyes of all, Cain was sent away—banished from his home by his parents. And although the life he asked of God was granted him, yet it was a life of ignominy, branded with an infamous mark of homicide; not only that he himself might be perpetually reminded of the sin he had committed, to his own confusion, but also that others might be deterred from the crime of committing murder. Nor could this mark be effaced by repentance. Cain was compelled to bear about this sign of the wrath of God upon him as a punishment in addition to his banishment, the curse, and all the other penalties.

233. It is worthy of observation that the original verb used above is *harag*, which signifies "to kill." But the verb here found is *nakah*, which means "to strike." God, therefore, here gives to Cain security, not only from death, but also from the danger of death. This security, however, as we have observed, is a legal security only; for it merely commands that no one shall slay Cain, threatening a sevenfold punishment upon the person who should do so. But God does not promise that all men will obey his command. It was far better for Cain, however, to have this legal promise made him, than to be without any promise at all.

V. 16. *And Cain went out from the presence of Jehovah, and dwelt in the land of Nod, on the east of Eden.*

234. This also is a very remarkable text, and it is a wonder that the fancy of the rabbins did not run riot here as usual. Moses leaves it to the thoughtful reader to reflect how miserable and how full of tears this departure of Cain from his father's house must have been. His godly parents had already lost their son Abel; and now, at the command of God, the other son departs from them into banishment, loaded with the divine curses, on account of his sin—the very son whom his parents had hoped to be the only heir of the promise, and whom they therefore had devotedly loved from his cradle. Adam and Eve, nevertheless, obey the command of God, and in conformity therewith they cast out their son.

235. Accordingly, this passage rightly praises obedience to God, or the fear of God. Adam and Eve had, indeed, learned by their own experience in paradise that it was no light sin to depart from the command of God; therefore they thought: Behold, our sin in paradise has been punished with death, and with an infinite number of other calamities into which we have been thrown since we were driven out of paradise. And now that our son has committed so atrocious a sin, it behooves us not to resist the will of God and his righteous judgment, however bitter we feel them to be.

236. The story of the woman of Tekoah is well known, whom Joab instructed

to intercede for the banished Absalom. She pleads as an argument before the king, that as she had lost one son, it would be wicked in the extreme to deprive her of the other also. Also Rebecca said to Jacob, her younger son, after she had perceived the wrath of Esau against his brother: "Why should I be bereaved of you both in one day?" Gen 27, 45. Adam and Eve overcame this same pain in their bosoms, and thus mortified their paternal and maternal affections. For not only did they feel it to be their duty to obey the will of God, but they had also learned wisdom from former obedience. They had been driven out of paradise for their sin of disobedience. They feared, therefore, that if they now retained their son with them, contrary to the will of God, they should be cast out of the earth altogether.

237. This part of the history of Adam and Eve, therefore, is a beautiful lesson in obedience to God, and a striking exhortation to fear God. This is also Paul's principal object in his first Epistle to the Corinthians, nearly all of which is written against the self-confidence of the human heart. For, although God is merciful, yet men are not therefore to sin; he is merciful to those only who fear and obey him.

238. As it was bitter in the extreme for the parents to lose their son, this departure from his home was, I have no doubt, most bitter also to Cain himself. For he was compelled to leave, not only the common home, his dear parents and their protection, but his hereditary right of primogeniture, the prerogative of the kingdom and of the priesthood, and the communion of the Church.

Hence it is that we have the expression in the text, that Cain "went out from the presence of Jehovah." We have above shown what the Scriptures term "the face of Jehovah," namely, all those things and means by which Jehovah makes himself known to us. Thus the face of Jehovah, under the Old Testament, was the pillar of fire, the cloud, the mercy-seat, etc. Under the New Testament, the face of Jehovah is baptism, the Lord's Supper, the ministry of the Word, etc. For by these things, as by visible signs, the Lord makes himself known to us, and shows that he is with us, that he cares for us and favors us.

239. It was from this place, therefore, in which God declared that he was always present, and in which Adam resided as high priest, and as lord of the earth, that Cain "went out;" and he came into another place, where there was no "face of God," where there was no visible sign of his presence by which he could derive the consolation that God was present with his favor. He had no sign whatever, save those signs which are common to all creatures, even to the beasts, namely, the uses of sun and moon, of day and night, of water, air, etc. But these are not signs of that immutable grace of God contained in the promise of the blessed seed. They are only the signs of God's temporal blessings and of his good will to all his creatures.

240. Miserable, therefore, was that going out of Cain indeed. It was a departure full of tears. He was compelled to leave forever his home and his parents, who now gave to him, a solitary man and a "vagabond," their daughter as his wife, to live with him as his companion; but they knew not what would become either of their son or of their daughter. In consequence of losing three children at one time their grief is so much greater. No other explanation suggests itself for the subsequent statement "Cain knew his wife."

241. Where, then, did Cain live with his wife? Moses answers, "in the land of Nod," a name derived from its vagabond and unsettled inhabitant. And where was this land situated? Beyond paradise, toward the east, a place indeed most remarkable. Cain came into a certain place toward the east, but when he came there, he was insecure and unprotected, for it was the land of Nod, where he could not set foot with certainty, because "the face of God" was not there. For this "face" he had left with his parents, who lived where they had paradise on their side, or toward the west. When Cain fled from his home he went toward the east. So the posterity of Cain was separated from the posterity of Adam, having paradise as a place of division between them. The passage, moreover, proves that paradise remained undestroyed after Adam was driven out of it. In all probability it was finally destroyed by the deluge.

242. This text greatly favors the opinion of those who believe that Adam was created in the region of Damascus, and that, after he was driven out of paradise for his sin, he lived in Palestine; and hence it was in the midst of the original paradise that Jerusalem, Bethlehem and Jericho stood, in which places Jesus Christ and his servant John chiefly dwelt. Although the present aspect of those places does not altogether bear out that conclusion, the devastations of the mighty deluge were such as to change fountains, rivers and mountains; and it is quite possible that on the site which was afterward Calvary, the place of Christ's sacrifice for the world's sin, there stood the tree of the knowledge of good and evil, the same spot being marked by the death and ruin wrought by Satan and by the life and salvation wrought by Christ.

243. It is not without a particular purpose, therefore, that Daniel uses the striking expression: "The end thereof (of the sanctuary, the sacrifice and the oblation) shall be with a flood," Dan 9, 26. As if he had said, The first paradise was laid waste and utterly destroyed by the mighty deluge, and the other, future paradise, in which redemption is to be wrought, shall be destroyed by the Romanists as by a flood.

244. We may carry the analogy further by stating that as Babel was the cause of the destruction of the Jewish people, so this disaster had its beginning with Cain and his offspring, who settled in that part of the earth where, at a later day, Babylon was founded. These are my thoughts and views, derived partly from the fathers. Though they may not be true, they are yet probable, and have nothing ungodly in them. And there can be no doubt that Noah, after the flood, saw the face of the whole earth altogether changed from what it was before that awful visitation of the wrath of God. Mountains were torn asunder, fountains were made to break forth and the courses of the rivers themselves were wholly altered and diverted into other channels, by the mighty force of the overwhelming waters.

VII. GENERATIONS OF CAIN AND OF THE RIGHTEOUS.

I. IN GENERAL.

1. Why Cain's generations were described before those of the righteous.

2. How the Holy Spirit is interested more in the generations of the righteous than in those of Cain.

3. Why the Holy Spirit gives this description of both.

4. The relation of the two to each other.

5. How the generations of the righteous are attacked and conquered by those of the godless.

* Of Cain's marriage.

   a. Who was his wife, and the question of his being married before he committed the murder.

   * How to read the writings of the Jews.

   b. The question of his being married after the murder.

   * That some of his posterity were saved.

VII. THE GENERATIONS OF CAIN AND THE GENERATIONS OF THE GODLY.

A. The Posterity of Cain in General.

V. 17. *And Cain knew his wife; and she conceived, and bare Enoch: and he builded a city, and called the name of the city, after the name of his son, Enoch.*

245. It is worthy of admiration that Moses describes the generation of the sons of Cain before the generation of the sons of God. But all this is done according to the fixed counsel of God. For the children of this world have in this life and in this their generation the advantage of the children of God (Lk 16, 8) with reference to the first promise. The spiritual seed of the woman indeed possess the spiritual blessing, but the seed of the serpent arrogate to themselves the corporal, or temporal, blessing, and they bruise the heel of the blessed seed. In this respect the temporal has precedence over the spiritual.

246. But a great difference comes to the surface at a later day. Although Moses records the history of the posterity of Cain before the posterity of the righteous, yet we afterwards see that the latter are more especially the care of the Holy Spirit. He does not confine himself to a bare registration of their names, but he carefully numbers their years, makes mention of their death, and not only chronicles their own doings, as he chronicles in this passage those of the sons of Cain, but also the transactions and the conversations which Jehovah had with them, the promises he made, the help rendered in danger, and the blessings vouchsafed.

247. None of these things are recorded of the wicked posterity of Cain. When Moses has said that Cain begat a son named Enoch, and that he built a city to which he gave the name of his son, calling it Enoch, the sacred historian immediately cuts off the memory of Cain altogether and, as it were, buries him forever with these few short words of record. He seems to entertain no further care or concern for either his life or his death. He merely records temporal blessings — that he begat a son and that he built a city. For as the gift of reproduction was not taken

away from the murderer Cain, neither was the gift of dominion taken from him. But he lost all the rich blessings of the earth because it had drunk the blood of his brother, as we have shown above.

248. The Holy Spirit records these things in order that we may see that there was, from the very beginning, two churches: one the church of the sons of Satan and of the flesh, which often makes sudden and great increase; and the other the church of the sons of God, which is usually weak and makes slow progress. Although the Scriptures do not relate how these two churches lived together in the beginning, yet, as it was declared by God to Satan, "I will put enmity between thy seed and her seed," it is certain that the church of Cain was ever hostile to the Church of Adam. And the present text fully shows that the sons of men so increased and prevailed that they almost completely perverted and destroyed the Church of the sons of God. For in the great flood, only eight souls of them were saved; all the rest of the human race perished in the waters on account of their sin.

249. And this is a calamity of the true Church, common to all ages: as soon as she begins to increase, she is compelled to oppose with all her might Satan and the ungodly. She is at length tired out by the wickedness of her enemy, and is then either obliged to yield to her enraged foe, overcome by the cross and its afflictions, or she sinks under the seductions of pleasures and riches. So it was with the posterity of Adam. Broken down, at length, under so long a war with the sons of men, they yielded, being reduced at last to eight souls only, who were saved. Ungodliness having so far prevailed, and the godly losing ground, the Lord at length interposes and saves the few righteous remaining; but all the rest, both the seduced and the seducers, he punishes, including them in the same judgment. And we hope and believe the Lord will do the same in the judgment at the last day.

250. Many questions arise here. Some inquire respecting the circumstances connected with the wife of Cain: at what time the murder was committed; whether Cain murdered his brother before he was a husband, or after he was married. And the Jews, moreover, say that Eve brought forth twins at every birth, a male and a female; and they assert that Cain married his sister Calmana, and Abel his sister Debora. Whether these things be true or not I cannot affirm. I know not. But they are not vital to the interests of the Church, and there is nothing certain known concerning them. This one thing is certain, that Cain had a sister for his wife. But whether or no he had her as his wife when he committed the murder, cannot with certainty be proven. However, the text before us greatly tends to the conclusion that Cain was married when he committed the murder of his brother; for it intimates that the inheritance was divided between the two brothers when it affirms that the care of the cattle was committed by the father to Abel and the tilling of the ground to Cain. I, therefore, am inclined to believe that both of the brothers were married.

251. This conclusion is favored also by the statement made above, that Cain and Abel "in the process of time" brought their offerings. This has been explained in the following manner: At the end of the year, the two newly married husbands brought as offerings the new fruits which God had given them in this first year of their marriage; Cain brought the first fruits of the earth, and Abel the first fruits

of his flock. And the time was probably the autumn of the year, the time when the fruits of the earth are gathered, the same season in which the Jews afterwards held the feast of expiation. Moses, in his Levitical law, seems carefully to have noted and collected the ancestral patterns, and to have reduced them to a code. When, therefore, the new husbands came to render their thanks to God for his blessings and to offer their gifts, and Abel's offering was accepted of God and not the offering of Cain, Cain's heart was immediately filled by Satan with hatred of his brother; and upon this hatred afterwards followed the horrible murder. This is the opinion of the Jews, which I thus relate because it does not appear to be at all far from the truth. But, as I have often said, the interpretations of the Jews are to be read with critical discrimination, so that in their teachings, we may retain the things consistent with the truth, but condemn and refute all fictions of their own making.

252. If Cain was not married when he slew his brother, it is still more wonderful that after such a wicked deed he obtained a wife at all; and certainly that damsel was worthy the highest praise who married such a man. For how could the maiden rejoice in a marriage with her brother who was a murderer, accursed and excommunicated? She, on her part, no doubt supplicated her father, and expostulated with him and asked how he could give her, an innocent one, in marriage to a man thus accursed, and force her into banishment with him. Nay, the very example of her brother's murder must have naturally filled her with terror, lest the crime which her husband committed on his brother he might also dare to commit on her, his sister and his wife.

253. In bringing about this marriage, Adam obviously had to exercise marvelous eloquence. It was for him to convince his daughter that the father's command was not to be disobeyed, and that while Cain, curse-ridden, would have to bear the penalty of his sin, God would still preserve and bless her, the innocent one.

Nor do I entertain the least doubt that God conferred many personal blessings upon Cain, down the whole line of his posterity, for the sake of his wife, who, from motives of faith toward God and of obedience toward her parents, had married her murderous brother.

As Christ was the minister of the circumcision for the truth of God, to establish the certainty of the promise made unto the Jewish fathers; and as, in the absence of a promise, he was the minister of the Gentiles, because of the mercy of God, (Rom 15, 8-9), so the like uncovenanted mercy was shown also to the posterity of Cain. These two opinions have been expressed concerning the marriage of Cain, but which is the truth I know not. If Cain was married after he committed the murder, his wife is most certainly worthy of all praise and of all fame, who could thus yield to the authority of her parents, and suffer herself to be joined in marriage with an accursed murderer.

254. To myself, the first opinion appears to be much nearer the truth, that he murdered his brother after his marriage with his sister; because we have so clear a testimony in the text concerning the division of the inheritance. And in that case, the necessity lay on the wife to follow her husband. As wife and husband are one

body and one flesh, Adam had no desire to separate them; moreover, the wife is bound to bear her part of the calamities of her husband. Just in the same manner as the posterity of Cain enjoyed a part of those blessings which were bestowed of God upon the innocent wife, Pharaoh, king of Egypt, was saved in the time of Joseph, and the King of Nineveh was saved in the time of his calamity, although neither of them belonged to the people of God. And so I also believe that some were saved out of the posterity of Cain, although Cain himself had utterly lost the promise concerning the blessed seed.

B. THE POSTERITY OF CAIN IN DETAIL.

II. IN DETAIL.

A. THE GENERATIONS OF CAIN.

* The names were given to the descendants of Cain, not by accident, but by special thought and with a definite meaning.

1. Of Enoch.

    a. The meaning of his name.

    b. Is the first in Cain's posterity and the beginning of the temporal blessing.

    * Why Cain built a city.

2. Irad and the meaning of his name. It was not given without a purpose.

3. Mehujael and the meaning of his name.

    * The means the false church uses to suppress the true Church.

4. Methushael and the meaning of his name.

5. Lamech.

    a. What his name signifies.

    * Cain's descendants persecute the true Church. Yet some of Cain's posterity were saved.

    b. The reason he took two wives.

    c. Who were his wives.

    d. His sons, Jabal, Jubal, Tubal-cain, and his daughter Naamah.

    * Why Moses mentions the various arts of Cain's descendants.

    * Whether poverty drove Cain's descendants to the arts.

    * As the false church was before the flood so is she still, and will remain so to the end of the world.

    * How the Cainites increased and oppressed the true Church.

    * Why the Scriptures do not mention that some of the Cainites were saved.

    e. Of his haughty speech, "I have slain a man etc."

(1) This is difficult to understand, and has been poorly treated by interpreters.

(2) The fable explanation of these words by the Jews refuted.

(3) How others explained them.

(4) Luther's understanding of them.

f. Whether Lamech slew Cain, and thereby made himself famous.

g. How he attempted to be ruler upon Adam's death.

* How the Church is oppressed from both sides.

* Why Moses mentions the blood descendants of Cain with such care.

h. Cain is not sorry for his deed, but even boasts of it.

* The nature of the Cain church.

i. How he seeks to avoid being slain by others.

* The pope has the conscience of Cain and Lamech.

j. He is a type of all the children of this world.

* How the devil drives the Cainites to rage against the Church under the guise of being holy.

* The true Church from the very beginning had to shed her blood.

* The tyranny of Popes Julius II and Clement VII.

* God at all times severely punished the persecutors of his Church.

k. How Lamech still wished to defend his deed.

l. He had no Word of God, but was filled with pride.

B. The Posterity of Cain in Detail.

255. As regards the names of Cain's offspring, I believe that, in common with those of the holy patriarchs, they indicate not an absence of purpose or a random selection, but a definite purpose and a prophecy. Thus "Adam" signifies a man of, or taken out of, the red earth. "Eve" signifies the mother of life, or of the living. "Cain" signifies possession. "Abel" signifies vanity. And we find that also among the Gentiles many names have such a significance; not seldom names are found which are truly prophetic. "Enoch" is a prophetic name, expressive of hope in the future as a relief to Cain's mind, or rather to his wife's, for it was the latter who called the son she bore Enoch, from the Hebrew *Hanach*, which signifies, "she dedicated," or "she devoted."

256. This is a word frequently used by Moses. As when he says, "What man is there that hath built a new house, and hath not dedicated it? let him go and return to his house, lest he die in the battle, and another man dedicate it," Deut 20, 5. The verb in this passage, which signifies originally to dedicate, here signifies to possess, or to enjoy; and when this possession or enjoyment begins, it is attended with happy signs and auspicious invocations. So when the wife of Cain brought forth her first son, she said to her husband, Enoch; that is, "Dedicate him, devote him:"

for the verb is in the imperative mood. As if Cain had said himself, May this our beginning be happy and prosperous. My father Adam cursed me on account of my sin. I am cast out of his sight. I live alone in the world. The earth does not yield me her strength; she would be more fruitful to me, had I not thus sinned. And yet God now shows me uncovenanted mercy in giving me this son. It is a good and happy beginning.

As in the generation of Cain the corporal blessings begin with Enoch, so it is another Enoch in the generation of the righteous under whom religion and spiritual blessings begin to flourish.

257. That which is added by Moses concerning the city Cain thus built belongs to history. But I have before observed that Cain, when separated from the true church and driven into banishment, hated the true church. When, therefore, Cain thus first built a city, that very act tended to show that he not only disregarded and hated the true Church, but wished also to oppose and oppress it. For he reflects thus: Behold I am cast out by my father and I am cursed by him, but my marriage is not a barren one; therefore I have in this the hope of a great posterity. What, therefore, is it to me that I am driven by my father from beneath his roof? I will build a city, in which I will gather a church for myself. Farewell, therefore, to my father and his church. I regard them not.

258. Accordingly, it is not through fear, or for defense, that Cain "built a city," but from the sure hope of prosperity and success, and from pride and the lust of dominion. For he had no need whatever to fear his father and mother, who at the divine command had thrust him out to go into some foreign land. Nor had he any more ground of fear from their children than from themselves. But Cain was inflated with pride through this uncovenanted mercy of God, as I have termed it; and, as the world ever does, he sought by means of his "city" an opportunity of emerging from his present state into future greatness. The sons of God, on the contrary, are only anxious about another city, "which hath foundations, whose builder and maker is God," as we have it described in the Epistles to the Hebrews 11, 10.

V. 18a. *And unto Enoch was born Irad.*

259. What opinion to form concerning this name, I really know not, for its origin is very obscure; and yet I believe the name is not accidental but prophetic. In the book of Joshua we have a city called Ai; and this same term is used elsewhere as an appellative. Now, the proper name Ai signifies, "a heap," as a heap of fallen buildings. And if with this name you compound the verb *Irad*, the word thus compounded will signify increase. Although the posterity of Cain, on account of their excommunication, were at that time like a great heap of ruins, it was his prayer that they might not altogether perish, but be preserved and greatly increased by means of this son Irad. If anyone can offer a better interpretation, I will by no means despise it; for on obscure points like the present, conjecture is quite allowable.

V. 18b. *And Irad begat Mehujael.*

260. This name is formed from the verb *mahah*, which signifies "to destroy," and from *jaal*, "he began," or "he attempted or dared." Accordingly this name sig-

nifies that the posterity of Cain should now enter upon so mighty an increase as to dare to set itself in array against the true Church and to despise it and persecute it; so mightily should it prevail by its wealth, wisdom, glory and numbers. These, indeed, are for the most part the influences through which the true Church is always overcome by the world and the false church.

V. 18c. *And Mehujael begat Methushael.*

261. *Meth* signifies "death," and *schaal* means "to ask," or "to demand." Hence we have the name Saul; that is, demanded. This name indicates a spirit haughtier than any of the others. I understand it to signify that Methushael threatens that he will avenge his parents, who are dead, whom the other church—that is the true Church—has punished with excommunication and exile.

V. 18d. *And Methushael begat Lamech.*

262. Hitherto the Cainites seem to have insulted the true Church with impunity and to have triumphed over them. But the name "Lamech" signifies that God, at the time in which Lamech was born, inflicted on the posterity of Cain their due punishment. The name Lamech is derived from the verb *makak*, which signifies to humble, to diminish, to suppress. Or, it may be understood actively, to mean that in the time of Lamech the posterity of Cain so greatly increased that the true Church was quite overwhelmed by them.

263. Such was the posterity of Cain; men, no doubt, renowned for their wisdom and greatness. And I also believe that some of them were saved by the uncovenanted mercy of God, as I have above explained. But far the greater part of them most bitterly hated and persecuted the true Church. They could not brook inferiority to the sons of Adam, the true Church; therefore they set up their own forms of worship, and introduced many other new things for the sake of suppressing the church of Adam. And because the false church was thus kept separate from the true Church, I believe that Cain married to each other his sons and daughters. Accordingly, about the time of Lamech, Cain's posterity began to multiply exceedingly. And it is for this reason, I believe, that Moses here terminates the list.

V. 19. *And Lamech took unto him two wives; the name of the one was Adah, and the name of the other Zillah.*

264. Here again a twofold question arises. In the first place divines dispute whether Lamech married these two wives on account of lustful passion or for some other cause. My belief is that polygamy was not entered into for the sake of lust, but with the object of increasing his family, and from the lust of dominion, and especially so if, as his name imports, the Lord at that time had been punishing the Cainites, or the posterity of Cain, by pestilence, or by some other calamity. In this case, Lamech probably thought by such expedient to retrieve his greatness. Thus barbarous nations retain polygamy to strengthen and establish both home and State.

265. As regards the names of these two wives, the name of one is Adah; that is, adorned, or, having chains on the neck. *Adi* signifies a neat, or elegant woman, and *adah*, the verb, signifies to adorn, or, to put on. And perhaps this name was

given to her, not only because she was the mistress of the house, elegantly adorned or clothed, but because she was also beautiful. The name of the other wife, Zillah, signifies, his shade.

V. 20. *And Adah bare Jabal; he was the father of such as dwell in tents and have cattle.*

266. The name Jabal is derived from the verb *jabal*, which signifies to bring forward, or to produce.

V. 21. *And his brother's name was Jubal; he was the father of all such as handle the harp and pipe.*

267. And the name Jubal has the same origin and signification; for it means produced, or introduced. Both these names, therefore, contain a wish or prayer of Lamech concerning the increase of his family. The posterity of Cain always entertained the object and expectation of surpassing in numbers. And, no doubt, the Cainites held up this temporal blessing in the face of the true Church as an evident proof that they were not cast off by God, but were the very people of God.

V. 22. *And Zillah, she also bare Tubal-cain, the forger of every cutting instrument of (an artificer in every workmanship of) brass and iron; and the sister of Tubal-cain was Naamah.*

268. Tubal-cain signifies, produce property. So the Romans gave such names as "Valerius" (from valeo), and "Augustus" (from augeo). And Naamah received her name from her sweetness, or beauty. This posterity of Cain increased infinitely; hence Moses breaks off at this point.

269. Now, when he not only chronicles names but makes mention also of the deeds and labors of each one, the Jewish explanation is to be rejected that the offspring of Cain was compelled to follow other occupations because the earth was cursed, and hence gained their livelihood, one as a shepherd, another as a worker in brass, and another as a musician, obtaining grain and the other fruits of the earth from the offspring of Adam. But if the Cainites had been so severely pressed by hunger, they would have forgotten the harp, organ and other instruments of music in their extremity; for the enjoyment of music is not characteristic of the hungry and thirsty.

270. Their invention of music and their efforts in the discovery of other arts is proof that they had the necessaries of life in abundance. The reason, therefore, that the descendants of Cain turned to these pursuits and were not contented with the simple food the earth produced, like the descendants of Adam, was that they wished to rule, and aimed at the high praise and glory of being men of talent. I believe, however, that some of them passed over to the true Church and followed the religion of Adam.

271. And such as Moses here describes the generation of the wicked, or the false church, to be, from the beginning down to the mighty flood of waters, so we find it ever, and such it will remain until the final flood of fire. "The sons of this world are for their own generation wiser than the sons of the light," Lk 16, 8. Therefore it is that they ever advance and increase, and commend themselves and their own, and thus acquire riches, dignities and power; while the true Church, on

the other hand, always lies prostrate, despised, oppressed, excommunicated.

V. 23-24. *And Lamech said unto his wives: Adah and Zillah, hear my voice; ye wives of Lamech, hearken unto my speech: for I have slain a man for wounding me, and a young man for bruising me. If Cain shall be avenged sevenfold, truly Lamech seventy and sevenfold.*

272. Thus far Moses has given us a history of the generation of the children of this world, and having brought down the list to the time of Lamech and his wives and children, he buries them, as it were, altogether in silence, leaving them without any promise, either of the life which is to come or of the life that now is. For except that uncovenanted blessing of offspring and of food, the Cainites possessed nothing whatever. Yet they so increased in power and in multitude that they filled the whole world, and at length overturned and ravaged to such an extent the righteous nation of the children of God which possessed the promise of the future and eternal life, and sunk them into so deep a hell of wickedness, that eight men only remained to be saved when the flood came upon the whole world of the ungodly. And though there is no doubt that some of the generation of Cain were saved both before the flood and in the flood, yet the Scriptures do not mention them, to the end that we might the more fear God and walk according to his Word. But hard as the diamond are those human hearts which fail to be moved by such an example as the flood, than which nothing more dreadful is to be found in the whole chain of time.

273. Moses, therefore, having buried in silence the entire generation of Cain, records only one unimportant fact respecting Lamech, but what the real import of that fact is, Moses does not explain. I know not that any other passage in the Holy Scriptures has been so diversely interpreted, and so rent and wrested, as this text. For ignorance at least, if eloquence is not, is fruitful of surmises, errors and fables. I will mention some of the vulgar views upon the passage now before us.

274. The Jews compose the fable that Lamech, when he had grown old and was blind, was led by a youth into the woods to hunt wild beasts, not for the sake of their flesh but for their skins; circumstances which are altogether absurd, and at once prove the whole fable to be a lie. And they hold that Cain was there, concealed among the bushes, and in that solitude he not only exercised repentance but sought security for his life. The young man who directed the spear for Lamech, thinking he saw a wild beast in a certain thicket, told Lamech to hurl his spear, and Lamech hurled his spear and, contrary to all thought, pierced Cain. And they add that after Lamech had been made conscious of the murder he had committed, he immediately speared the youth himself, who also died under the wound he received. It was thus, say the Jews, that the "man" and the "young man" were slain by Lamech. But such absurdities as these are utterly unworthy of refutation. Indeed, Moses himself completely refutes them; he records the fact that Cain, far from fleeing into solitude and concealment, "built a city," which implies that he governed a State and thereby established for himself a kind of kingdom. Moreover, the ages of Cain and Lamech would not accord with this explanation, for it is not at all probable Cain lived to the time Lamech became old and blind.

275. There is still another Jewish invention. After Lamech had killed Cain, his wives would no longer live with him, through fear of the punishment they foreboded would come upon him, and therefore Lamech, to comfort himself and to induce his wives to live with him, prophesied that whosoever should kill him would assuredly be punished "seventy and sevenfold." The Jews invent like absurdities also concerning the sons of Lamech, whom they say he taught to fabricate arms for the destruction of men. Other commentators, again, will have it that the sense of this text is to be taken negatively, thus: If I had killed a man, as Cain killed his brother, I should have been worthy of your reprobation.

276. My interpretation, accordingly, is that the words, "If Cain shall be avenged sevenfold," etc., are not to be taken for the Word of God. For that generation did not have the Word; how, then, could Lamech be believed to have been a prophet? Thus, even such a man as Jerome produces the vagary that, inasmuch as, according to Luke, seventy-seven generations can be counted between Adam and Christ, it was after this space of time that Lamech's sin was taken away by Christ. If such vaporings are legitimate, anything can be proved from the Scriptures. Jerome even forgets that Lamech represented the seventh generation from Adam! The word under consideration then, is not to be placed upon the same level with the former, spoken to Cain; for that was the Word of God. It is, on the contrary, the word of a wicked murderer; not true, but an audacious fiction, based upon that spoken by Adam to Cain. But why does he deliver his discourse not before his church but at home, and only before his wives?

277. It is probable that the good and pious women were greatly alarmed on account of the murder committed by their husband. The wicked murderer, therefore, to appear equally safe with Cain, endeavored in this way to reassure his wives concerning his safety from death. This is what the wicked church is accustomed to do; it prophesies out of its own head. But all such prophecies are vain. This one thing, however, we can gather from the present text, that Lamech did not utter the contents of his prophecy from the Word of God, but out of his own brain.

278. In respect to Cain, I do not think that he was killed by Lamech, but that he died long before the time of Lamech. And as there were continual animosities between the Cainite church and the Church of Adam—for the Cainites could not brook their being treated as outside of the true communion—my opinion is, that Lamech killed some eminent man and some distinguished youth of the generation of the righteous, just as Cain, his father, had killed Abel. And I believe that, having committed such murders, he wished to protect himself from being killed by uttering the words of the text, after the manner of the protection vouchsafed by God to his father Cain. For Lamech was no doubt a man of very great abilities and the chief man in his day and State. He had also strengthened his cause by a novel venture, for he was the first man who married two wives. And he harassed the Church of the godly in various ways, as men are wont to do who combine talent with malice. Therefore he furnished his men with arms, riches, and pleasures, that he might overcome the true Church on every side, which alone held the holy faith, the pure Word, and the pure worship of God. To all else he paid little attention.

279. It is very probable that the patriarch Adam died about this time, this being

the first patriarchal death; and there is no doubt that Lamech seized this opportunity of transferring the whole government of the world at that time to himself, that he might have all things under his own rule. This is the manner in which the world acts to this day. The Church of God, therefore, placed as it were in the midst, is oppressed on either side; by tyrants and blood-thirsty men on the one hand, and by those who are devoted to the concerns and pleasures of this world on the other. As tyrants use violence and the sword to destroy the Church, so the latter entice her by their allurements.

280. Hence it is that Moses makes a special point of recording that the blood-thirsty seed of the Cainites gave themselves up to pleasures and to other worldly pursuits. And hence it is, also, that Christ expressly shows that much blood was shed even before the flood, by testifying "that upon you may come all the righteous blood shed on the earth, from the blood of Abel the righteous unto the blood of Zachariah son of Barachiah, whom ye slew between the sanctuary and the altar," Mt 23, 35. Moses testifies subsequently (Gen 6, 1-13), that the earth before the flood was filled with iniquities; and he is not speaking of the iniquities and violent deeds of thieves and adulterers, but describes particularly the tyranny of the Cainite church, which pursued with all the violence of the sword the holy posterity of Adam. And it is for this same reason that the sacred historian describes the descendants of Cain by the name "giants." These are the reasons which lead me to conclude that Lamech followed in the footsteps of his father Cain and slew some distinguished man of the holy patriarchs and his son.

281. It was certainly an evidence of the greatest tyranny in Lamech, that, when he had been discovered by his wives, he did not grieve for what he had done, but held in contempt the punishment which he had just cause to dread. As if he had said: I have killed a man 'tis true, but what is that to you? The wound of that belongs to me; I shall be wounded for it, not you. I have indeed killed a young man, but it is to my own hurt. I shall be punished for it, not you. What utterances could evince more contempt than these in the face of open sins?

These are my thoughts on the passage now before us. The text shows that the Cainites were tyrannical men, proud of their success, and given to pleasure; and the very words of Lamech prove him to be a proud man, not grieving at all for the murder he had committed, but glorying in it as in a righteous cause. The Cainite church always excuses that tyranny which it exercises over the godly, as Christ says: "Whosoever killeth you shall think that he offereth service unto God," Jn 16, 2. This is expressed in the additional words of Lamech:

V. 24. *If Cain shall he avenged sevenfold, truly Lamech seventy and sevenfold.*

282. Here Lamech sets himself above his father Cain, making it appear that he had a more righteous cause for the murder he had committed, and fortifying himself against those inclined to avenge the murders perpetrated by him. For the words of the text are not the words of the Lord, as we have said, but the words of Lamech himself. Just so the pope fortifies himself by violence, tyranny, threats and anathemas, to make himself secure against avengers, for he has the conscience of a Cain and a Lamech. Let him, says the pope, who shall do anything contrary to

these my decrees know that he shall incur the indignation of St. Peter and St. Paul.

283. Lamech, therefore, is an example of this world, and Moses points to him to show what kind of a heart, will and wisdom the world has. Just as if he had said in reference to Lamech: Such are the actions of the seed of the serpent and such are the children of this world. They gather riches, follow their pleasures, increase their power, and then abuse all these things by their tyranny, making use of them against the true Church, the members of which they persecute and slay. And yet in the midst of all these mighty sins, they fear not, but are proud and secure, boasting and saying, "What can the righteous do?" (Ps 11, 3): "Our lips are our own: who is lord over us?" (Ps 12, 4): "He (the wicked) saith in his heart: God hath forgotten, he hideth his face, he will never see it," (Ps 10, 11): and other like sentiments.

284. That such is the meaning of the passage in question the facts recorded prove, though the words of the text do not so clearly express that meaning. The true Church has ever Satan as its great enemy, and he drives the Cainites into fury, disguised as devotion, against their brethren, the Abels; as Christ also says, affirming that the devil was a murderer from the beginning, Jn 8, 44. It is declared throughout the Scriptures concerning the true Church, that the wicked are ever shedding its blood. The various passages in the Psalms speak the same things, "Precious shall their blood be in his sight," Ps 72, 14. Again, "Precious in the sight of Jehovah is the death of his saints" Ps 116, 15. And again, "For thy sake are we killed all the day long" Ps 44, 22.

285. As, therefore, the Church of God has at all times, and in all ages, given her blood to be shed by the wicked and by false brethren, so also, in that first age of the world she had to suffer from her enemies, whom the Scriptures call "giants," and affirm that those "giants" filled the earth with "violence." Among these giants was also this Lamech now before us, who was one perhaps like Pope Julius II or Clement VII who although they exercised cruelty in the highest degree, yet wished to be called and appear as most holy saints. Just so Lamech here wishes to make it appear that he had a most righteous cause for the murder he had committed, and therefore he threatened greater vengeance on the man who should kill him than God himself had threatened on the person who should slay his father, the murderer Cain.

286. In this manner, the Church was vexed with the cross and with persecutions from the very beginning of the world until God, compelled by the wickedness of man, destroyed the whole world by the flood. Just so, also, when the measure of Pharaoh's malice was full he was drowned with all his host in the Red Sea. Just so, again, when the measure of the malice of the Gentile nations was full they were all uprooted and destroyed by Moses and Joshua. In the same manner afterwards when the Jews raged against the Gospel they were so utterly destroyed that not one stone was left upon another in Jerusalem. Other instances are the Babylonians, the Medes, the Persians, the Grecians, and the Romans.

287. The Scriptures therefore do not record whom Lamech killed. They only record that two murders were committed by him, and that Lamech, in his impenitence, wished to protect himself in the same manner as his father Cain had been

divinely protected, by issuing his proclamation, thereby making it appear that he had righteous cause for the murder he committed. And if this interpretation be not the true one, it is at least certain that the generation of the Cainites was a blood-thirsty generation, and hated and persecuted the true Church.

288. And it is, moreover, true that Lamech had not the Word, and that, accordingly, his utterance is not to be considered in the same light as that word which was spoken to his father Cain; for the latter was the voice of truth, but the word of Lamech was the voice of his own pride, expressive of the rule of Satan and of a church of hypocrites, which sins securely and yet glories in its sins as if they were deeds of righteousness.

C. THE POSTERITY OF THE RIGHTEOUS IN DETAIL.

B. THE GENERATIONS OF THE RIGHTEOUS.

1. Of Seth.
    a. Why Seth is described in detail.
    b. Why Eve at Seth's birth recalled Cain's murder.
    *   How and why the first parents after Abel's death refrained from bearing children.
    c. Seth's birth was announced before in a special way by God.
    *   The uncovenanted grace of the Cainites. Also, why God did not mention that some of them would be saved.
    d. How Eve manifested special faith and obedience in Seth's birth.
    *   Why the Romish church never canonized Eve.
    *   The idle fables of the Jews about Lamech and his wives, and about Adam's abstinence and Cain's increase, are to be rejected.
    e. A new generation springs from Seth, in which the promise shall be fulfilled.

2. Of Enoch.
    a. What his name means, and why it was given to him.
    *   The names of the holy patriarchs originated not by chance.
    b. How true worship began under Enoch.
    *   Of true worship.
        (1) In what it consists.
        (2) Why it was not in use before.
            *   The meaning of "the name of Jehovah" or the proclaiming of the name of Jehovah.
        (3) The right course to take in the doctrine concerning divine worship.
            *   God always ministered comfort to his Church under the cross.
        (4) What is the true worship according to the first table of the law.

(5) How true worship according to the second table follows from the first.

(6) People are to be instructed first and chiefly in the worship of the first table.

(7) Whether visible signs were present in these days in their worship, and to what end they were necessary.

(8) The worship of which Moses speaks is to be understood not of the Cainites but of Seth's posterity.

* A summary review of the contents of the fourth chapter of Genesis.

* Why the fifth chapter was written.

* Why the Jews cannot see the unity in the first five chapters of the Bible.

C. The Posterity of the Righteous in Detail.

V. 25. *And Adam knew his wife again; and she bare a son, and called his name Seth: For, said she, God hath appointed me another seed instead of Abel; for Cain slew him.*

289. Hitherto Moses has spoken of the generation of the wicked only, the whole of which he buries as it were with the above brief catalog. The historian now turns to the description of the godly and of the true Church. And first of all, we are to observe the manner of expression Moses uses in reference to the name given by Eve to her son: "And she called his name Seth." Moses does not speak thus concerning Cain when he was born, nor concerning righteous Abel, nor with reference to Enoch, nor with reference to any of the others. By this particular expression regarding Seth and his name Moses would signify that this was the first son in whom flowed the stream of the promise which had been made to the parents in paradise. So Eve is to be understood when she assigns the reason for giving her son this name. Eve manifests her surpassing godliness and faith in giving her son such a name.

290. The fact that Eve recalls the murder by wicked Cain of his brother Abel proves that there had existed a fierce enmity between these two churches, and that she had witnessed and suffered many evils and indignities from the Cainites. Because of this she now called to mind the awful murder which had been committed, whereby Cain wished to destroy the righteous seed that he might reign alone. But thanks be to God, says she, who hath appointed me another seed instead of Abel.

291. Moses here, as is his usual manner, embraces in the fewest possible words the mightiest things, that he may incite the reader to the most diligent consideration of the works of God. Of the pain and righteous grief of the parents at the murder of Abel by his brother we have spoken before. I see no reason why we should not believe that after the perpetration of that horrible murder no son was born to Adam until the birth of Seth; for it is most probable that the awful peril of a recurrence of a calamity like that which they had just experienced, induced the godly parents to abstain from connubial intercourse. I believe, therefore, that by a particular promise made to them by an angel, their minds were again comforted and confirmed, and that they were influenced to believe that a son of the descrip-

tion of Seth would now be born unto them, who should hold fast the promise; and that, although the generation of Cain should utterly perish by their sin, the generation of him about to be born should be preserved until the promised blessed seed should come into the world.

292. It is a proof of some like particular promise having been revealed to the parents by an angel that Eve adds to the name she gave to her son a kind of short sermon, and that Moses when recording this circumstance makes use of an expression not otherwise adopted by him in connection with the names Adam or Eve gave to their children: "And she called his name Seth." Seth is derived from the Hebrew verb *sath*, which signifies he placed, or he established, and was intended to show that this son would be, as it were, the foundation on which the promise concerning Christ would rest, even though many other sons should be born unto the parents. Eve does not give him an exalted name, such as "Cain," yet she gives him a name signifying that the posterity of Seth should never be suppressed or destroyed.

293. The Cainites, cast out from the sight of their parents, are left under a curse, without any promise whatever, and have only so much mercy as they receive from the generation of the righteous as beggars, not as heirs. This is the mercy we above called uncovenanted mercy. But who, of the posterity of the Cainites, obtained that mercy, Moses does not mention, and his design in this omission is to keep separate the two churches: the one the Church of the righteous, which had the promise of a life to come, but in this life was poor and afflicted; the other the church of the wicked, which in this life is rich and flourishing.

294. Eve, the mother of us all, is highly to be praised, as a most holy woman, full of faith and charity, because in the person of her son Seth she so nobly lauds the true Church, paying no regard whatever to the generation of the Cainites. For she does not say, I have gotten another son in the place of Cain. She prefers the slain Abel to Cain, though Cain was the first-born. Herein praise is due, not only to her faith but to her eminent obedience; for she is not only not offended at the judgment of God concerning righteous Abel, but she also changes her own judgment concerning God. When Abel was born she despised him, and magnified Cain as the first-born, and as the possessor, as she thought, of the promise. But now she acts in all things quite the contrary. As if she had said: After God's acceptance of him and of his offering, I had placed all my hopes on my son Abel, because he was righteous; but his wicked brother slew him. But now God hath appointed me another seed instead of Abel.

295. She does not indulge her maternal affection for Cain. She does not excuse or lessen the sin of her son. But she herself excommunicates him, already excommunicated of God; and she banishes him, together with all his posterity, among the polluted mass of the Gentiles who live without any sure mercy of God, laying hold only as they can of that uncovenanted mercy which, as we have said, they receive as beggars, not as heirs.

296. It is a great marvel, surely, that the church of the pope, having made up so great a list of saints, has not yet inserted in that catalog Saint Eve, a woman full

of faith and love, and with an infinite number of crosses! But perhaps we are to gather from this omission that it would rather follow the church of the Cainites than the holy Church.

297. I am inclined to say nothing here about that absurd and idle fable of the Jews, that Lamech brought his disobedient wives to Adam as judge, and that when Adam commanded them to render to their husband due benevolence the wives in reply asked Adam why he did not do the same to Eve. These fablers say that Adam, who had refrained from the bed of his wife from the murder of Abel to that time, again lived with her as man and wife, in order that he might not by his example induce others to maintain perpetual continence, and thus prevent mankind from being multiplied. All these fables show how impure the thoughts of the Jews were. Of the same description is the like argument of these Jews, who hold that when Seth was born, which was within a hundred years after the death of Abel, the children of Cain had increased unto the seventh generation. Such absurdities do wicked men invent to bring reproach upon the Holy Scriptures. And of precisely the same description is the opinion that Cain was born in paradise, while, as yet, the original righteousness of his parents remained. What is the object of this lying invention but to cause us to do away with Christ altogether? For take away original sin, and what need is there of Christ at all? These things are indeed, as we have intimated, unworthy of being mentioned here. But they are worthy the enemies of Christ and the enemies of grace.

298. In Seth, therefore, we have a new generation, which arises from and comes to pass in accordance with the great original promise, that the seed of the woman should bruise the serpent's head. Appropriately the name Seth is bestowed, so that Eve may felicitate herself upon the fact that this seed is established, safe from overthrow. David uses the same verb: "If the foundations be destroyed, what can the righteous do?" Ps 11, 3. And the Hebrew word forms a perfect rhyme with its German equivalent: "Seth—steht."

V. 26a. *And to Seth, to him also there was born a son; and he called his name Enosh.*

299. The verb *yikra*, he called, is in the masculine gender, by which you are to understand that it was the father who gave this name to his son. In the former case the verb was feminine, because Eve gave to her son Seth his name. The expression in each case is different, which difference of gender in a verb the Latin language does not indicate.

Enosh signifies a man afflicted or full of calamity. "What is man that thou art mindful of him," Ps 8, 4. Seth, accordingly, intimates that at that time there was some persecution or affliction of the Church. That "old serpent," who had cast man out of paradise and had killed Abel, the man beloved of God, was neither asleep nor idle. Therefore, upon the consolation enjoyed in the birth of Seth there soon follows another trial or tribulation, which the godly parents Adam and Eve signalize by giving the name Enosh to their son. The names thus given are by no means to be considered accidental. They were either prophetical or commemorative of some particular event.

V. 26b. *Then began men to call upon the name of Jehovah.*

300. The rabbins understand this as having reference to idolatry. They think that about this time the name of Jehovah began to be given to creatures: to the sun, the moon, etc. But Moses is not here speaking of what the generation of Cainites did, but what the godly generation of Adam did. The sacred historian is testifying that after the birth of Enosh there began the true worship of God, the calling upon the name of Jehovah.

301. Here Moses most beautifully defines what it is to worship God, to call upon the name of Jehovah; which is, as it were, the work of the first table and concerns the true worship of God. Now, calling upon the name of Jehovah embraces the preaching of the Word, faith, or confidence in God, confession, etc. Paul beautifully joins these things together in the fourteenth verse of the tenth chapter of his Epistle to the Romans. True, the works of the second table also belong to the worship of God, but these works do not refer directly and only to God as do the works of the first table.

302. After the confusion made in the house of Adam by Cain, the generation of the godly began to multiply by degrees and a little Church was formed, in which Adam as the high priest governed all things by the Word and by sound doctrine. Moses here affirms that this took place about the time of the birth of Enosh. Although this name implies that the Church had been overwhelmed by some terrible disaster, yet God raised her up again by his grace and mercy, and added the great spiritual blessing of godly assemblage in a particular place, with preaching, prayer and the offering of sacrifices, blessings which had hitherto perhaps been either hindered or forbidden by the Cainites. We have here, then, another evidence of the promised seed warring with the serpent and bruising its head.

303. Furthermore, as Moses does not say: Jehovah began to be called upon, but the name of Jehovah, the reference to Christ recommends itself to our approval, since also in other passages the Schem Jehovah (the name of Jehovah) is so to be understood. This expression, "then men began to call upon the name of Jehovah," contains a meaning most important. It signifies that Adam, Seth, and Enosh taught and exhorted their posterity to expect redemption and to believe the promise concerning the seed of the woman, and to overcome by that hope the snares, the crosses, the persecutions, the hatred and the violence of the Cainites, and not to despair of salvation, but rather to give thanks unto God, assured that he would at some time deliver them by the seed of the woman.

304. What could Adam and Seth teach greater or better than that the great deliverer, Christ, was promised to their posterity? And this is quite in keeping with the proper principle to be observed in religious instruction. The first care should ever be directed to the first table. When this table is well understood, the right understanding of the second table will soon follow; yea, it is then easy to fulfil the latter. For how is it possible that, where pure doctrine is taught, where men rightly believe, rightly call upon the name of Jehovah, and rightly give thanks unto God, the second and inferior fruits can be wanting?

305. In this manner did it please God at that time to comfort the afflicted church of the godly and to prevent their despair concerning the future. We see throughout

the pages of sacred history a perpetual succession and change of consolations and afflictions. Joseph in Egypt keeps alive his parents and his brethren when divinely visited by famine. After this, when these people were oppressed by wicked kings, they were again delivered from their cruel bondage. And Cyrus delivers them when captives in Babylon. When God permits his own people to be oppressed by the violence and guile of the devil and the world, he always lifts them up again and gives them prophets and godly teachers to restore his sinking church, and to break for a while the fury of Satan.

306. Furthermore, it is the intention to lay down a logical definition when it is claimed that the worship of God does not consist in ceremonies devised and transmitted by men, in the erection of statues, or the performance of other sport suggested by reason, but in calling upon the name of Jehovah. Worship in its truest meaning, well-pleasing to God, and subsequently made mandatory in the first commandment, embraces the fear of God, trust in God, confession, prayer and preaching.

307. The first commandment of the Law demands faith, that we believe God is the only helper in time of need, Ps 9, 9. The second commandment demands confession and prayer, that we call upon the name of Jehovah in times of peril and give thanks unto God. The third commandment requires that we teach the truth, and that we guard and defend sound doctrine.

These are the true and appropriate acts of the worship of God, and they are those which God requires. He requires not sacrifices nor money nor anything of the kind. As regards the first table, he requires that we hear, consider and teach the Word; that we pray to God and fear him.

308. Where these things exist, the observances and works required by the second table follow, as it were, of their own accord. It is impossible that he who does the works and performs the worship of the first table should not do and perform those of the second table also. David saith: "His delight is in the law of Jehovah; and on his law doth he meditate day and night. And he shall be like a tree planted by the stream of water; that bringeth forth its fruit in its season, whose leaf also doth not wither." Ps 1, 2-3. These things are evident consequences of the right worship of God, according to the commandments of the first table. He who believes God, who fears God, who calls upon God in tribulation, who praises God and gives thanks unto him for his mercies, who gladly hears the Word of God, who continually contemplates the works of God, and who teaches others to do the same things—do you think that such a one will harm his neighbor, or disobey his parents, or kill, or commit adultery?

309. The first table, therefore, is to be set forth first of all, and instruction as regards the true worship is to receive precedence to all else. This means, first to make the tree good on which good fruit is to grow. Now, our adversaries take the diametrically opposite course; they want to have the good fruit before they have even the tree.

310. Moreover, I believe that about this time there was added some visible ceremony of divine worship, for God is ever wont thus to do. He always joins

with the Word some visible sign. When Abel and Cain presented their offerings God showed by a visible sign from heaven that he had respect unto Abel and his offering, but not unto Cain and his offering. And so, in all probability, it was in this case and at this time. When the Church began to flourish and the Word of God was publicly taught with considerable success, God added also some visible sign, that the Church might assuredly know that she pleased God.

311. But whatever that sign was, whether fire from heaven or something else, God withheld it until the third generation, that men might learn to be content with the Word alone. Afterwards, when men had comforted themselves by the Word alone against the Cainites, in all tribulations, God of his great mercy added to the Word some visible sign. He established a place and appointed persons and ceremonies to which the Church might gather for the exercise of faith, for preaching and prayer. By means of these things, the Word or the first table and then a visible sign ordained of God, a Church is constituted, in which men undergo discipline through teaching, hearing, and the partaking of the sacraments. Then upon these things will assuredly follow the works of the second table, which are acceptable, and acts of worship, only on the part of those who possess and practice the first table.

312. This gift of God, Moses sets forth in the few short words of the text before us, when he says, "Then began men to call upon the name of Jehovah." For this beginning to call upon the name of Jehovah was not on the part of the Cainites, as the Jews explained the passage, but on the part of the godly posterity of Adam, which alone was then the true Church. If any of the posterity of Cain were saved, it must of necessity have been by joining this Church.

313. The sum of the first four chapters of Genesis is that we are to believe in a resurrection of the dead after this life, and a life eternal through the Seed of the woman. This is the blessed portion of the godly, of them that believe, who in this life are filled with afflictions and subject to injuries at the hands of all men. To the wicked, on the contrary, are given, as their portion, the riches and power of this world, which they use against the true Church of God.

In the first chapter it is shown that man was created unto immortality, because he was created "in the image of God."

The teaching also of the second chapter sets forth the same thing, "In the day that thou eatest thereof, thou shalt surely die." It follows that the first created man and woman could not have died if they had not eaten of that fruit. By their sin of eating they fell from immortality to mortality, and they begat an offspring like unto themselves.

In the third chapter immortality is set forth anew, as restored by the promise of the Seed of the woman.

In the fourth chapter we have an especial example of immortality set before us in Abel, who, after he had been slain by his brother, was received into the bosom of God, who testified that the voice of the blood of Abel cried unto him from the ground.

314. And the fifth chapter, which now follows, is expressly written to set forth the immortality of Enoch, who was taken up into heaven by the Lord. Although the following chapter is necessary as a chronicle of the number of the years of the generation of the righteous, yet its most remarkable feature is its record that Enoch did not die like Adam, nor was slain like Abel, nor carried away, nor torn to pieces by lions and bears, but was taken up into heaven and translated into immortality by the Lord himself; all which was written that we might believe in the Seed of the woman, Christ our Redeemer and Satan's conqueror, and that through him we also might expect a life immortal after this mortal and afflicted life.

315. This harmony of these five chapters the Jews see not, for they are destitute of that sun which sheds light upon these things and makes them manifest; which sun is Christ, by whom we have the remission of sins and life immortal.

CHAPTER V.

I. THE BOOK OF THE FIRST GENERATIONS OF MAN, AND THE GLORY OF THE CAINITES.

A. THE BOOK OF THE FIRST GENERATIONS OF MAN.

1. The reasons why Moses records the generations of Adam.
2. Why he so particularly gives the years, and in the case of each patriarch adds "and he died".
3. Why Enoch is placed in the records of the dead.
 * Was Enoch a sinner, and do sinners have hope of eternal life.
 * Of death.
    a. How we are to comfort ourselves against death.
    b. How reason views death, and how the best heathen philosophers viewed it.
    c. The knowledge the Scriptures give us of death.
4. How we may be greatly profited by the book of the generations of the ancient world.
5. Why the book of the generations of Cain is larger than that of Seth's.
 * How terrible that both lines were totally destroyed, except eight persons.
6. The aim of Moses in writing this book of the generations of Adam.
 * The glory of the first world.
    a. What was this glory.
    b. Why this glory was revealed.
    c. Profitable and interesting to meditate upon it.
    d. The patriarchs of the first world the most holy of all martyrs.

B. THE GLORY OF THE CAINITES.

1. The Cainites greatly tormented God's Church, especially after Adam's death.
2. To what end their hatred and persecution served the holy patriarchs.
 * Why Moses did not record the zeal of the holy fathers against the Cainites.
 * Why Moses gives such a short description of the deluge.
 * The character of the first world.

* Luther's lamentation over the character of the last world; its approaching destruction, and an earnest prayer to God.

I. THE RECORDS OF THE GENERATIONS OF MAN AND THE GLORY OF THE CAINITES.

A. *The Records of the Generations of Man.*

V. 1. *This is the book of the generations of Adam.*

1. This chronicle has been arranged by Moses for two reasons. First, on account of the promise of the seed made to Adam; and second, on account of Enoch. Moses writes still another genealogy in the tenth chapter, after the flood, from a far different motive than the present. In the present chapter, he gives the number of the years of the righteous and adds with a special purpose in the case of each one, the words, "and he died."

2. This little phrase may at first thought appear superfluous. After the historian has said, "All the days that Adam lived were nine hundred and thirty years," what seems to be the use of his adding the few words, "and he died"? The statement as to the number of his years connotes also the time of his death; for had he lived longer, the additional years would have been contained in the enumeration.

Moses, however, does this with the definite purpose of pointing out the unspeakable wrath of God against sin, and the inevitable punishment of it, inflicted by him on the whole human race, on the righteous as well as on the wicked. So does the Apostle Paul pursue his argument, drawn from this very portion of the Holy Scripture: "As through one man sin entered into the world, and death through sin; and so death passed upon all men, for that all sinned," Rom 5, 12. This is a consequence perpetuated through all generations. Adam died, therefore Adam was a sinner. Seth died, therefore Seth was a sinner. Infants die, therefore infants partake of sin and so are sinners. This is what Moses intends to set forth when he says, concerning the whole line of patriarchs, that, though they were all sanctified and renewed by faith, yet, "they died!"

3. Nevertheless, from this line of the dying there flames starlike a most lovely light of immortality when Moses here records concerning Enoch that "he was not;" that is, he no longer appeared among men, and yet he did not die but was taken up into heaven by the Lord himself. By this glorious fact is signified that the human race is indeed condemned to death on account of sin, and yet the hope of life and immortality is left us, that we need not abide in death forever.

4. For this cause God thought it needful, not only that the promise of life should be given to the original world, but that immortality should be demonstrated by an object lesson. Accordingly Moses said of each patriarch that he fulfilled so many years of life and "died": that is, suffered the punishment of sin, or, was a sinner. But the divine historian does not use these expressions concerning Enoch. Not because that patriarch was not a sinner, but because, even unto such sinners as he, there was left a hope of eternal life through the blessed seed. Therefore all the patriarchs, who died in the faith of this seed, held fast the hope of eternal life.

Enoch, therefore, is the second object lesson by which God makes it manifest that it is his will to give unto us life eternal after this life. The Lord says that Abel, who was killed by his brother, still lived, and that his voice cried from the ground. In the present instance, Enoch is taken up by the Lord himself into heaven.

5. We will not despair, therefore, though we see death, derived from Adam, extend to every one of the whole human race. We must, indeed, suffer death because we are sinners. But we shall not abide in death. We rather have a hope in a divine purpose and providence whereby God designs our deliverance from death. This deliverance has begun with the promise of the blessed seed, and has been demonstrated by Abel and Enoch as object lessons. Wherefore we possess the first fruits of immortality. The Apostle Paul says, "For in hope were we saved," Rom 8, 24. Hope saves us until the fullness of immortality shall be brought unto us at the last day, when we shall see and feel that eternal life which we possessed here in faith and hope.

6. Now, the flesh does not understand this. The flesh judges that man dies like a beast. Men, occupying the front rank of philosophers have felt accordingly that by death the soul is separated and delivered from the prison of the body, to mingle, free from all bodily infirmities, in the assembly of the gods. Such was the immortality dreamed of by the philosophers, though steadfastness of grasp and of vision was out of the question. The Holy Scriptures, however, teach differently concerning the resurrection and eternal life; they place this hope so plainly before our eyes as to leave no room for doubt.

7. Next in order, we find in this chapter a reflection of the condition of the primitive world. The ten antediluvian patriarchs belonging to the lineage of Christ, with their descendants, are enumerated. Nor is it a useless study to put these data before one's eyes on paper, according to the directions given by Moses, to see who the patriarchs were, who were their contemporaries, and how old they became, as I have taken the time to do. Cain also has his line, as Moses has shown in the preceding chapter, and I have no doubt that the posterity of Cain was far more numerous than that of righteous Seth.

8. From these two families, as from roots, was the world peopled, down to the deluge, in which both branches, with their two classes of descendants (that is, the posterity of the wicked and that of the righteous) were rooted out of the earth, eight souls only being left, and even among them one was wicked. Accordingly, as in this chapter a magnificent picture of the primeval world is presented to our view, so we behold also the incalculable wrath of God, and the horrible event of the reduction of the total offspring of these patriarchs to eight souls.

9. We will reserve this awful record for its proper time and place. Let us now do that which Moses does in the present chapter, who wants us to consider the exceeding splendor of this primeval age of the world. Adam lived beyond the age of his grandson Enoch, and died but a short time before Noah was born. A hundred and twenty years only intervened between the death of Adam and the birth of Noah. Seth died only fourteen years before Noah's birth. Enosh and the rest of the patriarchs, except Enoch, lived at the same time with Noah. Thus by a comparison

of the figures, we shall ascertain that quite a number of gray-headed patriarchs, of whom one lived seven hundred, and another nine hundred years, were contemporaries, and teaching and governing the Church of the godly.

10. The exceeding glory of the primitive world consists in this, that it contained so many good and wise and holy men. We are by no means to think that all these are merely common names of plain and simple men. They were the greatest heroes and men of renown that the world ever witnessed, next to Christ and John the Baptist. In the last day we shall behold and admire the real majesty of all these worthies, and then we shall truly behold the mighty deeds which these mighty men wrought. Yes, it will then be made manifest what Adam did, what Seth did, what Methuselah did, and the others; what they suffered from the old serpent; how they comforted and fortified themselves, by their hope in the promised seed, against all the harm and violence of the world, that is, of the Cainites; what craft they experienced; what injuries and hatred and contempt they bore for the glory of the blessed seed to be born from their lineage. We are assuredly not to imagine that these great and holy men lived without severe afflictions and innumerable crosses. All these things, I say, shall be revealed at the last day.

11. And it is an undertaking, as I said, full of profit and pleasure now to contemplate with our minds, as with open eyes, that happy age, in which so many patriarchs lived contemporaneously, nearly all of whom, except Noah, had seen and known their first father, Adam.

B. *The Glory of the Cainites.*

12. Also the Cainites had their glory. Among them were men most eminent in the liberal arts, and the most consummate hypocrites, who gave the true Church a world of trouble, and harassed the holy patriarchs in every possible way. We may justly call all those who were thus oppressed by them most holy martyrs and confessors. The Cainites, as Moses before intimated, very soon surpassed the other descendants of Adam in numbers and activity. Although they were compelled to revere their father Adam, yet they adopted all possible means of oppressing the Church of the godly, and especially so after the death of the first patriarch, Adam. By such wickedness, these Cainites helped to bring on the flood as retribution.

13. This power and malice of the Cainites caused the holy patriarchs to teach and instruct their Church with increased zeal and industry. What numerous and powerful sermons may we suppose were preached by them in the course of these most eventful years! There is no doubt that both Adam and Eve testified of their original state of innocence, described the glory of paradise and warned their posterity to beware of the serpent, who, by tempting them to sin, had caused all these great evils. How constant may we suppose them to have been in explaining the promise of the blessed seed! How earnestly must they have exhorted the hearts of their followers to be moved neither by the splendor of the Cainites nor by their own afflictions.

14. All these particulars Moses omits to record, both because they could not be described on account of their infinite variety of detail and because the revelation

of them is reserved for that great day of deliverance and glory!

15. Likewise the flood, in spite of its horror, is described with the greatest brevity because he wished to leave such things to the meditation of men.

16. For the same reasons Moses has purposely given us, in these first five chapters, as briefly as possible, a picture of the original and primeval world. It was an admirable condition of life, and yet that primeval age contained a multitude of the worst of men, in consequence not more than "eight souls" were saved from the destroying flood! What then, may we conclude, will be the state of things before the last day shall come, seeing that even now, under the revealed light of the Gospel, there is found so great a host of despisers of it that there is cause to fear that they will fill the world ere long with errors and prevail to the extinction of the Word altogether.

17. Awful is the voice of Christ when it utters the words, "Nevertheless, when the Son of man cometh, shall he find faith on the earth?" Lk 18, 8. And in Matthew 24, 37-38, our Lord compares the last days with the days of Noah. These utterances of our Lord are indeed most awful. But the world, in its security and ingratitude, is a despiser of all the threats as well as all the promises of God. It abounds in iniquities of every kind and becomes daily more corrupt. From the time that the popes ceased to rule among us, who had ruled the whole world by means of the mere dread of their vengeance, sound doctrine has been despised, and men have degenerated into all but brutes and beasts. The number of holy and godly preachers of the Word is becoming less and all men are indulging their desires. The last day, however, shall assuredly come upon the world as a thief, and will overtake these men in all their security, and in the indulgence of their ambition, tyranny, lust, avarice, and vices of every kind.

18. And let it be remembered that it is Christ himself who has foretold these things, and we can not possibly imagine that he would lie. If the primitive world, which contained so mighty a multitude of the greatest patriarchs, was so wholly corrupted, what may we not have cause to dread in the weakness of our nature? May the Lord our God grant that we may be gathered, as soon as possible, in the faith and confession of his Son Jesus Christ, unto these our fathers; yea, if it please him, that we may die within the next twenty years, and not live to see the miseries and calamities, both temporal and spiritual, of the last time! Amen!

II. ADAM AND HIS SON SETH.

1. The name Adam, and why given to the first man.

2. The Jews' fables of Adam's cohabitation with Eve.

  * Purity of doctrine cannot be expected from the Jews.

3. Why Moses so carefully describes the times of Adam.

4. Why it is said of Adam that he was created in the likeness of God.

  * The likeness of God.

    a. The difference between "Zelem" and "Demuth".

    b. How the likeness of God was lost and how it is restored.

    c. Whether it can be fully restored in this life.

5. The prating of the rabbins about the name Adam.

 * Why Moses here mentions the blessing.

 * Why he did not refer to the blessing in the descriptions of Cain and Abel.

6. How long it was before Adam begat Seth.

 * Abel's age when murdered.

7. How and why Adam mourned so long for his son Abel, and therefore refrained from bearing children.

8. The Jews' fable of Adam's vow of chastity refuted.

9. How we are to understand that Adam begat a son in his own likeness.

10. Whether Adam's son Seth had God's likeness.

11. How Adam acquired again the lost image.

12. How Seth secured the likeness of God.

13. Why Adam gave his son the name Seth; its meaning.

 * The long lives of the first men.

    a. Longevity a part of the happy state of the first world.

    b. The causes of such long lives.

   * Men's bodies were much stronger and healthier than ours.

    c. Whether the climate, food and holy living contributed to this end.

   * The creatures given to man for food after the flood were inferior to those before, and they injured the body more than nourished it.

    d. Luther's thoughts on this theme.

14. Which is the first or chief branch born from Adam and Eve.

15. How long Adam lived after Seth's birth.

 * The glory of the first world.

 * The histories of the first world were most excellent, but they were destroyed in the flood.

 * Eve's age and experiences.

 * The age of the first world is called the golden age.

II. ADAM AND HIS SON SETH.

    V. 1a. *This is the book of the generations of Adam.*

19. "Adam," as will be stated further on, is the common name of the whole human race, but it is applied to the first man more expressly as an appellation of dignity, because he was the source, as it were, of the whole human family. The Hebrew word *sepher*, "a book," is derived from *saphar*, which signifies "to narrate" or "to enumerate." Wherefore this narration or enumeration of the posterity of Adam

is called "the book of the generations of Adam."

V. 1b. *In the day that God created man, in the likeness of God made he him.*

20. This clause of the sacred text has induced the blind Jews to fable that Adam slept with Eve as his wife in paradise on the same day in which he was created, and that she conceived in that same day. Fables of this kind are numerous among them, nor may anything sound or pure in the matter of scriptural interpretation be expected of them.

21. The intent of Moses, in this clause, is to record the complete age of Adam, and to number the days of his life from the day of his creation, and, at the same time, to show that before Adam there was no generation. Generation is to be clearly distinguished from creation. There was no generation before Adam, but creation only. Adam and Eve were not born but created, and that directly by God himself. Moses adds, "In the likeness of God made he him." We are to understand, then, that when he afterwards mentions that Adam begat Seth, he numbers his years from the very day of his creation.

22. In respect to Adam's having been made in the likeness of God, we have shown above in its place what that "likeness" of God was. Although almost all commentators understand the expressions, "the likeness of God," and "the image of God," to mean one and the same thing, yet so far as I have been able from careful investigation to reach a conclusion, there is a difference between the two terms. *Zelem* properly signifies "an image," or "figure," as when the Scripture says, Ye shall break down their images, Ex. 23, 24, in which passage the original term signifies nothing more than the figures, or statues, or images erected by men. But *demuth* signifies "a likeness," or "the perfectness of an image." For instance, when we speak of a lifeless image, such as that which is impressed on coins, we say, This is the image of Brutus or of Cæsar. That image, however, does not reproduce the likeness, nor exhibit every single feature.

23. Accordingly, when Moses says that man was created also in the likeness of God, he points out that man resembles God not only in the possession of reason, or of intellect and will, but that he has also the likeness of God, that is, a will and an intellect, with which he knows God and wills what he wills.

24. If man, having been created both "in the image" and "in the likeness" of God, had not fallen, he would have lived forever, full of joy and gladness, and would have possessed a will joyfully eager to obey the will of God. But by sin both this "likeness" and this "image" were lost. They are, however, in a measure, restored by faith, as we are told by the apostle, Col 3, 10; Eph 4, 24. For we begin to know God, and the spirit of Christ helps us, so that we desire to obey the commandments of God.

25. Of these blessed gifts we possess only the first-fruits. This new creation within us is only as yet begun; it is not perfected here in the flesh. The will is in some measure stirred to praise God, to give him thanks, to confess sin, and to exercise patience, but all this is only the first-fruits. The flesh, obeying the law of its nature, still follows the things of the flesh, while it opposes the things of God. The result is that the restoration of such gifts in us is only in the initial stage; but the full

tithe of this likeness in all its perfection shall be rendered in the future life, when the sinful flesh shall have been destroyed by death.

V. 2. *Male and female created he them, and blessed them, and called their name Adam, in the day when they were created.*

26. I have above observed that the general name "Adam" was applied to Adam alone, by reason of his superiority. I omit to mention those vagaries of the rabbins, who say that no man can be called "Adam" unless he has a wife. Likewise, no woman can be called "Adam" unless married. The thought may have been drawn from the teachings of the fathers, but the Jews have corrupted it by their foolish fancies and opinions.

27. Moses aims to show this blessing was not taken from man because of his sin, since the blessing of bearing children and ruling them continued with Cain though he had murdered his brother.

28. Moses mentions not Abel, for he had died without an heir and is presented to us as an example of the resurrection of the dead. Neither is Cain mentioned, who because of his sin was cut off from the true Church.

29. Scripture says nothing of what Adam and Eve did during the one hundred years. Some of our writers add a hundred years longer Adam should have lived with Eve before Cain slew his brother Abel, which makes Adam two hundred and thirty years of age when Seth was born. It seems to me plausible that the godly parents passed one hundred years in sorrow and mourned the great dishonor that befell their family. After Adam was expelled from paradise did he first beget children, sons and daughters, who were like him, and Abel was perhaps thirty years of age when he was slain. It appears the children were not much younger than their parents, who were not born, but created.

30. I believe, accordingly, that the godly parents indulged their grief, and abstained from connubial intercourse. This abstinence, however, was not maintained with the intent which the Jews fable, who absurdly affirm that Adam vowed perpetual chastity, like our monks, and that he would still have kept his vow had he not been commanded by an angel from heaven to live together with his wife. Such a story as this is only fit to be told to a Roman pontiff of the age of forty, who alone is worthy of listening to such fables. No, Adam was not so wicked as thus to refuse the gift and command of God! Such abstinence would have been taking vengeance on himself for the grief he had endured, and it would have meant to reject the gift of that blessing which God had been pleased to leave to nature even in its fallen state.

Moreover, this was a matter not left in the power of Adam. As Moses has clearly shown, God had created him a male. He had, therefore, need of a female, or wife, because the instinct of procreation was implanted in his nature by God the Creator, himself. If therefore Adam abstained, he did so for a reason only, intending to return to his Eve after giving vent to his grief for a time.

31. Moses here expressly adds, concerning Adam, that he "begat a son in his own likeness, after his image." Theologians entertain various opinions as to the

real meaning of those expressions. The simple meaning is, that Adam was created "in the image" and "after the likeness" of God, or that he was the image of God, created, not begotten; for Adam had no parents. But in this "image of God" Adam continued not; he fell from it by sin. Seth, therefore, who was afterwards born, was begotten, not after the image of God, but after the image of his father Adam. That is, he was altogether like Adam; he resembled his father Adam, not only in his features, but he was like him in every way. He not only had fingers, nose, eyes, carriage, voice, and speech, like his father, but he was like him in everything else pertaining to body and soul, in manners, disposition, will and other points. In these respects Seth did not bear the image of God which Adam possessed originally, and which he lost; but he bore the likeness of Adam, his father. But this likeness and image were not of God by creation, but of Adam by generation.

32. Now, this image included original sin, and the punishment of eternal death on account of sin, which God inflicted on Adam. But as Adam, by faith in the seed that was to come, recovered the image of God, which he had lost, so Seth also recovered the same after he grew up to man's estate; for God impressed again his own "likeness" upon him through the Word. Paul refers to this when he says to the Galatians, "My little children, of whom I am again in travail until Christ be formed in you," Gal 4, 19.

33. Of the name Seth I have spoken above. It denotes command, and voices the sentiments of one praying and prophesying good news, as if Adam had said: "Cain has not only himself fallen, but also caused his brother to fall. May God, therefore, grant that this my son Seth shall stand as a firm foundation which Satan shall not overthrow." Such blessing or prayer is implied in the name.

V. 4-5. *And the days of Adam after he begat Seth were eight hundred years and he begat sons and daughters. And all the days that Adam lived were nine hundred and thirty years and he died.*

34. This is another part of the happiness of that age, that men attained to so long life. Such longevity, when compared with the length of our lives, seems quite incredible. A question naturally arises as to the cause and theory of such old age. I am not at all displeased with the reasons assigned by some, that the constitutions of men were then far better than ours are now, and also that all things then used for food were more healthful than those now used. To these particulars we must add that important requisite for a long life, the greatest moderation in the use and enjoyment of food. To what extent the latter conduces to health, is needless to explain.

35. Though the body was sounder than at present, yet the general vigor and strength of limb which men had in paradise before the advent of sin, had passed away. It is true, however, that their bodily well-being was enhanced when, after the fall, they were renewed and regenerated through faith in the promised seed. For the same reason, also, sin was weakened through faith in the seed. As for us, we have lost their strength and vigor just in proportion as we have departed from their righteousness.

36. With reference to food, who cannot easily believe that one apple, in that

primeval age, was more excellent and afforded a greater degree of nourishment than a thousand in our time? The roots, also, on which they fed, contained infinitely more fragrance, virtue and savor, than they possess now. All these conditions, but notably holiness and righteousness, the exercise of moderation, then the excellence of the fruit and the salubrity of the atmosphere—all these tended to produce longevity till the time came for the establishment of a new order by God which resulted in a decided reduction of the length of man's life.

37. Now, if we turn to consider thoughtfully our present mode of life, we find that we are much more corrupted than nourished by the meat and drink we consume. In addition to the immoderation characterizing our life, how much have the fruits themselves lost in excellence? Our first parents lived moderately, and chose only those things for their meat and drink calculated to nourish and refresh their bodies. There can be no doubt that after the deluge all the fruits of the earth deteriorated greatly. Even so, in our own age, we find all things deteriorate. The Italian wines and fruits differ no more from our own at the present day than the fruits before the deluge differed from those produced amid that brackishness and foulness made by the sea.

38. These causes, with others which many assign for the great longevity of the primeval patriarchs, I by no means disapprove. But this one reason is quite sufficient, in my opinion, that it pleased God to give them such length of life in the best part of the world. Yet we see, as Peter strikingly says, that God willed not to spare the old world, no, not even the angels in heaven that sinned; so horrible a thing is sin. Sodom and Gomorrah were the choicest portion of the earth, and yet, on account of sin, they were utterly destroyed. In the same manner the Holy Scriptures everywhere set forth the greatness of sin, and exhort to the fear of God.

39. We have now the root, or rather the source, of the human race, namely Adam and his Eve. From these Seth is born, the first branch of this tree. But as Adam lived eight hundred years after the birth of Seth, Adam saw himself in possession of numerous progeny. This was the period of the restoration of righteousness through the promise of the seed to come. Afterwards, however, when men increased, and the sons of God mingled with the daughters of men, the world gradually became corrupt, and the majesty of the holy patriarchs became an object of contempt.

40. It is an attractive sight, to view the number of gray-headed patriarchs living at the same time. Only a little ciphering is required to do it. If you compute carefully the years of our first parent, Adam, you will see that he lived over fifty years with Lamech, Noah's father. Accordingly, Adam saw all his descendants down to the ninth generation, having an almost infinite number of sons and daughters. These, however, Moses does not enumerate, being satisfied to number the trunk and the immediate branches down to Noah.

41. There were, without doubt, in this mighty multitude, many very distinguished saints, whose history, if we possessed it, would exceed in marvelousness all the histories of the world. Compared with it, the exodus of the children of Israel from Egypt, their passage through the Red Sea and through Jordan, their captivi-

ties and returns, would be as nothing. But as the primeval world itself perished, so did its history. In consequence, the first place in the annals of history belongs to the account of the flood, in comparison with which the others are only as sparks to the fire. Of the former world we have nothing but names, but these are, so to speak, great histories in miniature.

42. It is probable that also Eve lived to the age of 800 years and saw this great posterity. What must have been her concern, how great her labors, how devoted her toils, in visiting, in teaching, and in training her children and grandchildren. And what must have been her crosses and sighs, when the generation of the Cainites opposed with so much determination the true Church, although some of them were even converted by the uncovenanted mercy of God.

43. Truly that primeval time was a "golden age," in comparison with which our present age is scarcely worthy of being called the age of mud. During those primeval centuries, there lived at the same time nine patriarchs, together with their posterities, and all of them in harmony concerning the faith in the blessed seed! All these glorious things Moses just mentions, but does not explain; otherwise this would be the history of histories.

III. ENOCH.

1. Why Moses writes the history of Enoch and not that of the other patriarchs before the flood.

2. How it is to be understood that Enoch led a godly life and how the monks interpret this falsely.

3. Enoch's prophecy cited by Jude and where Jude received it.

4. Enoch's exceptional courage and how he opposed Satan and the world.

5. The length of time he led a godly life; and Moses justly praises him.

6. Why Enoch is so greatly praised.

7. The tenor of his preaching.

8. He by no means led the life of a monk.

9. How he was missed. "He was not".

  * Enoch's ascension a proof of the resurrection of the dead.

10. The effect of his ascension upon his father and grandfather.

11. Whether the other patriarchs living then at once knew that he ascended; and how such news affected them.

  * The cross must always precede consolation.

12. Why God took Enoch.

  * The news of Enoch's ascension must have quickened the holy patriarchs.

13. Enoch's ascension a sign that a better life is offered to man.

14. How Enoch walked and lived before God.

15. Enoch a man as we are and yet God took him.

* The great sorrow of the patriarchs at Enoch's disappearance and their great joy over such an experience.

* Seth at the time was high priest, old and tired of life, and died soon after Enoch was taken.

* What Luther would do if he knew in advance the day of his death.

* This temporal life full of want and misery.

* The results of Seth's preaching after Enoch's ascension.

* The longing of the holy fathers for eternal life, and how it should serve us.

* Lamentation over the great corruption inherent in our flesh.

16. Enoch's ascension was great comfort to the holy patriarchs in meeting death.

  * Of death.

    a.   It is not death to believers, but a sleep.

    b.   In what way death is a punishment of sin, and how it is sweetened.

  * Luther's thoughts of Enoch's ascension.

17. Enoch's ascension extraordinary, and well worthy of consideration by all.

18. The rabbins' foolish thoughts of Enoch's ascension refuted.

19. Enoch doubtless had many temptations.

20. Enoch ascended even bodily, and not with that life which he now lives.

  * How and why God willed that the world should have in all times a sign of the resurrection, and hence in the first world Enoch ascended, in the second Elijah, and in the third Christ.

  * Lamentation over the unbelief of the world.

  * Christ's ascension more significant than Enoch's or Elijah's.

  * The chief doctrine of the first five chapters of Genesis.

  * How and why death and the resurrection of the dead are set forth.

III. ENOCH.

44. There is one history, however, that of Enoch, the seventh from Adam, which Moses was not willing to pass over for the reason of its being extraordinarily remarkable. Still, even in this case he is extremely brief.

In the case of all the other patriarchs he mentions only the names and the number of their years. Enoch, however, he delineates in such a manner that he seems, in comparison, to slight the other patriarchs and, as it were, to disparage them as if they were evil men, or at least slighted of God. Did not Adam also, and Seth, and Cainan, together with their descendants—did not all these, also, walk with God? Why, then, does Moses ascribe this great honor to Enoch only? And is the fact that God took Enoch to be understood as if the other patriarchs are neither with God nor living? Yes, they all, like Enoch, now live with God, and we shall behold them all, at the last day, shining equally with Enoch, in the brightest glory!

45. Why, then, does Moses discriminate in favor of Enoch? Why does he not bestow the same praise upon the other patriarchs? Although they died a natural death, and were not taken by God, yet, also they "walked with God." We have heard above concerning Enosh that in his times, likewise, mighty things were done. It was in his days that "men began to call upon the name of Jehovah," that is, that the Word and worship of God began to flourish; and as a result holy men once more "walked with God." Why is it then, we repeat, that Moses does not laud Enosh equally with Enoch? Why does he bestow such high praise on the latter only? For his words are these:

V. 21-24. *And Enoch lived sixty and five years, and begat Methuselah. And Enoch walked with God after he begat Methuselah three hundred years, and begat sons and daughters. And all the days of Enoch were three hundred sixty and five years. And Enoch walked with God: and he was not; for God took him.*

46. When Moses says that Enoch "walked with God," we must beware of taking the monastic view in the premises, as if he had kept himself secluded in some private corner, and there lived a monastic life. No, so eminent a patriarch must be placed on a candlestick, or, as our Saviour Christ expresses it, set as a city on a hill, that he may shine forth in the public ministry.

47. It is as a bearer of such public office the Apostle Jude extols him in his epistle, when he says: "To these also Enoch, the seventh from Adam, prophesied, saying, Behold, the Lord came with ten thousands of holy ones, to execute judgment upon all, and to convict all the ungodly of all their works of ungodliness, which they have ungodly wrought, and of all the hard things which ungodly sinners have spoken against him," Jude vs. 14, 15. From what source Jude obtained these facts I know not. Probably they remained in the memory of man from the primitive age of the world; or it may be that holy men committed to writing many of the sacred words and works of the patriarchs as they were handed down from age to age by tradition.

48. It is this public ministry that Moses lauds, exalting the pious Enoch as a sun above all the other patriarchs and teachers of the primeval world. Wherefore, we may gather from all these circumstances that Enoch possessed a particular fullness of the Holy Spirit, and a preeminent greatness of mind, seeing that he opposed with a strength of faith excelling that of all the other patriarchs, Satan and the church of the Cainites. To walk with God, is not, as we have before observed, for a man to flee into a desert, or to conceal himself in some corner, but to go forth in his vocation, and to set himself against the iniquity and malice of Satan and the world, and to confess the seed of the woman; to condemn the religion and the pursuits of the world, and to preach, through Christ, another life after this.

49. This is the manner of life led for three hundred years by the greatest prophet and high priest of his generation, Enoch, the man who had six patriarchs for his teachers. Most deservedly, therefore, does Moses extol him as a disciple of greatest eminence, taught and trained by many patriarchal masters, and those the greatest and most illustrious; and, moreover, so equipped with the Holy Spirit that he was

the prophet of prophets and the saint of saints in that primeval world. The greatness of Enoch, then, consisted in the first place in his office and ministry.

50. In the second place, he receives preeminent praise because it was the will of God that he should be an example to the whole world in verifying, and showing the comfort of, the faith in the future life. This text, therefore, is worthy of being written in letters of gold and of being deeply engraven in the inmost heart.

51. Here we have another view of what it means to walk with God. It is to preach the life beyond this present life; to teach concerning the seed to come, concerning the serpent's head that is to be bruised and the kingdom of Satan that is to be destroyed. Such was the preaching of Enoch, who nevertheless was a husband, and the father of a family; who had a wife and children, who governed his household, and procured his subsistence by the labor of his own hands. Wherefore say or think no more about living in a monastery, which has merely the outward show of walking with God. When this godly man had lived, after the birth of Methuselah, 300 years in the truest religion, in faith, in patience and in the midst of a thousand crosses, all of which he endured and overcame by faith in the blessed seed to come, he appeared no more.

52. Mark how pregnant these words are with power! He does not say, as he expresses himself concerning the other patriarchs, "and he died," but "he was not," an expression that all scholars have come to regard as a pure proof of the resurrection of the dead. In the Hebrew this meaning is most strikingly brought out. And Enoch walked with God, and *veenenu*, "he was not." The original signifies that Enoch was lost or disappeared, contrary to the thought or expectation of all the other patriarchs, and at once ceased to be among men.

53. Without doubt, at the severe loss of so great a man, both his father and his grandfather were filled with grief and consternation; for they well knew with what devotion he had taught the true religion, and how many things he had suffered. When they had thus suddenly lost such a man as Enoch, who had strong testimony of his godliness both from men and from God himself, what do you think must have been their feelings?

54. Find me, if you can, a poet or a fluent orator to do justice to this text and to treat it with power! Enosh, Seth, and all the other patriarchs knew not by whom or whither Enoch was taken away; they sought him, but found him not. His son Methuselah sought him, and his other children and his grandchildren sought him, but they found him not. They suspected, no doubt, the malice of the Cainites, and they probably thought that he was killed, as Abel was, and secretly buried.

At length, however, they learned, through a revelation made to them of God by an angel, that Enoch was taken away by God himself, into paradise. This fact they probably did not know the first or the second day after the translation, and perhaps not till many months, or it may be many years, afterwards. In the meantime the holy men bewailed his wretched lot, as if he had been slain by the Cainite hypocrites. It is always the divine rule that the cross and affliction should precede consolation. God never comforts any but the afflicted, just as he never quickens unto life any but the dead, nor ever justifies any but sinners! He always creates all things out of nothing.

55. It was a severe cross and affliction to the patriarchs when they saw taken away from them, to appear nowhere among them, him who had governed the whole world by his doctrine, and who had done so many illustrious deeds in the course of his life. While these patriarchs were mourning and bewailing the misfortune of the holy man, behold! consolation was at hand, and it was revealed to them that the Lord had "translated" Enoch! Such an expression we have not concerning any other man than Enoch, except Elijah. God willed, therefore, to testify by an object lesson, that he has prepared for his saints another life after this life, in which they shall live forever with God.

56. The Hebrew verb *lakak* does not signify "translated" according to the impression conveyed by our use of the word, but "received to himself." These words are, accordingly, words of life, revealed by God through some angel to the patriarch Enoch, and to the whole of that generation of saints, that they might have the consolation and promise of eternal life, not only through a word, but also through an act, as before in the case of Abel. How delightful must have been to them this proclamation, when they heard that Enoch was not dead, nor slain by wicked men, nor taken away from them by the fraud or snares of Satan, but translated; that is, "received to himself" by the living and omnipotent God.

57. This is that bright gem which Moses sought to display in the present chapter—that the omnipotent God did not take unto himself geese, or cows, or blocks of wood, or stones, but a man, even Enoch, to teach there was reserved for men another and better life than this present one, so filled with evils and calamities of every kind. Although Enoch was a sinner, yet the manner of his departure from this life proved that God had prepared for him and brought him to another and eternal life; for he entered upon the life with God, and God took him to himself.

58. Accordingly, Enoch's walking with God signifies that he was in this life a faithful witness of eternal life to be gained after this life through the promised seed. This is what living with God means, not the mere animal life subject to corruption. Inasmuch as Enoch constantly preached this doctrine, God verified and fulfilled this preaching in the patriarch himself, that we might fully and surely believe it; in that Enoch, a man like unto ourselves, born of flesh and blood, as we also are, of the seed of Adam, was taken up into heaven by God, and now lives the life of God, that is, an eternal life.

59. Before the generation of patriarchs knew the facts in the case, it was appalling to them to hear that so holy a man as Enoch had disappeared so completely that his whereabouts or manner of death was beyond everybody's ken. Great, therefore, was the grief of the pious parents and elders. But afterwards incredible joy and consolation were theirs when they heard that their son lived with God himself and had been translated by God to an angelic and eternal life.

60. This consolation God made known to Seth, who was the greatest prophet and high priest after his father Adam had fallen asleep in the faith of the blessed seed fifty-seven years before, Seth having then arrived at about his eight hundred and sixtieth year. Seth, being now an old man and full of days and without doubt

fully confirmed in the faith of the blessed seed to come, and anxiously awaiting deliverance from the body and earnestly desiring to be gathered to his people, died with greater joy about fifty-two years afterward, because of the translation of his son Enoch. Fifty-two years were indeed but a short time for an old man wherein to make his will and visit all his grandchildren, and preach to them and exhort them to persevere in the faith of the promised seed and to hope in that eternal life unto which his son and their father Enoch had been translated to live with God. In this manner, doubtless, the aged saint employed his time among his descendants, bidding farewell to and blessing each one. Full of years and full of joy, he no doubt thus taught and comforted both himself and them.

61. If I knew that I were appointed to die in six months' time, I should scarcely find time enough wherein to make my will. I would remind men of what had been the testimony of my preaching, exhort and entreat them to continue and persevere therein, and warn and guard them as far as my powers of mind could do so, against the offense of false doctrine. All these things could not be done in one day, nor in one month. Those fifty years during which Seth lived after the translation of Enoch, formed but a very short period for him (for spiritual men have an altogether different method of calculating time than the children of this world) in which to instruct all his family in the nature of this glorious consolation — that another and eternal life is to be hoped for after this life, a hope which God revealed to his saints by the marvelous fact of his having taken to himself Enoch, who was of the same flesh and blood with ourselves.

62. "Follow not," said he, "the evil inclinations of your nature, but despise this present life and look forward to a better. For what evil exists that is not found in this present life? To how many diseases, to what great dangers, to what dreadful calamities, is it not subject? to say nothing now of those evils which are the greatest of all afflictions, those spiritual distresses which burden with anguish the mind and conscience, such as the Law, sin, and death itself.

63. "Why is it then, that ye so anxiously expect such great consolations from this present life as to seem incapable of ever being completely satisfied? Were it not for the fact that God wants us to live to proclaim him, to thank him, and to serve the brethren, life is such as to suggest its voluntary termination. This service, therefore, let us render unto God, with all diligence. Let us look forward with continual sighs to that true life to which, my children, your brother Enoch has been translated by the glorious God."

These and like things the aged saint taught his people after his great consolation had been revealed. There is no doubt that after it was understood that Enoch was translated alive into immortality, they longed for the time when they also might be delivered out of this afflicted life, in the same manner, or at least by death.

64. If, then, those godly patriarchs of old so anxiously looked forward to the eternal life and desired it to come, on account of Abel and Enoch, whom they knew to be living with God, how much greater ought to be our expectation and desire, who have Christ for our leader unto eternal life, who is gone before, as Peter says

in Acts 3, 20-26. They believed in him as one to come; we know that he has become manifest, and has gone to the Father to prepare for us a home, and to sit at the right hand of the Father to intercede for us. Ought we not, therefore, to sigh for those future things, and to hate those of the present? It is not an Enoch or an Abel who sets before us, as those patriarchs did before their people, the hope of a better life to come; but Christ, the leader and author of life himself. It becomes us, therefore, firmly to despise this life and world, and with swelling breast to pant after the coming glory of eternal life.

65. Herein we feel how great is the infirmity of our flesh which lusts after these present things with eager desire but fails to rejoice in the certainties of the life to come. How is it possible that a fact should not be most certain which has for witnesses not only Abel and Enoch and Elijah, but also Christ himself, the head and the first fruits of those that rise? Most worthy, therefore, the hatred of both God and men are the wicked Epicureans; and most worthy our hatred also is our own flesh, when we wholly plunge into temporal cares and securely disregard the eternal blessings.

66. Worthy of note and carefully to be remembered is the statement that Enoch was taken up and received, not by some patriarch or angel, but by God himself. This was the very consolation which rendered the deaths of the patriarchs endurable; yea, which enabled them to depart from this life with joy. They saw that the seed which had been promised them warred, even before he was revealed, with Satan, and bruised, through Enoch, his head. Such was the hope entertained by them concerning themselves and all their believing descendants, and, in perfect security, they despised death as having ceased to be death, as having become a sleep from which they were to awaken into life eternal. "To them that believe," death is not really death, but a sleep. When the terror, the power, and the sting of death are taken away, it can no longer be considered death. The greater the faith of the dying man, the weaker is death. On the other hand, the weaker the faith of the dying man, the more bitter is death.

67. In this text we are also reminded of the nature of sin. If Adam had not sinned, we should not have been dying men, but, like Enoch of old, we should have been translated, without fear or pain, from this animal life to that better and spiritual life. But although we have forfeited that life, the present history of the patriarch Enoch assures us that the restitution of paradise and of eternal life is not to be despaired of. Our flesh cannot be free from pain, but where conscience has obtained peace, death is no more than a swoon, by means of which we pass out of this life into eternal rest. Had our nature remained innocent, it would not have known such pain of the flesh. We should have been taken up as if asleep, presently to awaken in heaven, and to lead the life of the angels. Now, however, that the flesh is defiled by sin, it must first be destroyed by death. As to Enoch, perhaps he lay down in some grassy spot and fell asleep praying; and sleeping he was taken up by God, without pain; without death.

68. Let us give proper attention to this text to which Moses attaches special importance as embodying an account of the most noteworthy event of the primitive world. What fact could possibly inspire more wonder and admiration than that

a man, a corrupt sinner, born of flesh and blood, as we are, and defiled as we are by that sin and corruption, so obtained the victory over death as not to die at all! Christ himself is man, and righteous, yet our sins caused him to suffer the bitterest of all deaths; but he is delivered on the third day, and lifts himself up unto life eternal. In Enoch there was the singular fact that he died not at all, but was caught up, without death intervening, to the life spiritual and eternal.

69. Emphatically deserving of aversion are the rabbins. The sublimest passages of the Scriptures they shamefully corrupt. As a case in point, they prate concerning Enoch that, while he was good and righteous, he very much inclined toward carnal desires. God, therefore, out of pity, prevented his sinning and perishing through death. Is not this, I pray you, a shocking corruption of the text before us? Why should they say concerning Enoch in particular, that he was subject to the evil desires of the flesh? As if all the other patriarchs did not experience the same. Why do they not notice the repeated testimony of Moses, that Enoch "walked with God"? That is certainly evidence that Enoch did not indulge those evil inclinations of his flesh, but bravely overcame them by faith. The Jews when speaking of the corrupt desires of the flesh have reference to lust, avarice, pride, and similar promptings. Enoch, however, without doubt, lived amid mightier temptations than these; like Paul, he felt that "thorn in the flesh"; day by day he wrestled with Satan; and when, at length, he was completely bruised and worn out with every kind of temptation, God commanded him to depart from this life to the blessed life to come.

70. What that life is which Enoch now lives, we who still continue to be flesh and blood cannot possibly know. It is enough for us to know that Enoch was translated in his body. This the patriarchs must have clearly understood by revelation, and about to die, they needed this comfort. This much we know also. But what that holy patriarch is now doing, where he is, and how he lives, we know not. We know that he lives; and we also know that the life he lives is not like unto this animal life, but that he is with God. This the text before us distinctly declares.

71. This fact, then, makes the narrative under consideration so memorable that God intended to use it for the purpose of setting before the old, primeval world the hope of a better life. Likewise, to the second world, which had the Law, God gave the example of Elijah, who also was taken up into heaven and translated by the Lord before the very eyes of his own servant Elisha. We are now in the New Covenant, in a third world, as it were. We have Christ himself, our great deliverer, as our glorious example, who ascended into the heavens, taking with him many of his saints.

It was God's will to establish for every age a testimonial of the resurrection of the dead, that he might thereby allure our minds by all possible attractions from this corrupt and in many ways wretched life, in which, however, we will gladly serve God as long as it shall please him, by the faithful performance of all public and private duties, and especially by instructing others in holiness and in the knowledge of God. But, as the apostle says, we have here "no certain dwelling-place," 1 Cor 4, 11. Christ, our forerunner, is gone before us, that he might prepare for us, the eternal mansions, Jn 14, 2-3.

72. Just as we find many among us by whom such things are considered absurd, and not sufficiently worthy of faith, so there is no doubt that this account was deemed ridiculous by most people. The world is ever the same. For that reason these things have by divine authority been committed to writing and recorded for the saints and the faithful, that these might read, understand, believe and heed them. They present to our sight a manifest triumph over death and sin, and afford us a sure comfort in Enoch's victory over the Law, and the wrath and judgment of God. To the godly nothing can yield more grace and joy than these antediluvian records.

73. But the New Testament truly overflows with the mercy of God. While we do not discard records like these, we have others far superior. We have the Son of God himself ascending to the skies, and sitting at the right hand of God. In him we see the serpent's head completely bruised, and the life lost in paradise restored. This is more than the translation of Enoch and of Elijah; still, it was God's will in this manner to administer comfort to the original world and also to the succeeding one, which had the Law.

74. The paramount doctrine contained in these five chapters is, accordingly, this: that men died and lived again. In Adam all men died. But believers lived again through the promised seed, as the history of Abel and Enoch testifies. In Adam, death was appointed for Seth and all others; hence it is written of every one: "And he died." But Abel and Enoch illustrate the resurrection from the dead and the life immortal. The purpose intended is that we should not despair in death but entertain the unwavering assurance that the believers in the promised seed shall live, and be taken by God, whether from the water or the fire or the gibbet, or the tomb. We desire to live, and we shall live, namely the eternal life through the promised seed, which remains when this is past.

IV. LAMECH AND HIS SON NOAH.

A. LAMECH.

1. He lived at the time Enoch was taken to heaven.

 * To what end Enoch's ascension served the holy patriarchs.

2. Why Lamech called his son Noah.

 * The erroneous comments of the rabbins taken by Lyra without any good reason.

3. On what Lamech's heart was centered at Noah's birth.

4. How and why Lamech erred in the case of his son as Eve did at Cain's birth.

 * The longing of the patriarchs for the Messiah was of the Holy Spirit.

 * Complaint of the world's ingratitude.

 * The patriarchs' greatest treasure and desire.

 * Comparison of the three worlds.

 * Why the present world so lightly esteems Christ, whom the patriarchs so highly revered.

* The first world was the best, the last the worst.

IV. LAMECH AND HIS SON NOAH.

A. Lamech.

V. 28-29. *And Lamech lived a hundred eighty and two years, and begat a son: and he called his name Noah, saying, This same shall comfort us in our work and in the toil of our hands, which cometh because of the ground which Jehovah hath cursed.*

75. Only incidentally Moses adverts in this account to the name of Noah, which certainly deserves a somewhat careful examination. Lamech was living when Enoch was taken away by God out of this life into the other immortal life. When the great glory of God had become manifest in the extraordinary miracle of the rapture from a lowly estate into life eternal of Enoch who was a man like us, a husband, a man with family, having sons, daughters, household, fields and cattle, the holy fathers were filled and fired with such joy as to conclude that the glad day was near which should witness the fulfilment of the promise. That Enoch was taken up living, to be with the Lord, appeared as a salient display of divine mercy.

76. As Adam and Eve, after the reception of the promise, were so absorbed in their hope that, in their joy to see a man like themselves, they identified Cain with the promised seed, so in my judgment Lamech committed a similar pious error when he gave his son the name Noah, and said: This same shall comfort us, and shall deliver us from the labors and sorrows of this life. Original sin, and the punishment thereof, shall now cease. We shall now be restored to our former innocent state. The curse shall now cease which rests on the earth on account of the sin of Adam; and all the other miseries inflicted on the human race on account of sin, shall also cease.

77. Such considerations as these prompted Lamech to base upon the fact of his grandfather's rapture into paradise unaccompanied by pain, sickness and death, the hope that presently the whole of paradise was to be ushered in. He concludes that Noah was the promised seed by whom the earth was to be restored. This notion that the curse is about to be lifted is expressed in unmistakable terms. Not so; neither the curse of sin nor its penalty can be removed unless original sin itself shall have been removed first.

78. The rabbins, those pestilent corrupters of the Scriptures, surely deserve aversion. This is their interpretation of the passage in question: He shall bring us rest from the toil and labor of our hands by showing us an easier way of cultivating the earth. With a plowshare, by a yoke of oxen, the earth shall be broken up; the present mode of digging it with man's hand shall cease.

I wonder that Lyra is satisfied with this interpretation, and follows it. He ought to have been familiar with the unchanging practice of the Jews to pervert Scripture by substituting a material meaning for a spiritual one, in order to gain glory among men. Could anything more derogatory to the holy patriarch be said than that he gave such expression to his joy over the birth of his son Noah on account of an advantage pertaining to the belly?

79. No; it was a much greater concern than this which filled his mind with anxiety. It was the wrath of God, and death, with all the other calamities of this life. His hope was that Noah, as the promised seed, would put an end to these evils. And therefore it was that he thus exulted with joy at the birth of this his son, predicted good things, and called upon others to join him in the same hope. His thoughts did not dwell upon the plow, nor upon oxen, nor upon other trivial things of the kind pertaining to this present life, as the blind Jews rave. He was really filled with the hope that this his son Noah was that seed to come which should restore the former blessed state of paradise, in which there was no curse. As if he had said: Now we feel the curse in the very labors of our hands. We toil and sweat in cultivating the earth, yet it yields us in return nothing but briers and thorns. But there shall arise a new and happy age. The curse on the earth which was inflicted on account of sin shall cease, because sin shall cease. This is the true meaning of the text before us.

80. But the holy father was deceived. The glory of bringing about that renewal belonged, not to the son of a man but to the Son of God. The rabbins are silly. Although the earth is not dug by the hands of men, but by the use of oxen, yet the labor of man's hand has not ceased. Enoch, by his translation, does not disclose the solace of bodily easement, agreeable to the belly, but deliverance from sin and death. Lamech hoped, in addition, for the restoration of the former state. He believed to see the inauguration of this change in his grandfather Enoch, and felt assured that the deliverance, or the renewal of all things, was close at hand. Just so Eve, as we have already observed, when she brought forth her first-born son Cain, said, I have gotten a man with the help of Jehovah, one who shall take away all these punishments inflicted on sin, and bring about our restoration. But, like Eve, the good and holy Lamech was deceived in his ardent longing for the restoration of the world.

81. All these anxieties plainly show how those holy patriarchs longed for, hoped for, and sighed for, that great "restitution of all things," Acts 3, 21. Although they herein erred, even as Eve erred and was deceived with respect to Cain, this desire for deliverance in itself, was of the Holy Spirit, and proved the truth and constancy of their faith in the promised seed. When Eve named her son Cain, and when Lamech called his son Noah, these names were but birth cries, as the apostle represents them, of the whole creation, groaning and travailing in pain together, and earnestly expecting the resurrection of the dead, deliverance from sin, the restoration of all things, and the manifestation of the sons of God, Rom 8, 19-23. The simplest and true meaning, accordingly, is that Lamech, after seeing the reality of the future life demonstrated by the translation of Enoch from the afflictions and toils caused by sin, has a son born to him, whom he calls Noah, which means rest, an expression of the hope that deliverance from the curse of sin and sin itself shall take place through him. This interpretation accords with the analogy of faith, and confirms the hope for a resurrection and a life eternal.

82. Such longing for the future life on the part of the holy men whose shoes we are unworthy to clean, contrasts strangely with the horrible ingratitude of our time. How great the difference between having and wishing! Those patriarchs

were men of transcendent holiness, equipped with the highest endowments, the heroes of the world! In them we behold the strongest desire for the seed which is to come; that is their greatest treasure; they thirst, they hunger, they yearn, they pant for Christ! And we, who have Christ among us, who know him as one revealed, offered, glorified, sitting at the right hand of God and making intercession for us — we despise him and hold him in greater contempt than any other creature! O, the wretchedness of it! O, the sin of it!

83. Note the difference between the several ages of the world! The primeval age was the most excellent and holy. It contained the noblest jewels of the whole human race. After the flood there still existed many great and eminent men — patriarchs, and kings, and prophets; and although they were not the equals of the patriarchs before the flood, yet in them also there appeared a bright longing for Christ, as Christ says: "For I say unto you, that many prophets and kings desired to see the things which ye see, and saw them not; and to hear the things which ye hear, and heard them not," Lk 10, 24. And then there is our own age, the age of the New Testament; to this Christ has been revealed. This age is, as it were, the waste and dregs of the whole world. It holds nothing in greater contempt than Christ, than whom a previous age knew nothing more precious.

84. What is the cause of this grave state of affairs? To be sure, our flesh, the world, and the devil. We altogether loathe what we have, according to the proverb:

> *Omne rarum carum; vilescit quotidianum.*
> "All that's rare, is dear; vile is what is here."

And apt is the poetic truism:

> *Minuit praesentia famam.*
> "Sight levels what fancy has exalted."

As far as the revelation is concerned, we are far richer than the patriarchs. But their devotion to a comparatively inferior revelation was greater; they were lovers of the bridegroom. We, on the other hand, are that fat, bloated, wanton servant, Deut 32, 15; for we have the Word and are overwhelmed by the abundance of it.

85. In the same degree as the first world was excellent and holy, the latter-day world is evil and wicked. In view of the fact, then, that God did not spare the first, primitive world, and destroyed the second world by overturning kingdom after kingdom, and government after government, what shall we expect to be the end of this latter-day world which in security despises the Christ, the desire of nations, as he is called by Haggai, in spite of the fact that he urges himself upon us to the point of weariness!

B. NOAH.

1. Remarkableness of the fact that Noah refrained so long from wedlock.
2. He was fit to marry, but had reasons for abstaining.
3. What his reasons were.
4. His chastity is highly praised by Moses in few words.

5. The Jews' lies about the reasons for his chastity refuted.

* The Jews' lies as to why Shem was called the first-born.

* Papists without reason take offense at Moses relating so much about the birth of the children of the patriarchs.

6. Noah shines like a bright star as an example of chastity among all the patriarchs.

7. Noah remained single, not because he despised marriage; and why he finally married.

8. How his sons were born one after the other.

* Why Shem was preferred to Japheth.

* How to meet the objections to the birth of Noah's sons.

9. Noah an excellent example of chastity.

* The threefold world.

a. The first world a truly golden age and the most holy. How and why it was punished by God.

b. The second world is full of idolatry, and will be severely punished by God.

c. The third world is the worst, and hence can expect the hardest punishment.

d. The punishment of these three worlds portrayed in the colors of the rainbow.

e. How believing hearts act upon considering sin and the world's punishment.

B. Noah.

V. 32. *And Noah was five hundred years old: and Noah begat Shem, Ham, and Japheth.*

86. Here again we meet with surprising brevity. As is his custom, Moses expresses in the fewest possible words the greatest and most important things, which the ignorant reader passes by unobserved. But you will say, perhaps, Of what import is it that Noah first begat sons when he was five hundred years old? Why, if Noah had no children all those 500 years, he either endured that length of time the severe trial of unfruitfulness or, as appears to me more likely, he abstained from marriage all those years, setting an example of most marvelous chastity. I do not speak here of the abominable chastity of the Papists; nor of our own. Look at the prophets and the apostles, and even at some of the other patriarchs, who doubtless were chaste and holy. But what are they in comparison with this man Noah, who, possessed of masculine vigor, managed to live a chaste life without marriage for five hundred years?

87. Now you will scarcely find one in a thousand among the men of our age who, at the age of thirty, has not known woman. Moreover, Noah, after he had lived a single life for so many centuries, at length took to himself a wife, and begat

children; which latter fact carries its own proof that he was in a state appropriate for marriage prior to this, and had a definite reason for practicing continence.

88. In the first place, it is evident that such unequaled chastity must necessarily have been a peculiar gift of God. It evinced a nature almost angelic. It does not seem a thing possible in the nature of man to live 500 years without knowing a wife. In the next place these five centuries of chastity in Noah manifest some signal displeasure with the world. For what other reason are we to conclude that he abstained from marriage than because he had seen the descendants of his uncle and aunt degenerate into giants and tyrants, filling the world with violence? He thought in consequence, that he would rather have no children at all than such as those. And my belief is that he would never have taken to himself a wife at all if he had not been admonished and commanded so to do either by the patriarchs or by some angel. He who had refrained from marriage for 500 years might have refrained during all the rest of his life.

89. In this manner Moses explains in brief words exceedingly weighty facts, and, what the ignorant reader would never observe owing to the failure of chastity being mentioned in express words, he commends the chastity of Noah above that of all the other inhabitants of the primeval world, setting him up as an example of all but angelic chastity.

90. The Jews, according to their custom, play the fool, and fable that Noah for centuries denied himself a wife because he knew that God would destroy the world by the flood. If, therefore, Noah had married, like all the other patriarchs, in the earlier part of his life—that is, when he was about a hundred years old or less—he himself would have peopled the world in the space of 400 years; and then God would have been compelled to destroy both the father himself and the whole of his progeny. To this fable they add the other, that Shem was called the first-born for the reason that he was the first to receive circumcision.

91. In a word, these Jews corrupt everything and twist it to suit their own carnal bent and ambition. If Noah abstained from marriage for the reason which they assign, why did not all the other patriarchs, for the same reason, abstain from marriage and fatherhood? These comments of the rabbins are accordingly frivolous and nonsensical. Why do they not rather urge the real cause, that it was a special gift that Noah, a vigorous man, abstained from marriage for five hundred years? Throughout the course of time no instance of such continence is found.

92. The book of Genesis highly offends the Papists because it mentions so often that the fathers begat sons and daughters. They say of this book that it is a book in which little more is contained than the record that the patriarchs were men of extravagant love for their wives; and they consider it obscene that Moses should make mention of such things with such attention to detail. But, in the impurity of their hearts, they can not refrain from befouling the most exalted chastity.

93. If you would really behold the brightest examples of chastity the whole world contains, read Moses as he relates that the patriarchs did not marry until they were of advanced age. Among them Noah shines forth a star of first magnitude, inasmuch as he did not marry until he had reached the five hundredth year

of his life. Where will you find such eminent examples of chastity in the papacy? Although there are some among the Papists who do not actually sin with their bodies, yet how foul and filthy are their minds! And all this is judgment upon their contempt for marriage, which God himself has designed to be a remedy for the corruption of nature.

94. Another reason why Noah refrained from marriage has been mentioned. He did not condemn marriage, nor did he consider it to be a profane or impure manner of life; but he saw that the descendants of the elder patriarchs had degenerated to the level of the ungodly generation of the Cainites. Such children as these he felt he could not endure; he rather waited, in the fear of God, the end of the world. When afterwards he did enter into marriage, and begat children, he no doubt did it by reason of some particular admonition and command of God.

95. Here a question naturally arises concerning the order in which Noah's sons were born. It will be worth our while to inquire into this matter, so that our computation of the years of the world may have a reliable basis. The common opinion is that Shem was the first-born of Noah, because his name is mentioned first in order. The testimony of Scripture, however, compels us to conclude that Japheth was the first-born, Shem the second, and Ham the last. The truth of this is proved in the following manner: Shem begat his son Arpachshad two years after the flood, when he was 100 years old, Gen 11, 10. Hence Shem was 98 years old when the flood came, and Noah, when Shem was born, was 498 years old. But Japheth was evidently born before Shem, for he was the elder brother, Gen 10, 21. It plainly follows, therefore, that only Ham, the youngest brother, was born when Noah was 500 years old.

96. The reason why Shem is mentioned before Japheth is not because he was first circumcised, as the Jews, who always are hunting carnal glory, falsely claim, but because it was through him that Christ, the promised seed, was to come. For the same reason, Abraham, the youngest, is given precedence to his brothers, Haran and Nahor.

97. But you will perhaps say, How does this agree with the text which positively says, "Noah was five hundred years old; and Noah begat Shem, Ham and Japheth"? Harmony is restored if you make out of the preterit a pluperfect, and read the passage thus:—When Noah was five hundred years old he had begotten Shem, Ham, and Japheth. Moses does not record the particular year in which each son was born, but merely mentions the year in which the number of sons born to Noah reached three. Thus the biblical record is reduced to harmony.

98. As conclusion to the fifth chapter Moses presents the finest and most noteworthy example of chastity. Saintly and continent throughout his career, Noah had just rounded out his fifth century when he began married life. Thus far, he had renounced matrimony, repelled by the licentiousness of the young, who were drifting into the depravity of the Cainites. Notwithstanding, at the call of God, he obediently entered upon marriage, although it was quite possible for him to remain chaste, as a celibate.

99. Such is the description given by Moses of the first, the original world, in

five brief chapters. But it is readily seen that in the beginning was the real golden age of which poets have made mention, their information being doubtless the traditions and the utterances of the fathers.

100. But as the sins of men increased, God spared not the old world, but destroyed it by a flood utterly, even as he did not spare it when under the dispensation of the Law. Because of its idolatry and the impiousness of its worship, he not only overturned one kingdom after another, but even his own people, the Jews, having been severely punished at his hands by various afflictions and captivities, were at length utterly destroyed by the Roman armies.

101. Our age, which is the third age of the world, although it is the age of grace, is so filled with blasphemies and abominations that it is not possible either to express them in language or to form a mental image of them. This age therefore shall not be punished by temporal punishment, but by eternal death and eternal fire, or, if I may so express it, by a flood of fire. The very rainbow even, with its colors, contains a prophetic intimation of these things. The first color is sea-green, representing the destruction of the first world by the waters of the flood, because of violence and lust; the middle color of the bow is yellow, prefiguring the various calamities by which God avenged the idolatry and wickedness of the second age; the third and last color of the bow is fiery red, for fire shall at length consume the world, with all its iniquities and sins.

102. Wherefore, let us constantly pray that God may so rule our hearts by his fear and may so fill us with confidence in his mercy, that we are able with joy to await our deliverance and the righteous punishment of this ungodly world. Amen. Amen.

CHAPTER VI.

I. THE SINS OF THE FIRST WORLD, THE CAUSE OF ITS DESTRUCTION.

* How this chapter and the preceding one are connected.

* It is terrible that God destroyed by a flood the first world, which was the best.

* Of pride and the proud.

1. How God humbles what is high and grand in the eyes of the world and has the best gifts.

   * How man can meet the judgments of God.

2. The more gifts man has the greater his pride.

3. The most terrible examples of punishment God gives in the case of the proud and such examples should be diligently pondered.

   * The complaint that the world is hardened by reason of God's judgments.

4. How the ancient world was misled into pride through its gifts.

5. Pride is the common weakness of human nature.

6. In what ways man is moved to pride.

   a. The chief sin of the old world.

   * Pride is the spring of all vices.

   b. How the old world sinned against the first table of the law, and brought on the sins against the second table.

   c. How and why God punished the old world.

   * From the punishment of the first world we conclude that the last world will be also punished.

   d. Whether the first world was wicked before Noah's birth; on what occasion its wickedness increased.

   * Noah the martyr of martyrs.

   * Why Lamech called his son Noah.

   e. How sin greatly increased in the days of Noah.

   * Why Noah remained unmarried so long, which was his greatest cross.

   f. When the wickedness of the old world began.

   * Concerning unchastity.

    (1)   It is the foundation of all want and misery.

    (2)   It is the spring of many other sins.

    (3)   How to remedy it.

    (4)   Whether bearing children is in itself to be reckoned as unchastity, and how far Moses denounces it.

    (5)   Unchastity makes the bearing of children difficult.

  g. The reason the sons of God looked upon the daughters of men.

  h. Why the sin of the first world was not so terrible as the sin of the second.

  i. How the first world changed through the marriages of Adam and the other patriarchs.

  * The sons of God.

    (1)   What is understood by them.

    (2)   The rabbins' fables about the sons of God, how to refute them.

     * What is to be held concerning the "Incubis" and "Succubis".

    (3)   How the deluge came because of the sons of God.

    (4)   To what end should the fall and punishment of the sons of God serve us.

     * Should the Romish church be called holy.

     * How the children of God became the children of the devil.

     * How Noah had to spend his life among a host of villains.

     * The conduct of the world when God sends it righteous servants.

I. THE SINS OF THE PRIMEVAL WORLD IN GENERAL THE CAUSE OF ITS DESTRUCTION.

1. In the first five chapters Moses describes the state of the human race in the primeval world and the wonderful glory of the holy patriarchs who governed it. In these five chapters the chronicles as in the first book, so to speak, the happiest period of the whole human race and of the world before the flood. Now we shall begin what may be termed the second book of Genesis, containing the history of the flood. It shows the destruction of all the offspring of Cain and the eternal preservation of the generation of the righteous; for while everything perishes in the flood, the generation of the righteous is saved as an eternal world.

2. It is appalling that the whole human race except eight persons is destroyed, in view of the fact that this was truly the golden age; for succeeding ages do not equal the old world in glory, greatness and majesty. And if God visited with destruction his own perfect creation and the very glory of the human race, we have just cause for fear.

3. In inflicting this punishment, God followed his own peculiar way. Whatever is most exalted he particularly overthrows and humiliates. Peter says in 2 Peter 2,

5: God "spared not the ancient world;" and he would imply that it was, in comparison with succeeding ages, a veritable paradise. Neither did he spare the sublimest creatures—the angels—nor the kings ruling his people, nor the first-born of all times. But the more highly they were blessed with gifts, the more sternly he punished them when they began to misuse his gifts.

4. The Holy Spirit says in the ninth verse of the second psalm, concerning kings: "Thou shalt break them with a rod of iron; thou shalt dash them in pieces like a potter's vessel." But is it not the Lord himself who has ordained kings and wills that all men should honor and obey them? Here he condemns and spurns the wisdom of the prudent and the righteousness of the righteous. It is God's proper and incessant work to condemn what is most magnificent, to cast down the most exalted and to defeat the strongest, though they be his own creatures. He does this, however, that abundant evidence of his wrath may terrify the ungodly and may arouse us to despair of ourselves and to trust in his power alone. We must either live under the shadow of God's wing, in faith in his grace, or we must perish.

5. After the fall it came to pass that the more one was blessed with gifts, the greater was his pride. This was the sin of the angels who fell. This was the sin of the primitive world, in which the grandest people of the race lived; but because they prided themselves in their wisdom and other gifts, they perished. This was the sin of the greatest kings. This was the sin of nearly all the first-born. But what is the need of so many words? This is original sin—that we fail to recognize and rightly use the great and precious gifts of God.

6. That the greatest men must furnish the most abhorrent examples is not the fault of the gifts and blessings, but of those to whom they are intrusted. God is a dialectician and judges the person by the thing,[1] meting out destruction to the thing or gift as well as to its possessor.

7. It is expedient to give heed to such examples. They are given that the proud may fear and be humbled, and that we may learn our utter dependence upon the guidance and will of God, who resisteth the proud but giveth grace to the humble. Lacking the understanding and practice of these truths, man falls continually—kings, nobles, saints, one after the other, filling the world with examples of the wrath and judgment of God. The Blessed Virgin sings: "He hath scattered the proud in the imagination of their heart. He hath put down the princes from their thrones, and hath exalted them of low degree." Lk 1, 51-53.

8. Full of such examples are all ages, all princely courts, all lands. Yet, by the grace of Saint Diabolus, the prince of this world, our hearts are so hard that we are not moved by all this to fear; rather to disdain, though we feel and see that we also shall incur destruction. Blessed are they, therefore, who heed, and are moved by such examples of wrath to be humble and to live in the fear of God.

9. Consider, then, the preeminence of the old world, that perished in the flood. It possessed apparently the best, holiest and noblest men, compared with whom we are as the dregs of the world. For the Scriptures do not say that they were wicked and unjust among themselves, but toward God. "He saw," says Moses, "that

---

[1] *ut arguat a conjugatis.*

they were evil." The eyes of God perceive and judge quite differently from the eyes of men. He says in Isaiah 55, 8-9: "Neither are your ways my ways.... For as the heavens are higher than the earth, so are my ways higher than your ways, and my thoughts than your thoughts."

10. These tyrants and giants were esteemed and honored among themselves as the wisest and most just of men. So in our day kings and princes, popes and bishops, theologians, physicians, jurists and noblemen occupy exalted places and receive honor as the very gems and luminaries of the human race. More deservedly did the children of God in the old world receive such honor, because they excelled in power and possessed many gifts. Nevertheless, falling into pride and contempt of God while enjoying his blessings, they were rejected by God and destroyed, together with their gifts, as if they had been the lowest and vilest of the human race.

11. And this is a common failing of our human nature. It necessarily puffs itself up and prides itself on its gifts unless restrained by the Holy Spirit. I have often said that a man has no more dangerous enemy than himself. It is my own experience that I have not without me so great cause for fear as within me; for it is our inner gifts that incite our nature to pride.

12. As God, who is by nature most kind, cannot refrain from gracing and showering us with various gifts: health, property, wisdom, skill, knowledge of Scripture, etc., so we cannot refrain from priding ourselves upon these gifts and flaunting them. Wretched is our life when we lack the gifts of God, but twice wretched is it when we have them; for they tend to make us doubly wicked. Such is the corruption of original sin, though all but believers are either unaware of its existence or regard it a trivial thing.

13. Such corruption is perceptible not only in ourselves but in others. How property inflates pride though it occupies relatively the lowest place among blessings! The rich, be they noblemen, city-dwellers or peasants, deem other people as flies. To even a greater extent are the higher gifts abused—wisdom and righteousness. Possession of these gifts, then, makes inevitable this condition—God cannot suffer such pride and we cannot refrain from it.

14. This was the sin of that primeval world. Among Cain's descendants were good and wise men, who, nevertheless, before God were most wicked, for they prided themselves upon their gifts and despised God, the author. Such offense the world does not perceive and condemn; God alone is its judge.

15. Where these spiritual vices exist and flourish, the lapse into carnal ones is imminent. According to Sirach 10, 14, sin begins with falling from God. The devil's first fall is from heaven into hell; that is, from the first table of the Law into the second. When people begin to be godless—when they do not fear and trust God, but despise him, his Word and his servants—the result is that from the true doctrine they pass into heretical delusions and teach, defend and cultivate them. These sins in the eyes of the world are accounted the greatest holiness, and their authors alone are reputed religious, God-fearing and just, and held to constitute the Church, the family of God. People are unable to judge concerning the sins of the first table. Those who despise God sooner or later fall into abominable adul-

tery, theft, murder and other gross sins against the second table.

16. The purpose of my statements is to make plain that the old world was guilty, not only of sin against the second table, but most of all of sin against the first table by making a fine, but deceptive and false show of wisdom, godliness, devotion and religion. As a result of the ungodliness which flourished in opposition to the first table, there followed that moral corruption of which Moses speaks in this chapter, that the people polluted themselves with all sorts of lust and afterward filled the world with oppression, bloodshed and wrong.

17. Because the ungodly world had trampled both tables under foot, God came to judge it, who is a consuming fire and a jealous God. He so punishes ungodliness that he turns everything into sheer desolation, and neither government nor the governed remain. We may, therefore, infer that the world was the better the nearer it was to Adam, but that it degenerated from day to day until our time, when the offscouring and lowest filth of humanity, as it were, are living.

18. Now, if God did not spare a world endowed with so many and great gifts, what have we to hope for, who, offal that we are, are subject to far greater misfortune and wretchedness? But if it please God, spare the Roman pontiff and his holy bishops, who do not believe such things! I now come to my text.

V. 1-2. *And it came to pass, when men began to multiply on the face of the ground, and daughters were born unto them, that the sons of God saw the daughters of men that they were fair; and they took them wives of all that they chose.*

19. This is a very brief but comprehensive account. The text must not be understood to mean that the world did not increase until the five hundredth year of Noah. The more ancient patriarchs are embraced in this statement. This is demonstrated by the fact that Noah had no daughters. The reference in the text to "daughters" certainly must be understood as referring to the by-gone age of Lamech, Methuselah, Enoch and others. The world, accordingly, was corrupt and evil before Noah was born, particularly when licentiousness began to prevail after the death of Adam, whose authority, as the first father, they feared.

20. I have said that Noah was a virgin above all others; I may add he was the greatest of all martyrs. Our so-called martyrs, compared with him, have infinite advantage in strength received from the Holy Spirit, by which death is overcome and all trials and perils are escaped. Noah lived among the unrighteous for six hundred years, and like Lot at Sodom, not without numerous and dire perils and trials.

21. This was, perhaps, one reason why Father Lamech gave his son the name Noah at his birth. When the holy patriarch saw evil abounding in the world, he entertained the hope concerning his son that he should comfort the righteous by opposing sin and its author, Satan, and restoring lost righteousness.

22. However, the wickedness that began then, not only failed to cease under Noah, but rather grew greater. Hence Noah is the martyr of martyrs. For is it not much easier to be delivered from all danger and suffering in a single hour than to live for centuries amid colossal wickedness?

23. The opinion before expressed I maintain, that Noah abstained from matrimony so long that he might not be compelled to witness and suffer in his own offspring what he saw in the descendants of the other saints. This sight of man's wickedness was his greatest cross, as Peter says of Lot in Sodom (2 Pet 2, 8): "That righteous man dwelling among them, in seeing and hearing, vexed his righteous soul from day to day with their lawless deeds."

24. Accordingly, the increase of humanity of which Moses speaks has not reference alone to the time of Noah, but also to the age of the other patriarchs. It was there that the violation of the first table commenced—in the contempt manifested for Jehovah and his Word. This was followed later by such gross offenses as oppression, tyranny and lewdness, which Moses explicitly mentions and names first as the cause of evil. Consult all history, study the Greek tragedies and the affairs of barbarians and Romans of all times, and you find lust the mother of every kind of trouble. It can not be otherwise. Where God's Word remains unknown or unheeded, men will plunge into lust.

25. Lust draws in its train endless other evils, as pride, oppression, perjury and the like. These sins can be attacked only as men, through the first table, learn to fear and to trust in God. Then it is that they follow the Word as a lamp going before in the dark, and they will not indulge in such scandalous deeds, but will rather beware of them. With violation of the first table, however, the spread of passions and sins of every description is inevitable.

26. But it seems strange that Moses should enumerate in the catalog of sins the begetting of daughters. He had found it commendable in the case of the patriarchs. It is even enjoyed by the ungodly as a blessing of God. Why, therefore, does Moses call it a sin?

I reply, he does not condemn the fact of procreation as such, but the abuse of it, resulting from original sin. To be endowed with royal majesty, wisdom, wealth and bodily strength is a goodly blessing. It is God who bestows these gifts. But when men, in possession of these blessings, fail to reverence the first table, and by means of these very gifts do violence to it, such wickedness merits punishment. Therein is the reason for Moses' peculiar words: "The sons of God saw the daughters of men that they were fair; and they took them wives of all that they chose," without consideration of God or of law, natural or statutory.

27. The first table having been despised, the second shares the same fate. Desire occupies the principal place and in contempt for procreation it becomes purely bestial; whereas God has instituted matrimony as an aid to feeble nature and chiefly for the purpose of procreation. But when lust in this manner has gained the upper hand, all commandments, those that go before and that follow, are ruthlessly broken and dishonored. Parental honor becomes insecure; men do not shrink from doing murder; from alienating property, speaking false testimony, etc.

28. The word *jiru*, "saw," does not merely signify "to view," but "to view with pleasure and enjoyment." This meaning often occurs in the psalms, for instance: "Mine eye also hath seen my desire on mine enemies," Ps 92, 11; that is, shall with pleasure see vengeance executed upon my enemies. The meaning here is that, after

turning their eyes from God and his Word, they turned them, filled with lust, upon the daughters of men. The sequence is unerring that, from the violation of the first table, men rush to the violation of the second. After despising God they despised also the laws of nature and, as they pleased, they married whom they chose.

29. These are rather harsh words, and yet it is my opinion that lust continued hitherto within certain limits, inasmuch as they neither committed incest with their mothers, as later the inhabitants of Canaan, nor polluted themselves with the vice of the Sodomites. Moses confines his charge to their casting aside the legal trammels set by the patriarchs and recognizing in their matrimonial alliances no law but that of lust, selecting only as passion directed and against the will of the parents.

30. It seems the patriarchs had strictly forbidden to contract alliances with the offspring of Cain, just as, later, the Jews could not lawfully mingle with the Canaanites. Though there are not wanting those who write that incestuous marriages existed before the flood, blood-relationship being held to be no barrier, I yet infer from the fact that Peter has extolled the old world, that such incestuous atrocities did not exist at that time, but that the sin of the ancient world consisted rather in men marrying whom they pleased, and as many wives from the Cainites as they chose, ignoring parental authority and controlled alone by passion. It is, therefore, a harsh word—"All which they chose."

31. I have shown, on various occasions, that the two generations, or churches, of Adam and Cain were separate. For, as Moses clearly states, Adam expelled the murderer from his association. Without doubt, therefore, Adam also exhorted his offspring to avoid the church of the evil-doers and not to mingle with the accursed generation of Cain. And for a while his counsel or command was obeyed.

32. But when Adam died and the authority of the other patriarchs became an object of scorn, the sons of God who had the promise of the blessed seed and themselves belonged to the blessed seed, craved from the tribe of the ungodly, intercourse and espousal. He tersely calls the sons of the patriarchs the "sons of God," since to them was given the promise of the blessed seed and they constituted the true Church. Yielding to the corruptions of the Cainite church they indulged the flesh themselves and took from the tribe of Cain, as wives and mistresses, whom and as many as they chose. This Lamech and Noah saw with pain, and for that reason, perhaps, deferred entering upon marriage.

33. In reference to this point the Jews fancy foolish things. They interpret the sons of God to signify demon-lechers by whom that impious generation was begotten, and that they were called the sons of God by reason of their spiritual nature. The more moderate ones, however, refute such folly and represent the sons of the mighty. This has been aptly disproved by Lyra; for the punishment of the deluge befell, not alone the mighty, but all flesh, as shall the doom at the last day.

34. But as regards the demon-lechers and strumpets (incubi and succubi), I do not deny—nay, I believe—that a demon may be either a lecher or a strumpet, for I have heard men cite their own experience. Augustine says that he heard this from trustworthy people whom he was constrained to believe. Satan is pleased when he

can deceive us in this manner, by assuming the form either of a young man or a young woman. But that anything may be begotten by a devil and a human being is simply false. We hear of monstrous births of demon-like features, and I have even seen some. I am of opinion, however, that they have been deformed by the devil, but not begotten: or that they are real devils with a human body either simulated or purloined. For if the devil, by divine permission, may take possession of the whole man and change his mind, is it strange that he may disfigure also his body, causing men to be born sightless or cripples?

35. Hence, the devil may so deceive frivolous people and such as live without the fear of God that when the devil is in bed, a young man may think that he has a girl with him, and a girl that she has a youth with her; but that anything may be born from such concubinage I do not believe. Many sorceresses have at one time or another been subjected to death at the stake on account of their intercourse with demons. If the devil can deceive eyes and ears so that they fancy they see and hear things which do not exist, how much easier is it for him to deceive the sense of touch, which is in this nature exceedingly gross! But enough! These explanations have no bearing upon the present text, and we have been led to them merely by Jewish babbling.

36. The true meaning is that Moses calls those men the sons of God, who had the promise of the blessed seed. This is a New Testament phrase and signifies the believers who call God, Father, and whom, God in turn, calls sons. The flood came not because the generation of Cain was corrupt, but because the generation of the righteous who had believed God, had obeyed his Word, and had possessed the true worship, now had lapsed into idolatry, disobedience to parents, sensuality, oppression. Even so the last day shall be hastened, not by the profligacy of Gentile, Turk and Jew, but by the filling of the Church with errors through the pope and fanatical spirits, so that those very ones who occupy the highest place in the Church exercise themselves in sensuality, lust and oppression.

37. It is a cause of fear for us all, that even those who were descended from the best patriarchs, began to grow haughty and depart from the Word. They gloried in their wisdom and righteousness, as later the Jews did in circumcision and Father Abraham. So did the popes glory in the title of the Church only to replace gradually their spiritual glory by carnal indulgence after forfeiting the knowledge of God, his Word and his worship. The Roman Church was truly holy and adorned by the grandest martyrs. We, at this day, however, are witnesses how she has fallen.

38. Let no one, therefore, glory in his gifts, however splendid! The greatest gift is to be a member of the true Church. But take care not to become proud on that account, for you may fall, just as Lucifer fell from heaven and, as we are here informed, as the sons of God fell into carnal pleasures. They are, therefore, no longer sons of God, but sons of Satan, having fallen alike from the first and the second table of the Law. So in the past, popes and bishops have been good and holy, but today they are of all men the worst and, so to speak, the dregs of all classes.

39. Among this rabble of decadent men who had departed from the piety and virtues of their ancestors, godly Noah lived in the greatest contempt and hatred

of everybody. How could he approve the corruption of such degenerate progeny? And they themselves were most impatient of reproof. While, therefore, his example shone and gleamed, and his holiness filled the whole earth, the world became worse from day to day, and the greater the sanctity and chastity of Noah, the more the world reveled in lust. This is the beginning; it invariably introduces ruin.

40. When God arouses holy men, full of the Holy Spirit, to instruct and reprove the world, the world, impatient of sound doctrine, falls with much greater zeal into sin and plies it with much greater persistency. This was the situation at the beginning of the world, and now, at the end of the world, we realize it is still the case.

II. GOD'S JUDGMENT AND GRIEF OVER THE FIRST WORLD; NOAH AND HIS PREACHING.

A. GOD'S JUDGMENT AND LAMENTATION OVER THE OLD WORLD.

1. The words of the lamentation.

    a. Interpreters have shamefully perverted these words.

    b. The Jewish interpretation, which Jerome follows.

    c. The Jews' interpretation refuted.

    d. The interpretation of Rabbi Solomon.

    e. The interpretation of others, especially of Origen.

    *   Why Augustine was especially pleased with the doctrine of the Manicheans.

    f. Rabbi David's explanation.

    *   The false idea of the Jews and some Christian interpreters that the true sense of Scripture is learned from grammar.

        (1)   Thus ideas most foreign to the sense of Scripture are defended.

        (2)   This method is false and led the Jews into many fantasies.

    g. The source of Rabbi David's awkward interpretation of these words.

    *   Why Luther has so much to say about the false interpretation of Scripture.

    *   What is necessary to interpret Scripture.

    h. The true sense of these words.

    *   Scripture definition of "to judge".

2. The author of this judgment and lamentation.

*   Man's conduct upon hearing God's Word preached.

3. From what kind of a heart does such judgment and lamentation spring.

*   What kind of grief is the grief of the Holy Spirit.

*   God's severest punishment.

*   What follows when man does not possess God's Word.

    * Why the heathen are so carnal.

4. The nature of this judgment and lamentation.

   * The lamentation and judgment of Luther over Germany because it lightly esteemed God's Word.

   * The spirit of grace and of prayer.

   * The office of the ministry.

     a. It requires two things.

     b. It is the greatest blessing of God.

     c. To despise it is a great sin, and what follows when it is taken from a people.

     d. A complaint of its neglect.

     e. This office is explained by the expression "to judge".

      * Every godly preacher is one who disputes and judges.

      * Luther's grief because of the stubbornness of the world.

      * Why Ahab called Elijah a troubler of Israel.

      * Why the world resents being reproved by sound doctrine. It is a good sign if a minister is reviled by the world.

  * The glory of people who boast of being the Church.

     a. Such glory avails nothing before God.

     b. Papists wish by all means to have this glory.

     c. Papists need this glory to suppress the Protestants.

     d. Christ will decide at the judgment day to whom this glory belongs.

     e. Although the first world adorned itself with this glory, it did not save them.

5. How and why this judgment and complaint are ascribed to God.

6. How they were published to the world by the holy patriarchs.

7. Why they were made.

8. In what way they have been published to the world.

9. How the world resented this judgment and complaint.

  * Time given to the first world for repentance.

     a. We are not to understand the 120 years as the period of a man's life.

     b. The 120 years the time given these people in which to repent.

10. Whether and to what end this time was necessary.

11. How the old world felt upon hearing this.

  * The complaint and judgment of the last world.

  * The nearer the world approaches its destruction the less it thinks of it.

* How the time of the flood is to be compared with the time God gives man to repent.

II. THE JUDGMENT AND LAMENTATION OF GOD OVER THE FIRST WORLD; NOAH AND HIS PREACHING.

A. God's Judgment and Lamentation Over the Old World.

V. 3. *Jehovah said, "My Spirit shall not strive with man forever, for that he also is flesh: yet shall his days be a hundred and twenty years."*

41. Moses here begins by describing Noah as the highest pontiff and priest, or, as Peter calls him, a preacher of righteousness. This text has been mangled in various ways, for the natural man cannot understand spiritual things. When, therefore, the interpreters, with unwashed feet and hands, rushed into the Holy Scriptures, taking with them a human bias and method, as they themselves acknowledge, they could not but fall into diverse and erroneous views. It has almost come to pass, that the more sublime and spiritual the utterances of Scripture, the more shamefully they have been distorted. This passage in particular they have managed so shamelessly that you would not know what to believe, if you followed the interpreters.

42. The Jews are the first to crucify Moses here, for this is their exposition: My Spirit, that is my indignation and wrath, shall not always abide upon man. I will not be angry with men, but spare them, for they are flesh. That means, being spurred by sin, they incline to sin. This meaning Jerome also adopts, who is of the opinion that here only the sin of lust is spoken of, to which we are all prone by nature. But his first error is that he interprets Spirit as wrath. It is the Holy Spirit Moses here speaks of, as the contrast shows. "For man," he says, "is flesh." The meaning is, therefore, that the flesh is not only prone to sin, but also hostile toward God.

43. Then the matter itself serves as refutation, for could anything more absurd have been devised? They see with their eyes the wrath of God swallowing the whole human race through the flood, and yet they expound that God does not wish to be influenced toward the human race by anger but by mercy, and this after a hundred and twenty years, the very time of the flood.

44. Rabbi Solomon expounds it thus: The Spirit which is in God shall no more strive and wrangle. As if God in his majesty would have disputed and wrangled about what should be done with man, whether to destroy or to spare him, finally, wearied by man's wickedness, determining upon his destruction, nevertheless.

45. Others understand this of the created spirit: My spirit that I breathed upon the face of man, that is the spirit of man, shall no longer strive and contend with the flesh, which is in subjection to its lusts, for I shall take away this spirit and free it from the flesh, so that when the latter has become extinct, it may create no more difficulties for the spirit. This is the understanding of Origen, and it does not differ much from the Manichean error which attributes sin not to the whole man, but only to a part. And Augustine says that this had pleased him most in the tenets

of the Manicheans, to hear that his depravity was not altogether his, but only of that part of the body which is evil from the beginning. The Manicheans posited two principles, the good and the bad, just as certain philosophers have posited enmity and friendship. Thus do men not only miss the mark, but they also fall into ungodly delusions.

46. Rabbi David cites Sanctes, and derives the word *jadon* from *nadan*, which means sheath, or shell. But as the interpretation is very clumsy, so he clothes it also in a very clumsy word: My Spirit shall not be inclosed in man as in a sheath. Has anything more unnatural ever been heard? But the Jews make a laughing-stock of modern Hebraists when they convince them that the Holy Scriptures can not be understood except through grammatical rules and an exact science of vowel-points. No exposition is so absurd but that they defend and polish it with their stale grammatical rules.

47. But tell me, what language has there ever been that men easily have learned to speak from grammatical rules? Is it not true that the very languages most thoroughly reduced to rules, like Greek and Latin, are learned rather by practice? What stupendous absurdity, therefore, it is to gather the sense of a sacred tongue, which is the repository of things theological and spiritual, from grammatical rules, and to pay no attention to the proper signification of things? And this is what the rabbis and their disciples do almost universally. Many words and verbs may be declined for which no use is seen in the language. While they make such things paramount and everywhere chase anxiously after etymology, they fall into strange fancies.

48. So here. Because the word in this passage can be derived from *nadan*, they construct from that a prodigious meaning. My spirit, they say, shall not be held back as in a sheath. They mean the spirit of man contained in the body as in a sheath. I shall not leave it in a sheath, they say, but I shall remove him and destroy the sheath. Such absurdities originate in the stale grammatical rules, whereas usage rather should be considered; it is that which trains the grammarian.

49. But I recite all this at length, in order to admonish you, when you come upon such silly commentators, not to follow them and admire such singular wisdom. For great men even have found delight in the folly of the rabbis. They are not unlike the Sacramentarians, who do not deny the words of Christ, This is my body, this is my blood; but explain it thus: Bread is bread, and yet the body of Christ, namely, his creature; this is my blood, namely my wine. This passion of distorting texts no sane man tolerates in the exposition of the fables of Terence, or of the eclogues of Virgil, and, forsooth, we should tolerate it in the Church!

50. We need the Holy Spirit to understand the Holy Scriptures. For we know that the same Spirit shall exist to the end of the world who existed before all things. We glory in possessing this Spirit through the grace of God, and, through him, we have faith, a moderate knowledge of Scripture and an understanding of the other things necessary to godliness. Hence we do not invent a new interpretation; we are guided not only by an analogy of Holy Scripture but also by faith.

51. Through the Holy Scriptures in its entirety, the verb judge, *dun*, signifies almost invariably a public office in the Church, or the office of the ministry, through

which we are corrected, reproved, instructed and enabled to distinguish the evil from the good, etc. Thus, Psalm 110, 6: *Jadin bagojim,* "He will judge among the nations;" which means: He will preach among the nations. The word found in this passage is evidently the same. And in the New Testament this phrase, originally Hebrew, is very much in vogue, especially in Paul's writings, who uses the Hebrew idiom more than the others.

52. I understand this passage therefore as words spoken by Lamech or Noah as a new message to the whole world. For it was a public message proclaimed at some public assembly. When Methuselah, Lamech and Noah saw that the world was hastening straight to destruction by its sins, they resorted to this proclamation: My Spirit shall no longer preach among men. That means: we teach in vain, we admonish in vain; the world has no desire to be better.

53. It is as if one in the present perverse times should say: We teach and make ample effort to summon the world back to sobriety and godliness, but we are derided, persecuted, killed, and all men, in the end, rush to destruction with blind eyes and deaf ears; therefore we are constrained to desist. These are the words of a soul planning appropriate action and full of anxiety, because it is clear that the human race, at the height of its peril, cannot be healed.

54. This exposition conforms to faith and Holy Scriptures. When the Word is revealed from heaven, we see that some are converted, who are freed from damnation. The remaining multitude despises it and securely indulges in avarice, lust and other vices, as Jeremiah says (ch 51, 9): "We should have healed Babylon, but she is not healed: forsake her, and let us go everyone into his own country."

The more diligently Moses and Aaron importuned and instructed, the more obstinate Pharaoh became. The Jews were not made better by even the preaching of Christ and the apostles. The same befalls us who teach in our day. What, in consequence, are we to do? Deplore the blindness and obstinacy of men we may, correct it we cannot. Who would rejoice in the eternal damnation of the popes and their followers? Who would not prefer that they should embrace the Word and recover their senses?

55. A similar exhibition of obstinacy Methuselah, Lamech and Noah saw in their day. Therefore there bursts from them this voice of despair: My Spirit, namely the Word of healing truth, shall no longer bear witness among men. For inasmuch as you refuse to embrace the Word—will not yield to healing truth—you shall perish.

These are the words of a heart filled with anxiety after the manner that the Scriptures say God is anxious; that is, the hearts of Noah, Lamech, Methuselah and other holy men who are filled with love toward all. Beholding this wickedness of men, they are troubled and pained.

56. Such grief is really the grief of the Holy Spirit, as Paul says, "Grieve not the Holy Spirit of God, in whom ye were sealed unto the day of redemption," Eph 4, 30. This means that the Holy Spirit is grieved when we miserable men are distracted and tormented by the wickedness of the world, that despises the Word we preach by the Holy Spirit. Thus Lot was troubled in Sodom, and the pious Jews

in Babylon under the godless king Belshazzar; also Jeremiah, when he preached to the ungodly Jews and exclaimed (Jer 15, 10): "Woe is me, my mother, that thou hast borne me." So in Micah 7, 1: "Woe is me! for I am as the grape gleanings of the vintage: there is no cluster to eat."

57. The wrath of God is most fearful as he recalls the Word. What man would not prefer pestilence, famine, war—these being mere bodily calamities—to a famine of the Word which is always joined to eternal damnation? An example of the horrible darkness into which Satan can lead men when God is silent and does not speak, is furnished by the Gentiles who have been bereft of the Word. Who is not horrified by the Romans, men of exemplary wisdom and famous before other nations by reason of their dignified discipline, who observed the custom of letting the worthy matrons worship and crown Priapus, the foul idol, and of leading bridal virgins before it? What is more ludicrous than that the Egyptians adored the calf Apis as the supreme godhead?

58. The Tripartite History gives an account of Constantine the Great being the first to abolish in Phoenicia and other places the shameless custom of using virgins, before their nuptials, for purposes of prostitution. Such monstrous infamies were accounted religion and righteousness among the Gentiles. There is nothing, in fact, so ridiculous, so stupid, so obscene, nothing so remote from all propriety, that it cannot be foisted as the very essence of religion upon men who have been forsaken by the Word.

59. This is, therefore, the greatest penalty, that God, through the mouths of the holy patriarchs, threatens no longer to reprove men by his Spirit; which means that henceforth he will not give his Word to men, since all teaching is vain.

60. Like punishment our times will bring also upon Germany. For we see the haste, the unrest, of Satan, and his efforts to defraud whom he may of the Word. How many sects has he roused during our lifetime, and this while we bent all our energies toward the maintenance of pure doctrine! What is in store after our death? Surely, he will lead forth whole swarms of Sacramentarians, Anabaptists, Antinomians, Servetians, Campanistans and other heretics who at present, conquered by the pure Word and the constancy of faithful teachers, keep out of sight, but are ready for every opportunity to establish their doctrines.

61. Those, therefore, who have the Word in its purity, should learn to embrace the same, to thank God for it and to call upon him while he may be found. For when the spirit of knowledge is taken away, the spirit of prayer is also gone. Zechariah says (Zech 12, 10): For the spirit of prayer is joined to the spirit of grace. It is the spirit of grace which reproves our sins and gives instruction concerning their remission, which condemns idolatry and instructs concerning the true worship of God, which condemns avarice, lust and oppression, and teaches chastity, patience and charity. This spirit, God here threatens, shall no longer continue his work of instruction, since men refuse to hear and are incorrigible. The spirit of grace having been taken away, the spirit of prayer has also been taken away. For it is impossible for him to pray who is without the Word.

62. Accordingly, the office of a priest is twofold; first, that he turns to God

and prays for himself and for his people; second, that he turns from God to men through instruction and the Word. Says Samuel: "Far be it from me that I should sin against Jehovah in ceasing to pray for you: but I will instruct you in the good and the right way," 1 Sam 12, 23. He is aware that this is his proper office.

63. Therefore, the ministry is rightly praised and esteemed as the highest favor. When this has been lost or has been vitiated, not only prayer becomes impossible, but men are simply in the power of the devil, and do nothing but grieve the Holy Spirit with all their deeds, and thus fall into mortal sin, for which it is not lawful to pray. Such other lapses as occur among men are trivial, for return is open and the hope of pardon is left. But when the Holy Spirit is grieved and men refuse to receive the witness and reproof of the Holy Spirit, the disease is desperate and incurable.

64. But how common is this sin today among all classes! Princes, noblemen, inhabitants of city and country, refuse to be reproved; they rather reprove and sit in judgment upon the Holy Spirit in his servants. They judge of the office of the ministry by the lowliness of the person. They reason thus: This minister is poor and despised; why then should he reprove me, a prince, a nobleman, a magistrate? Rather than endure this, they trample under foot the ministers, together with their office and their message. Should we not, then, fear the judgment of God, such as he here announces to the old world?

65. These, therefore, are the words of a father who disinherits his son, or of a severe schoolmaster in wrath ejecting a pupil, when God simply fixes a hundred and twenty years as the time in which opportunity is granted for repentance. He threatens, should it not be improved, his Spirit shall no longer reprove and strive.

This word pertains properly to the office of the ministry and, in a certain sense, describes it. For every preacher or servant of the Word is a man of strife and judgment, and is constrained, by reason of his office, to chide whatever is vicious, without considering the person or office of his hearer. When Jeremiah does this zealously, he incurs not only hate but also the gravest dangers. He is moved even to impatience, so that he wishes he had never been born, Jer 20, 14.

66. And if I had not been particularly strengthened by God, I should have been wearied and broken down ere this by the contumacy of an impenitent world; for the ungodly so grieve the Holy Spirit in us, that, with Jeremiah, we wish often we had never made a beginning of anything. Hence I often pray to God to let the present generation die with us, because, after our death, the most perilous times are to come.

67. For this reason Elijah is called by Ahab the godless king of Israel, the disturber of Israel; because he openly reproved the idolatry, violence and passions of his day. Likewise we today are deemed the disturbers of Germany.

68. But it is a good sign when men condemn us and call us authors of strife, for the Spirit of God strives with men, reproves and condemns them. But men are so that they wish to be taught only what gives them pleasure, as they frankly admit in Micah 2, 6-7: "Prophesy not to us; for confusion has not seized us, says the house of Jacob." The latter they use as an argument; because they look upon

themselves as the house of Jacob and the people of God, they decline chastening, and will not take to themselves penalties and threats. So today the pope and his accomplices plume themselves solely upon being the Church, and declare that the Church is incapable of error. But notice this text and it will appear how frivolous such an argument is.

69. Are not those whom God threatens to no longer judge by his Spirit likewise the sons of God? What can be more splendid than this name? Beyond doubt they gloried in this name and rebelled against the patriarchs when they opposed, or at least despised, their preaching. For it does not seem likely that God should be thrown into a rage against the whole human race on account of a few sins. But the magnificent name did not save them, nor did it avail that they were strong and great in number. Six hundred thousand marched out of Egypt, and two only entered the land of Canaan; all the others were prevented by death on account of their sins.

70. Evidently God will in no way inquire about the magnificent titles of the Church, pope and bishop. Other testimony will be needed when they desire to escape the wrath of God than to boast of being the Church. For it is written (Mt 7, 20): "By their fruits ye shall know them." And verse 21: "Not every one that saith unto me, Lord, Lord, shall enter into the kingdom of heaven."

71. If ever in the future a council shall be held—which I hardly believe—no one will be able to take from them the title of Church, but propped up by this alone they will condemn and oppress us. Different shall be the judgment, when the Son of man shall come in his glory. Then it shall appear that among the members of the holy Church have been John Huss and Jerome of Prague. The pope, however, and the cardinals, the bishops, doctors, monks and priestly mountebanks, shall appear as the church of evil-doers, enthroned in pestilence, and as veritable henchmen of Satan, rendering aid to their father in his lying and murdering.

72. Such judgment of God we see also here. He does not deny that the offspring of the saints are sons of God. This magnificent title in which they took pride and securely sinned, God leaves to them. And yet these very sons of God who took in marriage the daughters of men, he warns that he not only will take the Word from their hearts and minds, but that he will take from their eyes and ears also the ministering Spirit who preaches, prays, reproves, teaches and sighs in holy servants, and because they refuse to be chastened and reproved; knowing themselves to be the sons of God they despise the Word and its teachers. But they do not escape punishment because of their name. The same shall likewise befall the papists and other enemies of the Word.

73. In accordance with this I hold that the sentiments of pious men are here attributed to God himself, according to the usage of the Holy Scriptures; for instance in Malachi 3, 8, where the Lord says that he is pierced through, or, as the Hebrew has it, that violence is done to him because the people were unfaithful in rendering to the priests the first-fruits and the tenth.

74. But why, you may say, should God need to complain thus? Can he not when it pleases him suddenly destroy the whole world? He surely can, but does

not do so gladly. He says: "I have no pleasure in the death of the wicked; but that the wicked turn from his way and live," Ezk 33, 11. Such a disposition proves that God is inclined to pardon, to endure and to remit the sins of men, if only they will come to their senses; but inasmuch as they continue in obduracy, and reject all help, he is, as it were, tormented by this wickedness of men.

75. The words "And Jehovah said," I attribute to the holy fathers, who testified through a public decree that God should be compelled to exercise vengeance, for they taught by divine authority. When Noah and his ancestors had preached nearly a thousand years, and yet the world continued to degenerate more and more, they announced God's decision to an ungrateful world and disclosed this as his thought: Why should I preach forever and permit my heralds to cry in vain? The more messengers I send, the longer I defer my wrath,—the worse they become. It is therefore necessary for preaching to cease, and for retribution to begin. I shall not permit my Spirit, that is my Word, to sit in judgment and to bear witness forever, and to tolerate man's wickedness. I am constrained to punish their sins. Because man is flesh, he is opposed to me. He is earthly, I am spirit. Man continues in his carnal state, mocks at the Word, persecutes and hates my Spirit in the patriarchs, and the story is told to deaf ears. Hence it is necessary that I should cease and permit man to go his own way. This contrast he desires to indicate when he says: "For he is flesh."

76. Noah, Lamech and Methuselah were very holy men, full of the Holy Spirit. Accordingly they performed their office by teaching, admonishing, urging and entreating, in season and out of season; as Paul says, 2 Tim 4, 2. But they reproved flesh and did unprofitable labor, for the flesh would not yield to sound teaching. Should I, says he, endure forever such contempt for my Word?

77. This proclamation, therefore, contains a public complaint, made by the Holy Spirit through the holy patriarchs, Noah, Lamech, Methuselah and others, whom God took away before the flood that they might not be spectators of so widely diffused wrath. All these, with one voice and mouth, admonished the giants and tyrants to repent, and added the threat that God would not endure forever such contempt of his Word.

78. But the flesh remained true to its nature; they despised faithful exhortations in their presumption and carnal security, and the holy patriarchs they treated as men in dotage and as simpletons because of their threat that God would move in wrath even upon his Church, namely, the heirs of the promise of the coming seed.

79. The added clause, "yet shall his days be a hundred and twenty years," Jerome affirms must not be understood as referring to the years of human life, nor to the age of individual men; for it is certain that after the flood many exceeded the two hundredth year. If you refer it to the years allotted to individuals, the promise would be that individuals should complete so many years, which, however, is false. Therefore he speaks of the time conceded to the world for repentance until the flood should arrive.

80. This interpretation agrees with what precedes. God shows that he is dis-

pleased with the perversity of men. He is full of solicitude and quite ready to forbear. Against his will, so to speak, he permits the flood to rage. Therefore, he decided upon a fixed and adequate time for them to come to their senses, and to escape punishment. All this time Noah admonished men to repent, making it clear that God could not longer endure such wickedness, while he was yet so kind as to grant adequate time for repentance.

81. There is a beautiful cohesion between the words and their significance. A former proclamation threatens: I cannot endure longer contempt for my Word; my preachers and priests attain nothing with their infinite labor except derision. Nevertheless, as a father or good judge would gladly spare a son but is compelled by his wickedness to be severe, so, the Lord says, I do not destroy gladly the human race. I shall grant them one hundred and twenty years in which they may come to themselves, and during which I shall exercise mercy.

82. Horrible was the disaster, because neither the brothers nor the sisters of Noah were saved. It was necessary that the most earnest warning should precede, that, perhaps, they might be called back to repentance. To the Ninevites Jonah announces destruction within forty days, and they repent and are saved.

83. It is clear, therefore, that the heedlessness of the old world was very great, inasmuch as in the one hundred and twenty years of grace it obstinately persisted in its lusts, even deriding its pontiff Noah, the teacher of righteousness.

84. In our times, at the approach of the day of the Lord, almost the same condition obtains; we exhort to penitence the papists and our noblemen; the inhabitants of city and country we admonish not to continue despising the Word, since God will not leave this unavenged. But in vain we exert ourselves, as the Scripture says. A few faithful folk are edified and these are, one by one, gathered away from the face of sin, and "no man layeth it to heart," as is spoken in Isaiah 57, 1. But when God, in this way, has shaken out the wheat and gathered the grain in its place, what, think you, shall be the future of the chaff? Nothing else but to be burned with inextinguishable fire, Mt 13, 42. This shall be the lot of the world.

85. But the world does not understand how it can be that through the preaching of the Gospel the wheat should be separated from the chaff, to be gathered into the barn, while the chaff, that is, the throng of unbelievers sunk in idolatry and darkness, shall be consigned to the fire. It is written: "In a day of salvation have I helped thee; and I will preserve thee," Is 49, 8. Those who will neglect this day of salvation, will find God as an avenger, for he will not do useless labor in threshing empty chaff.

86. But the world is flesh; it does not obey. Yea, the nearer and more immediate the calamity, the more secure it is and the more readily it despises all faithful admonitions. Though this offense provokes the righteous, we should, notwithstanding, conclude that God does not reprove in vain the world through his Holy Spirit, nor that the Holy Spirit in the righteous is grieved in vain. Christ uses this as an example when he speaks of the wickedness and heedlessness of our age: "And as were the days of Noah, so shall be the coming of the Son of man," Mt 24, 37.

87. It is to be observed here what has been an object of difficulty for Jerome,

that the flood came a hundred years after the birth of Shem, Ham and Japheth, while here a hundred and twenty years are said to have been the time of the flood.

B. NOAH AND HIS PREACHING.

1. The time Noah began to preach.
2. Why the world took occasion to despise Noah's preaching.
   * Jerome's reckoning of the 120 years.
3. Why Noah married after living so long single, when the world was to be destroyed.
4. How and why Noah was the prophet of prophets and his the greatest of prophecies.
5. His preaching disregarded not only by the Cainites but by the sons of God.
   * To what end God's complaint of the first world should serve us.
   * When was the judgment of God announced.
   * The generation of the Cainites.
     a. Whether it still existed in the days of Noah.
     b. Why Moses does not record the generations of the Cainites and of their patriarchs.
     c. How the holy patriarchs warned their children against the Cainites.
     d. How the Cainites tormented the holy patriarchs.
6. Why God raised up Noah.
7. Noah's faith exceptionally strong.
8. What impelled Noah to continue his work, and not to turn to the world.
9. How Noah's age was the wickedest and he had to oppose its wickedness all alone.
   * Who of the patriarchs were still living in Noah's time.
10. What trials Noah had to experience.

B. Noah and his Preaching.

87. But this passage shows that Noah began preaching about the impending punishment of the deluge before his marriage, having hitherto led the life of a celibate.

88. Consider, therefore, what pastime he offered to a wicked world in its fancied security. He predicts destruction to the whole world through the flood, nevertheless, he himself marries. Why? Was it not sufficient for him to perish alone, that he must join to himself a companion for the disaster? Oh, foolish old man! Surely if he believed the world was to perish by a deluge, he would rather perish alone than marry and take the trouble to beget children. But if he himself will be saved, why, so shall also we.

In this manner they commenced to despise the preaching concerning the flood with the greater assurance because of the marriage of Noah, ignorant of the counsel of God, who moves in a manner altogether unintelligible to the world. How absurd to promise Abraham posterity through Isaac, and yet to command Isaac to be sacrificed!

89. The divine Jerome argues against the view that God had fixed the time for the flood at a hundred and twenty years, but saw himself compelled, later, when wickedness had waxed strong, to shorten the time.

90. But we shall not make God a liar; we rather give it as our conviction that Noah had hitherto preached, while in a state of celibacy, that the world was to be destroyed through the flood, and later, by a divine command, had taken a maid as a little branch, so to speak, from the race of women, and begotten three sons. Below it is written that he had found grace with the Lord; otherwise he who had refrained from marriage so long, might have continued to do so still longer. But God, in order to restrain his wrath, wants to leave a nursery for the human race; therefore, he commands marriage. This the wicked believe to be a sign that the world shall not perish; they live accordingly in security and despise the preacher, Noah. But the counsel of God is different—to destroy the whole world and to leave through this righteous Noah a nursery for the future world.

91. Noah was, therefore, the greatest prophet; his equal the world has not had. First he teaches the longest time; then he gives instruction concerning a universal punishment coming upon the world, and even fixes the year of its advent. Likewise Christ prophesies concerning the last judgment, when all flesh shall perish. "But of that day," he says in Mark 13, 32, "or that hour knoweth no one, ... but the father."

Jonah foretells punishment for the Ninevites within forty days; Jeremiah foretells seventy years of captivity; Daniel, seventy weeks until the coming of Christ. These are remarkable prophecies, in which time, place and person are accurately described.

But this prophecy of Noah surpasses all others, inasmuch as he foretells through the Holy Spirit that within a certain number of years the whole human race shall perish. He is worthy to be called the second Adam and the head of the human race, through whose mouth God speaks and calls the whole world to repentance.

92. It is terrible, however, that his message was despised with such assurance that not only none of the Cainites, but not even any one of Adam's progeny underwent a change. Therefore Noah was compelled to witness the destruction of brothers, sisters, relatives and kindred without number, and all these made a mock of the pious old man and of his message as an old woman's tale.

93. This awful example is held up to us lest we persist in sin. For if God did not spare the primitive world, which was so magnificent—the very flower and youth of the world—and in which had lived so many pious men, but, as he says in Psalm 81, 12, "gave them up unto their own hearts' lust," and cast them aside, as if they had no claim upon the promise made to the Church—if he did this, how much less will he spare us who do not possess such prerogatives?

94. Therefore, the decree cited in this passage that God would grant men a hundred and twenty years for repentance, was rendered and promulgated before Noah had begotten children.

95. With reference to the generation of the Cainites, no mention is made of their patriarchs at the time of the flood, nor does Moses even deem them worthy of being named. Previously he has brought down the generation of Cain as far as Lamech, but whether his sons or nephews lived at the time of Noah is uncertain. This much is certain, that the offspring of Cain existed to that time, and were so powerful as to mislead the very sons of God, since even the posterity of the holy patriarchs perished in the flood.

96. Before this time the holy patriarchs—the rulers of the true Church, as it were—admonished their families to beware of the accursed generation. But the Cainites, incensed at being condemned, made the attempt to overturn the righteous with every kind of mischief; for the church of Satan wars perpetually against the Church of God.

97. Therefore, as the righteous begin to waver and wickedness gains ground, God raises Noah to exhort to repentance and to be for his descendants a perpetual example, whose faith and diligent, patient devotion to teaching, his offspring might admire and imitate. A great miracle is it and a case of illustrious faith, that Noah, having heard through Methuselah and Lamech the decree that the world is to perish after a hundred and twenty years, through the flood, does not doubt its truth, and yet, when the hundred and twenty years have almost expired, marries and begets children. He might rather have thought: If the human race is to perish, why should I marry? Why should I beget sons? If I have refrained these many years, I shall do so henceforth. But Noah does not do this; rather, after making known God's purpose respecting the world's destruction, he obeys God, who calls him to matrimony, and believes God that, though the whole world may perish, yet he with his children shall be saved. An illustrious faith is this and worthy of our consideration.

98. There was in him first that general faith, in common with the patriarchs, concerning the seed which was to bruise the head of the serpent. He possessed also the singular virtue of holding fast to this faith in the midst of such a multitude of offenses, and not departing from Jehovah. Then, to this general faith he added the other, special faith, that he believed God as regards both the threatened destruction of the rest of the world and the salvation promised to Noah himself and his sons. Beyond a doubt, to this faith his grandfather Methuselah and his father Lamech earnestly incited him; for it was as difficult to so believe as it was for the Virgin Mary to believe that none but herself was to be the mother of the Son of God.

99. This faith taught him to despise the presumption of the world which derided him as a man in his dotage. This faith prompted him diligently to continue the building of the ark, a work those giants probably ridiculed as extreme folly. This faith made Noah strong to stand alone against the many evil examples of the world, and to despise most vehemently the united judgment of all others.

100. But almost unutterable and miraculous is this faith, burdened as it is with strange and most weighty obstacles, which the Holy Spirit shows in passing, without going into great detail, that we may be induced to meditate the more diligently upon its circumstances. Consider first the great corruption of the age. While the Church had before this time many and most holy patriarchs, it was now deprived of such rulers; Adam, Seth, Enos, Cainan, Mahalalel, Jared, Enoch are all dead, and the number of patriarchs is reduced to three—Methuselah, Lamech and Noah. These alone are left at the time the decree concerning the destruction of the world is published. These three are compelled to witness and suffer the incredible malice of men, their idolatry, blasphemy, violent acts, foul passions, until finally Methuselah and Lamech are also called out of this life. There Noah was the only one to oppose the world rushing to destruction, and to make an effort to preserve righteousness and to repress unrighteousness. But far from meeting with success, he had to see even the sons of God lapse into wickedness.

101. This ruin and havoc of the Church troubled the righteous man and all but broke his heart, as Peter says of Lot in Sodom, 2 Pet 2, 8. Now, if Lot was so distracted and vexed by the wickedness of one community, how must it have been with Noah, against whom not only the generation of Cain raged, but who was opposed also by the decadent generation of the patriarchs, and then even by his own father's house, his brothers, sisters, and the descendants of his uncles and aunts? For all these were corrupted and estranged from the faith by the daughters of men. As the text says, they "saw the daughters of men."

III. THE SINS OF THE ANCIENT WORLD IN PARTICULAR.

A. THE FORBIDDEN MARRIAGES ENTERED INTO.

1. Why this is said of the sons and not of the daughters of the holy patriarchs.
2. Why were the holy fathers so emphatically forbidden to let their sons marry the ungodly.
3. How this was the beginning of all evils.
   * What evils have in all times come through woman.
4. The sins here sprang from despising the first table of the law.
   * The sins of the second table follow when the first table is not kept.
5. Everything that is called sin is embraced in this sin.
6. How marriage with the children of the true Church was despised.
7. Their desire to marry thus resembled Eve's desire to take the forbidden apple.
8. Why the patriarchs' children took this step.
9. How these marriage alliances were formed.
10. Berosus' testimony concerning these forbidden marriages.

B. DISORDER IN ALL BRANCHES OF SOCIETY.

C. THE TYRANNY EXERCISED.

1. By the "giants" or tyrants.
    a. What is to be understood by tyrants.
     * The pope resembles the tyrants before the flood.
    b. The nature of these tyrants.
    c. Why called Nephilim.
    d. Whether they received their name from their size or from their cruelty.
     * How the Scriptures designate true rulers.
    e. These tyrants types of Antichrist.
    f. They were raging, powerful and criminal characters.
     * Of authorities.
        (1) How God wants us to honor the authorities though he terribly threatens them.
        (2) Why God wants them to be honored, when he himself does not honor them.
        (3) Godless rulers are God's swine and are rare birds in heaven.
    g. Whether these tyrants were rulers and why God called them by such a shameful name.
    h. Moses chose the word Nephilim, which in his day designated a wicked people, to express the tyrants of the first World.
2. By "the mighty men."
    a. How Jerome perverts this text.
    b. What is to be understood by "the mighty men that were of old".
     * The meaning of "Olam".
    c. Whence did they receive their power.
    d. Why called "mighty men".
     * The character of the true church.
3. By "the men of renown."
    a. Why they were thus named.
    b. Who they were.
     * They resembled the pope and bishops.
    c. Lyra's false explanation of it refuted.
     * How Antichrist is restrained from the world, and true doctrine maintained.

D. THE SIN AGAINST THE HOLY SPIRIT.

 * That one sin follows another until man reaches the highest degree of sin.

III. THE SINS OF THE OLD WORLD IN PARTICULAR.

A. The Forbidden marriages entered Into.

102. But, I ask, why is not complaint made also of the men, or why are not the daughters of God included in this complaint? He says merely that they "saw the daughters of men." It was surely for this reason, that the holy generation of Seth had received the peculiar injunction to beware of fellowship with the Cainites, inasmuch as they had been excluded from the true Church, and to mingle with them neither socially through marriage, nor ecclesiastically through worship, for the righteous should avoid every occasion of offense.

103. In prohibiting marriage with the Cainites it was the chief purpose of the pious fathers to maintain their generation pure; for daughters bring into the houses of their husbands the views and manners of the fathers. Thus, we read of Solomon in the Book of the Kings that he was led astray through a woman who was a stranger; and thus Jezebel introduced the wickedness of the Syrians into the kingdom of Israel.

104. The holy fathers saw the same would come to pass in their generation; therefore, after they were separated from the Cainites through the divine command, they resolved that the sons of the holy generation should not marry the daughters of men. The daughters of the race of the righteous could more readily be restrained from marriage with the Cainites, while the sons were independent and headstrong.

105. In this way Moses wishes to show the trouble began from the time the sons of God joined themselves to the daughters of men, seeing that they were fair. The sons of men who were proud and strong and passionately given to pleasure, without doubt despised the plain maidens of the pious race who had been reared by the holy patriarchs not delicately, but simply and modestly, being arrayed in homely garb. There was hence no necessity of making a law also for the maidens, inasmuch as they were in any case neglected by the noble Cainites.

106. If you study the history of nations you will find that women have been the occasion for the overthrow of the strongest kingdoms. Well known is the disgrace of Helen. The sacred writings demonstrate also that woman occasioned the fall of the whole human race. This, however, should be mentioned without reflection upon the sex, for we have a command, "Honor thy father and thy mother," Ex 20, 12. Likewise, "Husbands, love your wives," Col 3, 19. It is true that Eve was the first to pluck the apple; however, she first sinned by idolatry and fell from the faith, which faith, as long as it is in the heart, controls also the body; but when it has departed from the heart, the body serves sin. Guilt is not peculiar to sex but to sin, which man has in common with woman.

107. Thus Moses gives an account of the prevailing unrighteousness and lust. But he gives the reader to understand that, before sin was committed against the second table of the Law, the first had been violated, and the Word of God treated with contempt. Otherwise the sons of God would have obeyed the will of their pious parents forbidding marriage with those outside the Church.

108. Moses, therefore, concludes that, because the sons of God had forsaken the worship and Word of God and departed from the precepts of their parents, thereupon to fall into sensuality and lust, and to take to wife whom they pleased, they also became violent and appropriated the goods of others. The world cannot do otherwise. When it has forsaken God, it worships the devil; when it has despised the Word and fallen into idolatry, it rushes forth into all sins of passion, in which fierceness of anger and fierceness of desire by turns are aroused, and thus all the appetites are thrown into a state of the greatest disorder. When the righteous reprove this, the result is resentment and violence against them.

109. The sin of the flood, then, embraces everything that may be called sin, by the first as well as the second table. Wicked men first depart from God through unbelief; then they disregard obedience to parents, and finally become murderers, adulterers, etc.

110. I mention this to the end that no one may believe that sex or the marriage estate in themselves are to blame. It is chiefly transgression of God's commandments and disobedience to parents which are condemned. Owing to absence of fellowship between the Cainites and the true Church, pious parents desired also social separation from the Cainites, for fear they might be perverted by the manners of ungodly wives. But God's command being neglected, and the authority of parents despised, the younger generation lapsed into the passions of concupiscence and vehemence. In this way the honor of sex and the dignity of matrimony are conserved: accusation is brought solely against the unrighteousness which first departs from God and then manifests itself in injuring the saints.

111. This is the teaching of the words: "The sons of God saw the daughters of men that they were fair." Why did they not see the daughters of God and desire those in the Church and possess the promise of the seed? Are they not convicted of contempt for the sisters of their own generation, that is the true Church, and of mingling with the carnal and impious generation of Cain? They despise the simplicity and reserve of their sisters and prefer the smiles, the dress, the wiles of the daughters of Cain; the latter they crave and cultivate, the former they treat either with neglect or dishonor.

112. With such eyes as Eve viewed the apples when she fell into sin, the sons of God viewed the daughters of men. Eve had seen the forbidden tree before that, but with eyes of faith looking back to God's commandment; for that reason she did not crave, but rather she fled from the same. When, however, the eyes of faith were dimmed and she beheld the tree solely with carnal eyes, she stretched out her hand with desire and invited also Adam, her husband.

113. Likewise the sons of the patriarchs had seen long before that the daughters of the Cainites excelled in form, dress and elegance of manners. Nevertheless, they did not mingle with them, for the eye of faith looked back to the commandment of God and to the promise of the seed to be born from the generation of the righteous. But the eyes of faith having been lost, they saw no longer either the command or the promise of God, but followed merely the desire of the flesh. The simple, good and virtuous girls of their own generation they despised; the Cain-

ites they married, seeing they were polished, charming and pleasant.

114. It is not a sin, therefore, that they marry, nor is the sex in itself condemned. Condemnation lies in this, that with contempt of the divine commandment they marry unlawfully; that they permit themselves to be led astray by their wives from the true worship to the wicked worship of a false church; that, after the fashion of the Cainites, they pay no heed to parental authority and become guilty of violence, oppression and other sins.

Moses clearly reveals their sin when he says: "They took them wives of all that they chose," as if he said: To marry a wife is not an evil but a blessing, if it be done lawfully. But they sinned in that they married without judgment, against the will and purpose of the parents, marrying whom and as many as they pleased, regardless of their own estate, whether married or single.

115. This is a stern word, by which Moses characterizes it as a great sin that they arbitrarily married two wives or more, exchanged them, or snatched them from others, after the manner of Herod, who possessed himself of his brother's wife. It is this unbridled reign of evil lust that Moses discloses and condemns.

116. Berosus writes that incestuous marriages also took place among them, so that they married even their mothers and sisters. But I doubt whether they were so wicked as that. It is a sin sufficiently grave that in marrying they dispensed with judgment, the authority of their parents and even with the Word of God, following altogether the guidance of lust and desire. They took whom they pleased and whom they could, and by such license they brought chaos into domestic, public and churchly relations.

B. Disorder in all Branches of Society.

The sin of the primeval world was, therefore, an upheaval of all established order, inasmuch as the Church was demoralized by idolatry and false modes of worship. This condition was aggravated by those oppressors who cruelly persecuted the righteous teachers and holy men. Public discipline was destroyed by oppression and violent deeds, and domestic discipline by uncurbed lust. Upon such overturning of piety and integrity followed universal depravity; men were not merely evil but plainly incorrigible.

C. The Tyranny Exercised.

V. 4a. *The Nephilim* (giants) *were in the earth in those days,*

117. Moses continues the description of the sin and offense which provoked the deluge. The first point was that the sons of God had fallen from the fear of God, and the Word had become altogether carnal, perverting not only the Church but also the State and home. Now he adds that wickedness had grown to the extent of giants arising upon earth. He clearly states that there were born from the concubinage of the sons of God with the daughters of men, not sons of God, but giants; that is, bold men who arrogated to themselves at the same time both government and priesthood.

118. Just so the pope arrogates to himself at the same time the spiritual and the temporal sword. This would not be the height of evil, if he would only make use of his power for the preservation of State and Church; but the greatest sin is that he abuses his power for the establishment of idolatry, for a warfare against sound doctrine, and for purposes of oppression even in the State. When the Papists are reproved with the Word of God, they spurn such reproof, claiming that they are the Church and incapable of error. This class of people Moses calls "giants," men who arrogate to themselves power both political and ecclesiastical, and who sin most licentiously.

119. Such men are described in the Book of Wisdom who say: "Let unrighteousness be our law," 2, 11. Also in Psalms, 12, 4: "Who have said, With our tongue will we prevail; our lips are our own: who is lord over us?" Again in Psalm 73. "They scoff, and in wickedness utter oppression: they speak loftily," etc. Such were the giants who withstood the Holy Spirit to his face, who, through the mouth of Lamech, Noah and the sons of Noah, exhorted, implored, taught and reproved.

120. There are those who dispute the meaning of the noun Nephilim and derive it from *Naphal,* which signifies "to fall." They commonly take it in a passive sense, meaning that other men, seeing the uncouth forms and extraordinary size, fell down from fear. Let the rabbis vouch for the correctness of this; it is ridiculous to call them *"Nephilim"* because others fell. Some, however, suggest the etymology that they were thus called because they had fallen from the common stature of men, and allege as proof-passage Numbers 13, 33, from which it appears that giants possessed huge bodies like the Anakim and Rephaim. Which of these are right, I do not decide, especially since it is certain that a theory of all words can not be given, nor their origin demonstrated.

121. But here another question obtrudes itself: Why should those born from the sons of God and the daughters of men alone have differed from the ordinary stature of man? I have no other answer than that the text says nothing of stature in this place. In Numbers 13, 33 it is said: "There we saw the giants, the sons of Anak, who come of the giants: and we were in our sight as grasshoppers, and so we were in their sight." There hugeness of body is shown, but not here; therefore they may be called giants for some other reason than massive stature.

122. To give my opinion of the word, I hold it is to be taken neither in the sense of the neuter nor of the passive, but of the active, inasmuch as the word *"naphal"* is often used in the sense of the active, though it does not belong to the third conjugation, in which almost all transitive verbs are found. Thus in Joshua 11, 7: "So Joshua came, and all the people of war with him, against them by the waters of Merom suddenly, and fell upon them." If the verb is construed as neuter, as if Joshua and his men had fallen before the enemies, history will object; for the meaning is that they fell upon the enemies and suddenly overpowered them.

123. Therefore, this passage and other, similar ones prompt me to understand *"nephilim"* to designate not bulk of body, but tyranny and oppression, inasmuch as they domineered by force, making no account of law and honor, but merely indulging their pleasure and desire. Rightful rulers the Scripture calls shepherds

and princes, but those who rule by wrong and violence are rightly called "*Nephilim*," because they fall and prey upon those beneath them.

Thus in Psalm 10: "He croucheth and humbleth himself and *Venaphal Baa Zumaf Helkaim* (falls with his strong ones upon the poor)". The Holy Spirit speaks there of the reign of the Antichrist, whom he describes as raging so furiously as to crush what he can, and, at all events, to bend what he cannot crush, so that afterward he may suppress with all his strength what has been bent. For *baazuma* can be indifferently rendered by "with his strength," or "with his strong ones." This power, he says, he uses only against those who are *Hilkaim*, that is the poor, such as have previously been in some state of affliction. Others who excel in power, he worships so as to draw them over to his side.

124. Accordingly I interpret "giants" in this passage not as men of huge stature, as in Numbers 13, 33, but as violent and oppressive; as the poets depict the Cyclopeans, who fear neither God nor men, but follow only their desires, relying upon their strength and power. For the oppressors sit enthroned in majesty, sway empires and kingdoms, and arrogate to themselves even spiritual power, but use such power against the Church and the Word of God for the gratification of their lust.

125. Observe here the strange counsel of God, commanding us to fear the authorities, to obey, serve and honor them, while at the same time the threats and dreadful reproofs which he administers are almost invariably directed against those in authority, against kings and princes, as if God proceeded against them with a peculiar hatred. Scripture enjoins upon us to honor authority, but itself does not honor it; rather it destroys it with a threat of the gravest penalties. Scripture enjoins us to fear authority, but itself appears to despise authorities, inasmuch as it does not commend but threatens.

126. Does not Mary earnestly declaim in her song against princes, Luke 1, 51-53: "He hath scattered the proud in the imagination of their heart. He hath put down princes from their thrones, and hath exalted them of low degree. The hungry he hath filled with good things; and the rich he hath sent empty away"? If we believe this to be true, who would wish to be found among authorities, for whom so certain perdition is prepared and imminent? Who would not prefer to live on a lowly plane and suffer hunger? The second psalm accuses the authorities of the gravest crime when it says that they place themselves with united strength and efforts in opposition to God and his anointed and render violence to his kingdom. "Thou hast made of a city a heap, of a fortified city a ruin," Is 25, 2. The whole Bible abounds with like sentiments.

127. Thus, the Bible does not honor the authorities, but threatens them with danger, and drags them into manifest contempt; and still with consummate care it commands us to reverence and fear them, and to render them all manner of service. Why is this? Surely because God himself desires to punish them, and has reserved vengeance for himself instead of surrendering it to their subjects. Jeremiah argues in chapter 12, 1, concerning the prosperity of the way of the ungodly, and yet the Lord is righteous. But he concludes: "Thou, O Lord, fattenest them and

preparest them for the sacrifice."

128. So might it be said that the authorities are God's swine, as it were; he fattens them, gives them wealth, power, fame and the obedience of their subjects. They are not pursued, while they themselves pursue and oppress others; they suffer no injury, but they inflict it upon others; they do not give to others, but rob them until the hour comes when, like fattened swine, they are slaughtered. Hence the German proverb: A prince is a rare bird in the kingdom of heaven or, princes are wild game in heaven.

129. Accordingly, those whom Moses calls here "*Nephilim*," which is an odious and disgraceful name, were without doubt the lawful administrators of Church and State. But because they did not use their office as they should, God marks and brands them with this opprobious name. As we, in this corrupt state of nature, are unable to use the least gift without pride, so God, most intolerant of pride, thrusts the mighty from their throne, and leaves the rich empty.

130. I accept, then, the word "*Nephilim*" as having an active signification, being equivalent to tyrants, oppressors, revelers. I believe, furthermore, as has been the case with other languages also, that Moses has transferred the usage of this word from his own times to those before the deluge, after changing somewhat its meaning, inasmuch as these degenerate descendants of the sons of God abused their power and position for the oppression of the good, just as those Anakim were tyrants relying upon bodily strength, and so Moses will presently show.

V. 4b. *And also after that, when the sons of God came in unto the daughters of men, and they bare children to them; the same were the men that were of old, the men of renown.*

131. Jerome[2] renders: *Isti sunt potentes a seculo* (these are mighty men from the beginning). But the word *seculum* (olam) does not here signify duration of time, nor does it predicate extent. These giants did not exist from the beginning, they were not born until the sons of God had degenerated. But *seculum* (olam) connotes a second predicate, that of substance, so that Moses explains the nature of the power in which they trusted to have been secular or worldly. They despised the ministry of the Word as a vile office; therefore they seized upon another office, a secular one. The very same thing our Papists have done. It has pleased them better to hold ample revenues and worldly kingdoms than to be hated of all men for the sake of the Gospel.

132. As far as Moses is concerned, the noun *olam* designates the world itself, and also age or time. Hence it is to be carefully noted when *olam* (*seculum*) signifies duration of time, and when it signifies "world" in the Scriptures. Here it signifies of necessity "world," for they did not exist from the beginning.

133. This clause, then, aptly describes the power they had received, not from the Church, nor from the Holy Spirit, but from the devil and the world. It is, as it were, the counterpart of what Christ says before Pontius Pilate, John 18, 36: "My kingdom is not of this world." The servants of the Word struggle with hunger,

---

[2] So also the A. V. and the R. V., while Luther has by no means the philological science against him. **Mundus, seculum, aion**, and **olam** are used to express the same conception. Translator.

and they labor under the hate of all classes. In consequence, they cannot exercise tyranny; but those who possess kingdoms, who govern states, who possess castles and domains, are equipped for exercising tyranny.

134. This clause contains also a suggestive reference to the small Church with her few souls. These are cross-bearers without wealth; but they possess the Word. Their only wealth is what the world despises and persecutes. The Nephilim, on the other hand, or giants, usurp as the descendants of the patriarchs the splendid name of the Church, and possess also kingdoms. They exercise dominion, and pursue the miserable Church in their power. In accordance therewith Moses calls them mighty before, or in, the world; or worldlings and temporal potentates.

135. What Jerome renders *viri famosi* (famous men) is, in Hebrew, "men of name," that is, renowned or famous in the world. Moses touches here also upon the sin of the Cyclopeans, who, possessing everything in the world, possessed also a famous name and were renowned throughout the world; while, on the contrary, the true sons of God, namely Noah and his sons, were held in the greatest scorn and regarded as heretics, as sons of the devil, as a blot upon the grandeur of Church and State. So is it now with us. Christ testifies in Matthew 24, 37, that the last times resemble the times of Noah.

136. Moses had before testified that the Holy Spirit would be taken from the wicked and they would be sent in the ways of their own desire. They were, accordingly, such rascals as the pope today with his cardinals and bishops, who are not only styled princes and possess kingdoms, but also take to themselves the name of Church, so as to subject us as heretics to the ban, and securely to condemn us. They do not permit themselves to be called tyrants, nor wicked, nor temple-robbers. They wish to be styled most kind, holy and reverend gentlemen.

137. The meaning, therefore, is not that which Lyra follows when he understands "famous" as "notorious." As the world does not call the pope Antichrist, but ascribes to him the name of the greatest saint and admires him as if he and his carnal creatures were filled with the Holy Spirit and incapable of error, and therefore humbly worships whatever he commands or advises—exactly so those giants had a noble name and were held in admiration by the whole world. On the contrary, Noah with his followers was condemned as a rebel, as a heretic, as a traducer of the dignity of State and Church. So today do bishops regard us who profess the Gospel.

D. The Sin against the Holy Spirit.

138. This passage furnishes a description of the sins with which that age was burdened: Men were averse to the Word; they were given over to their own lusts and reprobate minds; they sinned against the Holy Spirit by persistent impenitence, by defending their ungodly behavior and by warring upon the recognized truth. Yet with all these blasphemies they retained the name and authority, not only of the State, but also of the Church, as if God had exalted them to the place of the angels. When this was the state of things, and Noah and Lamech with their pious ancestor Methuselah taught in vain, God turned them over to the desires

of their hearts (Ps 81, 12) and maintained silence until they should experience the flood, the prophecy of which they refused to believe.

139. This is falling away from God and Church and entering upon illicit marriage. One sin, unless corrected at once, will lead to another, and so on indefinitely until the state is reached which Solomon describes in Proverbs 18, 3, "When the wicked cometh, there cometh also contempt, and with ignominy Cometh reproach." They who thus sin, even if afterward rebuked, do not heed. They imagine they stand in need of no instructor, and think they represent a just cause. They do not believe in a life after this, or even hope for salvation, while living in open sin. Notwithstanding, scorn and shame shall overwhelm them. It was this persistent impenitence and consummate contempt for the Word that impelled God to visit all flesh with a universal flood.

IV. GOD'S REPENTANCE AND GRIEF THAT HE MADE MAN.

A. THE REPENTANCE OF GOD.

1. The Words, "The wickedness of man was great."

    a. How Luther used these words against the doctrine of free will; how the advocates of free will falsely interpreted them, and how they are refuted.

      * Concerning free will.

        (1) Augustine's doctrine of free will misinterpreted by the schools.

        (2) The schools unreasonably defend it.

        (3) Man has no free will and without the grace of the Holy Spirit can do nothing.

        (4) The reproving office of the Holy Spirit makes it clear that man has no free will.

        (5) Whether there is hope, if a council be held, that the Papists will abandon their false doctrine of free will.

        (6) How the true doctrine of free will leads us to a knowledge of sin and what we are to hold in reference to it.

        (7) Why we should guard against the false doctrine concerning free will.

            * The comfort for one who commits sins of infirmities.

            * All endeavors without the Holy Spirit are evil.

        (8) We are to distinguish in the doctrine of free will what is good politically from what is good theologically.

    b. These words are wrongly understood by the Jews and sophists.

      * How we should view the discussions of philosophers in regard to God and divine things.

    c. These words should be understood as spoken not only of the people before the flood, but of all men.

2. The Words, "It Repented Jehovah."

   a. How the repentance of God is to be reconciled with the wisdom and omniscience of God.

     (1) The way sophists answer this question.

     (2) Luther's answer.

       * How man should treat questions which lead us into the throne of the divine majesty.

       * How the passages of Scripture are to be understood which attribute to God the members of a human body.

       * Whether the Anthropomorphites were justly condemned.

       * Why God is represented to us as if he sprang from the temporal and the visible.

       * We cannot explore God's nature.

       * In what pictures God reveals himself in the Old Testament, and in the New.

       * The will of God in signs and the will of God's good pleasure, "signs" and "Beneplaciti."

         (a) How we can know God's will in signs.

         (b) Why we cannot know the will of God's pleasure, nor fathom it.

         (c) What is really to be understood by the will in signs.

   b. The way the schools explain these words.

   c. How they are to be rightly understood.

    * Disputing about God's majesty and omnipotence places man in a dangerous position.

    * How man should hold to the signs by which God revealed himself.

    * What the will of God's pleasure is, to what it serves and how it is revealed in Christ.

    * The will of good pleasure of which the fathers speak cannot comfort the heart.

    * The only view of the Godhead possible in this life.

   d. In what sense it can be said that "it repented Jehovah that he had made man".

IV. THE REPENTANCE AND GRIEF OF GOD
BECAUSE HE HAD MADE MAN.

A. The Repentance of God.

V. 5-6. *And Jehovah saw that the wickedness of man was great in the earth, and that every imagination of the thoughts of his heart was only evil continually. And it repented*

Jehovah that he had made man on the earth, and it grieved him at his heart.

140. This is the passage which we have used against "free will," of which Augustine writes that without the grace of the Holy Spirit it can do nothing but sin. The scholastics, however, the champions of free will, are not only hard beset by this clear passage, but also by the authority of Augustine, and they sweat. Of Augustine they say that his language is hyperbolical, as Basil writes of one who in refuting the other side had gone too far, that he did like the farmers; they when trying to straighten out crooked branches bend them a little too far on the other side; and so Augustine, in beating back the Pelagians, is asserted to have spoken more severely against free will in the defense of grace than the merits of the case warranted.

141. As far as this passage is concerned, it is slandered when it is held that it speaks only of the evil generation before the flood, and that now men are better, at least some who make good use of their freedom of will. Such wretched interpreters do not see that the passage speaks of the human heart in general, and that a particle is plainly added, *Rak*, which signifies "only." In the third place, they fail to see that after the flood the same declaration is repeated in the eighth chapter in almost precisely the same terms. For God says, "The imagination of man's heart is evil from his youth," Gen 8, 21. Here evidently he does not speak only of the antediluvians. He rather speaks of those to whom he makes the promise that henceforth another general flood of water shall never come, that is, of all the offspring of Noah. These are words of universal application: "The imagination of man's heart is evil."

142. We draw, therefore, the general conclusion that man without the Holy Spirit and without grace can do nothing but sin, and thus he unhaltingly goes forward from sin to sin. When in addition, he will not endure sound doctrine but rejects the word of salvation and resists the Holy Spirit, he becomes an enemy of God, blasphemes the Holy Spirit and simply follows the evil desires of his heart. Witnesses of this are the examples of the prophets, Christ and the Apostles, the primeval world under Noah as teacher, and also the example of our adversaries today, who cannot be convinced by anything that they are in error, that they sin, that their worship is ungodly.

143. Other declarations of Holy Scripture prove the same thing. Is not the statement of the fourteenth Psalm, verse 3, sweeping enough when it says: "Jehovah looked down from heaven upon the children of men, to see if there was any that did understand, and did seek after God. They are all gone aside?" Thus, Ps 116, 11, "All men are liars;" and Paul, "God hath shut up all unto disobedience," Rom 11, 32. These passages are most sweeping, and emphatically force the conclusion that we all, without the Holy Spirit, whose dispenser is Christ, can do nothing but err and sin. Therefore, Christ says in the Gospel, "I am the vine, ye are the branches: ... apart from me ye can do nothing," Jn 15, 5. Without me you are a branch cut off, dry, dead and ready for the burning.

144. And the very reason the Holy Spirit performs the office of reproving the world is that he may call the world back to penitence and the recognition of its de-

rangement. But the world remains consistent with itself; it hears not and believes it can please God with forms of worship of its own choosing and without the sanction of the divine Word, and does not permit itself to be undeceived.

145. If ever a council should be held, the final declaration and conclusion with reference to this very point, the freedom of will, will be that we should abide by the decisions of the pope and the fathers. We may clamor until we are hoarse that man in himself without the Holy Spirit is evil, that everything he does without the Holy Spirit or without faith is condemned before God, that his heart is depraved and all his thought; we shall effect nothing.

146. Therefore, the mind is to be grounded in this, and we are to hold fast the doctrine which lays before us our sin and condemnation. This knowledge of our sin is the beginning of salvation; we must absolutely despair of ourselves and give glory for righteousness to God alone. Why does Paul elsewhere complain, and in Romans 7, 18 freely confess that there is nothing good in him? He says plainly, "in my flesh;" so that we understand that the Holy Spirit alone can heal our infirmity. When this has been fixed in our hearts, the foundation of our salvation is largely laid, inasmuch as subsequently clear testimonies are given that God will not cast away the sinner, that is, one who recognizes his sin and desires to come to his senses and thirsts after righteousness and the remission of sin through Christ.

147. Let us, therefore, take care not to be found among those Cyclopeans who oppose the Word of God and proclaim their freedom of will and their own powers. Though we often err, though we fall and sin, still, upon yielding to reproof on the part of the Holy Spirit with an humble confession of our depravity, the Holy Spirit himself will be present, and not only not impute to us the sin we acknowledge, but the grace of Christ shall cover it and he will shower upon us other gifts necessary to this life as well as the future one.

148. But the words of Moses are to be more closely considered, for with a definite purpose he has used here a peculiar expression; he has not merely said, "The thoughts of man's heart are evil," but "the imagination of the thoughts of his heart." Thus he expresses the highest that man can achieve with his thoughts or with his reason and free will. "Imagination" he calls that which man with his strongest effort devises, selects, creates like a potter, and believes to be most beautiful.

But such imagination is evil, he says, and that not once, but always. For our reason without the Holy Spirit is altogether without knowledge of God. Now, to be without knowledge of God means to be entirely base, to dwell in darkness and to deem that very good which, in reality, is very bad.

149. But when I speak of good, I do so from the standpoint of theology, for we must distinguish between the theological and the civil standpoints. God approves also the rule of the ungodly; he honors and rewards virtue also among the ungodly: but only in regard to the things of this life and in things grasped by a reason which is upright from the civil standpoint; whereas the future life is not embraced in such reward. His approval is not with regard to the future life.

150. When we dispute about the freedom of the will, the question with us is

what it may do from the theological standpoint, not in civil affairs and in those subjects to reason. We believe that man, without the Holy Spirit, is altogether corrupt before God, though he may stand adorned with all heathen virtues, inasmuch as there are certainly distinguished examples of moderation, of liberality, of love of country, parents and children, of courage and humanity, even in the history of the Gentiles. We maintain that man's best thoughts concerning God, the worship of God, the will of God, are worse than Cimmerian darkness; for the light of reason, which has been given to man alone, understands only bodily blessings. Such is the wicked infatuation of our evil desires.

151. This declaration, therefore, should not be construed frivolously, as the Jews and sophists do, who believe that the lower part of man only is here meant, which is bestial, and that the reason longs for better things. "The imagination of the thoughts" they apply accordingly to the second table, like the Pharisee who condemns the publican and says that he is not like the other persons. The words the Pharisee uses are very fine, for to give thanks to God for his gifts is not a sin; and yet we declare this same thing to be ungodly and wicked, because it proceeded from gross ignorance of God, and it is truly prayer turned into sin, tending neither to the glory of God nor to the welfare of men.

152. You may observe that philosophers have at various times quite cleverly discussed God and the providence with which he rules all things. To some, such words have seemed so pious that they almost have placed Socrates, Xenophon and Plato in the same rank with the prophets; yet, because in these discussions the philosophers are ignorant of the fact that God has sent his only Son into the world to save sinners, these beautiful utterances are, according to the declaration of this passage, consummate ignorance of God and mere blasphemies, for the passage states unequivocally that all imagination and effort of the human heart is only evil.

153. The text speaks, accordingly, not only of the sins before the flood, but it speaks of the whole nature of man, his heart, his reason and his intellect, even when man pretends to righteousness and desires to be very holy, as do today the Anabaptists when they purpose in their heart so to excel as to fail in nothing, when for a show they attempt to attain the fairest virtues. The truth is that hearts without the Holy Spirit are not only ignorant of God, but naturally even hate him. How, then, can anything be aught but evil that proceeds from ignorance and hatred of God?

154. Another question is here raised. Moses speaks thus: "When Jehovah saw that every imagination of the thoughts of man's heart was only evil continually, it repented him that he had made man on the earth." If God foresees everything, why does the text say that he now first sees? If God is wise, how can regret for having created anything befall him? Why did he not see this sin or depraved nature of man from the beginning of the world? Why does Scripture thus attribute to God such things as a temporary will, vision and purpose? Are not the purposes of God eternal and unalterable, incapable of being regretted? Similar instances are found also in the prophets, where God threatens penalties, as for instance to the Ninevites, and yet pardons the penitent.

To this question the sophists have no other reply than this, that the Scripture speaks after the manner of men, that such things are ascribed to God accordingly through the use of a figure of speech. Hence they contend concerning a double will of God, the will expressed by signs (*voluntas signi*) and the will of his good pleasure (*voluntas beneplaciti*). The will of his good pleasure, they say, is constant and unchangeable, while the expressed will is subject to change. For the signs through which he expresses himself, he changes when he pleases. Thus he has abolished circumcision and instituted baptism, whereas the will of his good pleasure, fixed from eternity, abides.

155. While I do not condemn this interpretation, a simpler meaning of the Scripture seems to be that the Holy Scriptures express the thought of men in the ministry. For when Moses says that God sees and regrets, this is really done in the hearts of those who have the ministry of the Word. Thus he said above: "My Spirit shall not strive with man," but he does not say this simply of the Holy Spirit as existing in his own nature, or of the divine majesty, but of the Holy Spirit in the hearts of Noah and Methuselah, that is, the Holy Spirit as officiating and administering the Word through the saints.

156. In this manner God saw the wickedness of man and repented; that is, Noah, who had the Holy Spirit and was a minister of the Word, saw the wickedness of men and, seeing such things, he was moved by the Holy Spirit to grief. So Paul says in Ephesians 4, 30, that the Holy Spirit in the righteous is grieved by the ungodliness and malice of the wicked. Inasmuch as Noah is a faithful minister of the Word and an organ of the Holy Spirit, the Holy Spirit is said to grieve when Noah grieves and wishes that man rather did not exist than to be thus iniquitous.

157. The meaning, therefore, is not that God did not see these things from eternity; he saw everything from eternity; but inasmuch as this wickedness now manifests itself in all its fierceness, God now first reveals the same in the hearts of his ministers and prophets.

From eternity, therefore, God is firm and constant in his purpose. He sees and knows everything. But only in his own time does God reveal this to the righteous so that they, also, may see it. This seems to me the simplest meaning of this passage, nor does Augustine differ from it much.

158. However, I constantly follow the rule to avoid, whenever possible, such questions as draw us before the throne of the highest majesty. It is better and safer to stand at the manger of Christ, the man. To lose one's self in the labyrinths of divinity is fraught with greatest danger.

159. To this passage belong also other similar ones in which God is pictured as having eyes, ears, mouth, nose, hands and feet, as Isaiah, Daniel and other prophets saw him in their visions. In such passages the Bible speaks of God in the same manner as of a man. In consequence, the Anthropomorphites stood condemned of heresy because they attributed to the divine essence a human form.

160. Because the Anthropomorphites fancied such gross things, they have rightly been condemned. Their fancy is manifestly erroneous, for a spirit, as Christ says (Lk 24, 39), has not flesh and bone. I am rather of the opinion that the Anthro-

pomorphites intended to adapt the form of their doctrine to the plainest people. For in his substance, God is unknowable, indefinable, inexpressible, though we may tear ourselves to pieces in our efforts to discern or portray him.

161. Hence, God himself condescends to the low plane of our understanding and presents himself to us with childlike simplicity in representations, as in a guise, so that he may be made known to us in some way. Thus the Holy Spirit appeared in the form of a dove; not because he is a dove, but in this crude form he desired to be recognized, received and worshiped, for it was really the Holy Spirit. No one, to be sure, will say that the same passage defines God as a voice speaking from heaven, yet under this crude image, a human voice from heaven, he was received and worshiped.

162. When Scripture thus ascribes to God human form, voice, actions and state of mind, it is intended as an aid only for the uncultivated and feeble; we who are great and learned and of discernment in reference to Scripture, should likewise lay hold of these representations, because God has put them forth and revealed himself to us through them. The angels likewise, appear in human form, though it is certain that they are only spirits; spirits we cannot recognize when they present themselves as such, but likenesses we do recognize.

163. This is the simplest way of treating such passages, for the nature of God we cannot define; what he is not we can well define—he is not a voice, a dove, water, bread, wine. And yet in these visible forms he presents himself to us and deals with us. These forms he shows to us that we should not become wandering and unsettled spirits which dispute concerning God, but are completely ignorant concerning him, since in his unveiled majesty he can not be apprehended. He sees it to be impossible for us to know him in his own nature. For he lives, as the Scripture says in 1 Timothy 6, 16, in an inaccessible light, and what we can apprehend and understand he has declared. They who abide in these things will truly lay hold of him, while those who vaunt and follow visions, revelations and illuminations will either be overwhelmed by his majesty or remain in densest ignorance of God.

164. Thus the Jews also had their representations in which God manifested himself to them, as the mercy-seat, the ark of the covenant, the tabernacle, the pillars of smoke and fire. God says in Exodus 33, 20, "Man shall not see me and live," therefore he gives a representation of himself in which he so manifests himself to us that we may lay hold of him. In the new covenant we have Baptism, the Lord's Supper, absolution and the ministry of the Word.

165. These are what the scholastics call *voluntas signi*, the will expressed through signs, which we must view when we desire to know the will of God. Another is the *voluntas beneplaciti*, the will of his good pleasure, the essential will of God, or his unveiled majesty, which is God himself. From this our eyes are to be turned away. It cannot be laid hold of; for in God is nothing but divinity, and the essence of God is his infinite wisdom and almighty power. These are absolutely inaccessible to reason: what he has willed according to the will of his good pleasure, that he has seen from eternity.

166. Into this essential and divine will we should not pry, but should abso-

lutely refrain from it as from the divine majesty, for it is inscrutable, and God has had no desire to declare it in this life. He desires to show it under certain tokens or coverings, as Baptism, the Word and the Lord's Supper. These are the images of the deity and are his will as expressed through signs, by which he deals with us on the plane of our intelligence. Hence, we should look to these alone. The will of his good pleasure is to be left entirely out of contemplation, unless you happen to be Moses, or David, or some similarly perfect man, although even they so looked to the will of the divine good pleasure as never to turn their eyes from the will expressed by signs.

167. This will of God is called his activity (*effectus Dei*), wherein he comes out to us and deals with us garbed in the drapery of things extraneous to himself; these we can lay hold of—the Word of God and the ceremonies instituted by himself. This will of God is not that of his omnipotence, for though God in the ten commandments enjoins what ought to be done it is yet not done. Thus, Christ has instituted the Lord's Supper to strengthen in us faith in his mercy, and yet many receive it to their condemnation, that is, without faith.

168. But I return to Moses. He says that God sees man's wickedness and repents. The scholastics explain this: He sees and repents, namely, according to the expressed will, not that of his good pleasure, or the essential will.

169. We say that Noah's heart is moved by the Holy Spirit to understand that God is wroth with man and desires his destruction. This interpretation commends itself to our intelligence and does not draw us into discussions concerning the absolute will or majesty of God, which are very dangerous, as I have seen in many. Such spirits are first puffed up by the devil so that they believe themselves to be in possession of the Holy Spirit, neglect the Word to the point of blaspheming it and vaunt nothing but the Spirit and visions.

170. This is the first degree of error—that men, paying no heed to the Deity as imaged and incarnate, seek after the unveiled God. Afterward, when the hour of judgment comes, and they feel the wrath of God, God himself judging and searching their hearts, the devil ceases to puff them up and they despair and die. They go about in the untempered sunlight and forsake the shade that delivers from the heat, Is 4, 6.

171. Let no one therefore meditate upon divinity unveiled, but flee from such thoughts as from the infernal regions and the very temptations of Satan. But let us take care to abide in these symbols through which God has revealed himself to us—the Son, born of the Virgin Mary, lying among beasts in the manger, and the Word, Baptism, the Lord's Supper and absolution. In these images we see and find God in a way wherein we can endure him; he comforts us, lifts us up into hope and saves. Other thoughts about the will of the good pleasure, or the essential and eternal will, kill and damn.

172. However, to name this the will of "good pleasure" is a misnomer. For that deserves to be called the will of good pleasure which the Gospel discloses, concerning which Paul says, "that ye may prove what is the good will of God," Rom 12, 2. And Christ says, "This is the will of my Father, that every one that beholdeth

the Son should have eternal life," Jn 6, 40. Also, "Whosoever shall do the will of my Father who is in heaven, he is my brother," Mt 12, 50. Again, "This is my beloved Son, in whom I am well pleased," Mt 3, 17. This will of grace is correctly and properly called the will "of the divine good pleasure" and it is our only remedy and safeguard against that other will, be it called the "expressed will" or the "will of good pleasure," about the display of which at the flood and the destruction of Sodom the scholastics dispute.

173. On both occasions a terrible wrath is in evidence, against which no soul could find protection, except in that gracious will, keeping in mind that the Son of God was sent into the flesh to deliver us from sin, death and the power of the devil.

174. This will of the divine good pleasure has been determined from eternity, and revealed and published in Christ. It is a quickening, gracious and lovable will, and consequently it alone merits to be called "the will of good pleasure." But the good fathers almost pass the promises by; they do not press them, though they could properly be called "the will of the good pleasure."

175. Therefore, as they enjoin looking to the will expressed by signs, they do well, but this is in no wise sufficient; when we consider the ten commandments, are we not frightened by the sight of our sins? When those terrible examples of wrath are added which are also divine will as expressed by signs, it is impossible for the soul to be lifted up except by looking back to the will of the good pleasure, as we call it, that is, the Son of God, who portrays for us the spirit and the will of his Father, who does not hate sinners but desires to have compassion upon them through his Son. Christ says to Philip, "He that hath seen me hath seen the Father," Jn 14, 9.

176. The Son of God, therefore, who became incarnate, is that sign or veil of God in which the divine majesty with all its gifts so offers itself to us that no sinner is so wretched but he dare approach him in certain confidence of obtaining forgiveness. This is the only vision of Deity which in this life is expedient and possible. However, those who have died in this faith shall on the last day be so illumined by power from on high as to behold the majesty itself. In the meantime, it behooves us to approach the Father through the way, which is Christ himself. He will lead us safely and we shall not be deceived.

177. The additional statement of the text, "It repented Jehovah that he had made man on the earth," I believe to be meant to bring out the antithesis, that God has in mind not the earthly man, who is subject to sin and death, but the heavenly man, who is lord over them. He expresses his love for the latter, while he hates the former and plans his destruction.

B. THE GRIEF OF GOD.

1. This is not to be understood of the divine nature, but of the hearts of the patriarchs.
2. Abraham, Samuel and Christ grieved in like manner.
3. By whom such grief is awakened in the heart.

4. The cause of this grief.

 * The character of the children of God and of the world in the face of the approaching calamity.

 * How the patriarchs and the Church were walls of defense.

5. What made the grief of the holy patriarchs greater.

6. Moses describes this grief very carefully.

 * How we see the grief of God in his saints.

 * How all is ruined on account of sin.

 * Why Noah did not dare to reveal the great wrath of God to the world.

 * What prevents the world from believing God's threatenings.

 * To whom God's promises do and do not apply.

 * Why the old world did not believe the threat of the deluge.

 * The fate of true doctrine in our day is the same as it was in Noah's.

B. The Grief of God.

V. 6b. *And it grieved him at his heart.*

178. Such was the regret of God that he was pained in his heart. The word here is *azab*, which was used before when he said (Gen 3, 16), "In pain shalt thou bring forth children"; also in Psalm 127, 2, "the bread of toil." This expression must be understood according to the usage of Scripture. We must not think that God has a heart or that he can suffer pain, but when the spirit of Noah, Lamech or Methuselah is grieved, God himself is said to be grieved. We may understand such grief not of his divine nature, but of his conduct. Noah, with his father and grandfather, feels in his heart, through a revelation of the Holy Spirit, that God hates the world because of sin and desires its destruction; therefore they are grieved by this impenitence.

179. This is the simple and true meaning. If you refer these words to the will of the divine essence and hold that God has resolved this from eternity, a perilous argument is employed to which are equal only men who are spiritual and tested by trial, like Paul, for instance, who has ventured to argue concerning predestination. Let us take our stand on an humbler plane, one less open to danger, and hold that Noah and the other fathers were most grievously pained when the Spirit disclosed to them such wrath. These inexpressible groanings of the best of men are accordingly attributed to God himself, because they emanate from his Spirit.

180. An example of such groanings we see later in the case of Abraham, who interposed himself like a wall in behalf of the safety of the Sodomites and did not abandon the cause until they came down to five righteous ones. Without a doubt the Holy Spirit filled the breast of Abraham with infinite and frequent groanings in his attempts to effect the salvation of the wretched. Likewise Samuel—what does he not do for Saul? He cries and implores with such vehemence that God is compelled to restrain him: "How long wilt thou mourn for Saul, seeing I have rejected

him from being king over Israel?" 1 Sam 16, 1. So Christ, foreseeing the destruction of Jerusalem within a few years by reason of its sins, is most violently moved and pained in his soul.

181. Such promptings the Spirit of prayer arouses in pious souls. Present everywhere, he is moved by the adversities of others, teaches, informs, spares no pains, prays, complains, groans. Thus Moses and Paul are willing to be accursed for the sake of their people.

182. In this manner Noah, the most holy man, and his father and grandfather are consumed with pain at the sight of such terrible wrath of God. He is not delighted at this overthrow of the whole human race, but is filled with anxiety and the most grievous pain, while at the same time the sons of men live in the greatest security, mocking, boasting and taunting. Thus Psalms 109, 4, "For my love they are my adversaries: but I give myself unto prayer." Thus Paul, "I tell you even weeping." Phil 3, 18. And what else could holy men do but weep when the world would in no wise permit itself to be corrected?

183. It is always the appearance of the true Church that she not only suffers, not only is humiliated and trampled under foot, but also prays for her tormentors, is seriously disturbed by their dangers; on the contrary, others play and frolic in proportion as they approach their doom. But when the hour of judgment comes, God in turn closes his ears so completely that he does not even hear his own beloved children as they pray and intercede for the wicked. So Ezekiel laments that no one is found who will stand for Israel as a protecting wall, saying that this is the office of the prophets, Ezek 13, 5.

184. It is impossible for the ungodly to pray; let no one, therefore, entertain the hope concerning the papists, our adversaries, that they pray. We pray for them and plant ourselves like a wall against the wrath of God and, without doubt, it is by our tears and groanings that they are saved, if, perchance, they will repent.

185. It is a terrible example, that God has spared not the first world, for which Noah, Lamech and Methuselah set themselves like a wall. What, then, shall we expect where such walls do not exist, where there is no Church at all? The Church is always a wall against the wrath of God. She feels pain, is tormented in her soul, prays, intercedes, instructs, teaches, exhorts, as long as the judgment hour is not here but coming. When she sees these ministrations to be unavailing, what else can she do but feel grievous pain at the destruction of the impenitent? The pain of the godly fathers was augmented by the sight of so many relatives and kindred at one time going to destruction.

186. This pain Moses could not express in a better and more graphic description than to say that God repented of having made man. Before, when he describes man's nature as having been formed in God's image, he says that God beheld all that he had made and it was very good. God, then, is delighted with his creatures and has joy in them. Here he absolutely alters that statement by one altogether at variance with it—that God is grieved at heart and even repents of having created man.

187. It was Noah and the other fathers who felt this through the revelation

of the Holy Spirit; otherwise, they would have shared those thoughts of joy and would have judged according to the earlier prophecy that God had delight in all his works. Never would they have thought that the wrath of God was such as to destroy not only the whole human race, but also all living flesh of sky and earth, which surely had not offended, yea, the very earth also; for the earth, because of man's sin, had not retained after the flood its pristine excellence. Some have written, as Lyra reminds us, that by the flood the surface of the earth was washed away three hands deep. Certain it is that paradise has been utterly destroyed through the flood. Therefore, we possess today an earth more deeply cursed than before the flood and after the fall of Adam; though the state of the earth after the fall could not compare with the grandeur of its primeval state before sin.

188. These disasters, therefore, the holy fathers saw through the revelation of the Holy Spirit a hundred and twenty years before. But such was the wickedness of the world that it put the Holy Spirit to silence. Noah could not venture to reveal such threats without risk of the gravest dangers. With his father and grandfather, with his children and wife, he would discuss this great wrath of God. The sons of men, however, had no more inclination to hear these things than the papists today have to hear themselves called the church of Satan and not of Christ. Accordingly, they would vaunt their ancestors and over against Noah's proclamations they would plead the promise of the seed, believing it to be impossible for God, in this manner, to destroy all mankind.

189. For the same reason, the Jews did not believe the prophets nor even Christ himself when called to repentance, but maintained that they were the people of God, inasmuch as they had the temple and worship. The Turks today are inflated with victories which they believe to be the reward for their faith and religion because they believe in one God. We, however, are viewed as heathen and reputed to believe in three Gods. God would not give us such victories and dominions, they say, if he did not favor us and approve our religion. This same reasoning blinds also the papist. Occupying an exalted position, they maintain they are the Church and hence they have no fear of divine punishment. Devilish, therefore, is that argument whereby men take the name of God to palliate their sins.

190. But if God did not spare the first world, the generation of the holy patriarchs, which had the promise of the seed as its very own—if he saved only a very small remnant—the Turks, Jews and Papists shall boast in vain of the name of God. According to Micah 2, 7, the Word of God promises blessings to those who walk in uprightness. But those who do not walk in uprightness are cursed. Those he threatens, those he destroys. Neither does he take account of the name "Church", nor of their number, whereas he saves the remnant which walks in uprightness. But never will you convince the world of this.

191. In all probability the descendants of the patriarchs who perished in the flood abused quite shamefully the argument of the dignity of the Church, and condemned Noah for blasphemy and falsehood. To say, they argued, that God was about to destroy the whole world by a flood is equal to saying that God is not merciful, nor a Father, but a cruel tyrant. You proclaim the wrath of God, O Noah! Then God is not such a being as to promise deliverance from sin and death through

the seed of woman? The wrath of God, therefore, will not swallow the whole earth. We are the people of God. We have from God magnificent gifts; never would God have given these to us if he had resolved to act against us with such hostility. In this fashion the wicked are in the habit of applying to themselves the promises and trusting to the same. All warnings, however, they neglect and deride.

192. It is profitable to contemplate this diligently so that we may be safeguarded against such vicious heedlessness of the wicked. For what happened to Moses, now happens also to us. Our adversaries ascribe to themselves the name of God's people, true worship, grace and everything holy; to us, everything devilish. Now, when we reprove them for blasphemy and say that they are the church of Satan, they rage against us with every kind of cruelty. Hence we mourn with Noah, and commend the cause to God, as Christ did on the cross—what else could we do?—and wait till God shall judge the earth and show that he loves the remnant of those that fear him and that he hates the multitude of impenitent sinners in spite of their boast of being the Church, of having the promises, of having the worship of God. When God destroyed the whole original world, he manifested the promise of the seed to that wretched and tiny remnant, Noah and his sons.

V. NOAH ALONE WAS RIGHTEOUS; THE WORLD DESTROYED.

A. NOAH ALONE WAS FOUND RIGHTEOUS.

1. What comfort was offered Noah by his righteousness in the midst of his suffering.
* To find grace before God leads to faith and excludes works.
2. For what was righteous Noah especially praised by God.
* Many great men lived in the days of Noah.
3. How righteous Noah had to contend against so much all alone.
* By what means the Papists contend against the Evangelicals.
4. With what the world especially upbraided righteous Noah.
* People then were wiser and more ingenious than now.
5. Noah may be called both just and pious.
6. Righteous Noah led a godly life, possessed great courage and was a marvelous character.
7. By his piety Noah was a confessor of the truth.
* It is very difficult for one man to withstand the united opposition of many.
8. Being a preacher of righteousness Noah was in greater danger.
9. Noah an example of patience and of all virtues.
10. How he traveled and preached everywhere in the world, and preserved the human race temporally and spiritually.
11. The world takes offense at righteous Noah's marrying, and adds sin to sin.
12. The order of the birth of Noah's sons.

B. THE WHOLE WORLD DESTROYED.

1. Whether, as Lyra teaches, birds and animals were destroyed.

* Why the punishment of sin was visited also upon the animals.

2. The meaning of "the earth was corrupt before God".

* The sins against the first table of the law can easier be concealed than those against the second table.

* Where false doctrine is taught, godless living follows.

3. How the earth was corrupt in the light of the first table of the law.

4. How the earth was corrupt in the light of the second table.

* The meaning of "violence" in Scripture.

* The greatest violence can obtain under the appearance of holiness, as among the Papists and Turks.

* Moses beautifully traces the course God takes in his judgments.

* Who can pass the right judgment upon the pope that he is Antichrist.

* How Antichrist strengthens the courage of the godly, and whether they can check him.

5. Noah laments this corruption.

* Godlessness cannot be remedied when it adorns itself with the appearance of holiness.

6. How God views this corruption.

* Luther laments the wickedness of the enemies of the Gospel.

* How we should view God's delay in punishing the wickedness of his enemies.

* God's delay is very hard for believers.

7. The first world, although corrupt, was much better than the present world.

V. HOW NOAH ALONE WAS FOUND RIGHTEOUS, AND HOW THE WHOLE WORLD WAS DESTROYED.

A. Noah Alone Was found Righteous.

V. 8. *But Noah found grace in the eyes of Jehovah.*

193. These are the words through which Noah was lifted up and quickened again. For such wrath of the divine majesty would have killed him, had not God added the promise of saving him. It is likely, however, that his faith had a struggle and was weak. We cannot imagine how such contemplation of God's wrath weakens courage.

194. This novel expression of the Holy Spirit the heavenly messenger Gabriel also uses when speaking to the Blessed Virgin Lk 1, 30, "Thou hast found favor (grace) with God." The expression most palpably excludes merit and commends faith, through which alone we are justified before God, made acceptable and well pleasing in his sight.

V. 9. *These are the generations of Noah. Noah was a righteous man, and perfect in his generations; Noah walked with God.*

195. With this passage the Jews commence not only a new chapter, but also a new lesson. This is a very brief history, but it greatly extols our patriarch Noah; he alone remained just and upright while the other sons of God degenerated.

196. Let us remember many most excellent men were among the sons of God, of whom some lived with Noah well nigh five hundred years. Man in that age before the flood was very long-lived; not only the sons of God, but also the sons of men. A very wide and rich experience had been gathered by these people during so many years. Much they learned from their progenitors and much they saw and experienced.

197. Amid the corruption of all these stands Noah, a truly marvelous man. He swerves neither to the left nor to the right. He retains the true worship of God. He retains the pure doctrine, and lives in the fear of God. There is no doubt that a depraved generation hated him inordinately, tantalized him in various ways and thus insulted him: "Art thou alone wise? Dost thou alone please God? Are the rest of us all in error? Shall we all be damned? Thou alone dost not err. Thou alone shalt not be condemned." And thus the just and holy man must have concluded in his mind that all others were in error and about to be condemned, while he and his offspring alone were to be saved. Although his conviction was right in the matter, his lot was a hard one. The holy man was in various ways troubled by such reflections.

198. The wretched Papists press us today with this one argument: Do you believe that all the fathers have been in error? It seems hard so to believe, especially of the worthier ones, such as Augustine, Ambrose, Bernard and that whole throng of the best men who have governed Churches with the Word and have been adorned with the august name of the Church. The labors of such we both laud and admire.

199. But surely no less a difficulty confronted Noah himself, who alone is called just and upright, at a time when the very sons of men paraded the name of the Church. When the sons of the fathers allied themselves with these they, forsooth, believed that Noah with his people raved, because he followed another doctrine and another worship.

200. Today our life is very brief, still to what lengths human nature will go is sufficiently in evidence. What may we imagine the condition to have been in such a long existence, in which the bitterness and vehemence of human nature were even stronger? Today we are naturally much more dull and stupid, and yet men singularly gifted rush into wickedness. It is afterward said that all flesh had corrupted its way upon the earth, only Noah was just and upright.

201. From these two words we may gather the thought that Noah is held to be "just" as he honored the first table and "upright" as he honored the second. "Just" he is called, because of his faith in God, because he first believed the general promise with respect to the seed of woman and then also the particular one respecting the destruction of the world through the flood and the salvation of his own off-

spring. On the other hand he is called "upright" because he walked in the fear of God and conscientiously avoided murder and other sins with which the wicked polluted themselves in defiance of conscience. Nor did he permit himself to be moved by the frequent offenses of men most illustrious, wise and apparently holy.

202. Great was his courage. Today it appears to us impossible that one man should oppose himself to all mankind, condemning them as evil, while they vaunt the Church and God's Word and worship, and to maintain that he alone is a son of God and acceptable before him. Noah, accordingly, is a marvelous man, and Moses commends this same greatness of mind when he plainly adds "in his generation," or "in his age," as if he desired to say that his age was indeed the most wicked and corrupt.

203. Above, in the history of Enoch, we explained what it means to walk with God, namely, to advocate the cause of God in public. To be just and upright bespeaks private virtue, but to walk with God is something public—to advocate the cause of God before the world, to wield his Word, to teach his worship. Noah was not simply just and holy for himself but he was also a confessor; he taught others the promises and threats of God, and performed and suffered all that behooves a public personage in an age so exceedingly wicked and corrupt.

204. If it were I who had seen that so great men in the generation of the ungodly were opposed to me, I surely in desperation should have cast aside my ministry. For one cannot conceive how difficult it is for one man to oppose himself alone to the unanimity of all churches; to impugn the judgment of the best and most amicable of men; to condemn them; to teach, to live, and to do everything, in opposition to them. This is what Noah did. He was inspired with admirable constancy of purpose, inasmuch as he, innocent before men, not only regarded the cause of God, but most earnestly pressed it among the most nefarious men, until he was told: "My spirit shall not further strive with man." And the word "strive" finely portrays the spirit with which the ungodly heard Noah instruct them.

205. Peter also beautifully sets forth what it means to walk with God when he calls Noah a preacher, not of the righteousness of man, but of God; that is, that of faith in the promised seed. But what reward Noah received from the ungodly for his message Moses does not indicate. The statement is sufficient, that he preached righteousness, that he taught the true worship of God while the whole earth opposed him. That means the best, most religious and wisest of men were against him. More than one miracle, in consequence, was necessary to prevent his being waylaid and killed by the ungodly. We see today how much wrath, hate, and envy one sermon to the people may create. What shall we believe Noah may have suffered who taught not a hundred, not two hundred, but even more years, down to the last century, when God did not desire the wicked to receive instruction any longer lest they become still fiercer and more depraved.

206. Therefore we may conjecture from the condition and nature of the world itself, and of the devil, from the experience of the apostles and the prophets, and likewise from our own, what a noble example of patience and other virtues Noah has been, who was just and irreproachable in that ungodly generation and walked

with God—that is, governed the churches with the Word—and who, when the one hundred and twenty years were determined upon, after the lapse of which the world was to be destroyed by a flood, in face of such a terrible threat, entered into matrimony and begot children.

207. It is very probable that he traveled up and down the earth; that he taught everywhere; that everywhere he exhorted to worship God in truth; that he, hindered by many labors, refrained from matrimony on account of abundance of tribulations and in the expectation of the advent of a better and more religious age. But when he recognized this hope as unfounded and by a voice divine was warned that a time had been set for the world's destruction, then and not before, prompted by the Spirit, did he make up his mind to marry, in order to transmit to the new age seed out of himself. And thus the holy man preserved the human race, not only spiritually, in the true Word and worship, but also bodily, by begetting children.

208. As in paradise a new Church had its beginning, before the flood, through Adam and Eve's faith in the promise, so also here a new world and a new Church arise from the marriage of Noah—a nursery of that world which shall endure to the end.

209. I stated above (§88) that this marriage was an occasion of great offense to the ungodly and that they made the most extraordinary sport of it. How inconsistent that the world is to perish so soon, when Noah, five hundred years old, becomes a father! They deemed his act the surest evidence that the world was not to perish by a flood. Hence, they began to live even more licentiously, and in the greatest security to despise all threats. Christ says in Matthew 24, 38, that in the days of Noah they ate, they drank, etc. The world does not understand the plans of God.

210. Concerning the order of the sons of Noah, I said above that Japheth was first, that Shem was born two years afterward when Noah commenced to build the ark, and Ham two years later. This has not been clearly explained by Moses, but still it has been carefully noted.

B. Destruction of the Whole World.

V. 11. *And the earth was corrupt before God, and the earth was filled with violence.*

211. Lyra, perhaps under the influence of rabbinic interpretation, contends here that even the birds and other animals forsook their nature and mixed with those of another species. But I do not believe it, for the creation or nature of animals remains as it was fashioned. They have not fallen through sin, like man, but are, on the contrary, fashioned for this bodily life alone. In consequence they neither hear the Word, nor does the Word concern them. They are absolutely without the Law of the first and the second tables. Accordingly, this passage refers only to man.

212. But that the beasts bore the penalty of sin and perished at the same time with man through the flood was the result of God's purpose to destroy man altogether; not alone in body and soul, but with the possessions and dominion which were his at creation. Instances of similar retribution occur in the Old Testament.

In the sixth chapter of Daniel we see the enemies of Daniel cast into the lions' den, together with their wives, children and whole families. In the sixteenth chapter of Numbers a like incident is narrated in connection with the destruction of Korah, Dathan and Abiram. Similar is also an instance spoken of by Christ when the king commands to sell the servant together with wife, children and all his substance.

213. In this manner, evidently, not only men but all their goods were destroyed, so that punishment might be full and complete. Beasts, fields and the birds of heaven were created for man. They are man's property and chattels. Therefore, the animals perished, not because they had sinned, but because God wanted man to perish amid all his earthly possessions.

214. In this passage Moses' specific statement that "the earth was corrupt before God," is made to show that Noah was treated and esteemed in the eyes of his age as a stupid and good for nothing character. The world, on the contrary, appeared in its own eyes perfectly holy and righteous, believing it had just cause for the persecution of Noah, especially in regard to the first table of the Law and the worship of God. The second table is not without its disguise of hypocrisy, but in this respect it bears no comparison to the former. The adulterer, the thief, the murderer can remain hidden for a while, though not forever. But the sins of the first table generally remain hidden under the cloak of sanctity until God brings them to light. Godlessness never wishes to be godlessness, but chases after a reputation for piety and religion; and trims its cult so finely that in comparison with it the true cult and the true religion appear coarse.

215. The verb *shiheth* is very frequent and conspicuous in Holy Scripture. Moses uses it in the thirty-first chapter of Deuteronomy, verse 29: "For I know that after my death ye will utterly corrupt yourselves, and turn aside from the way which I have commanded you." And David says, "They are all gone aside; they are together become filthy," Ps 14, 3. Both passages speak particularly of the sins against the first table; that is, they accuse the apparently devoutest saints of false worship and false doctrine, for it is impossible for a righteous life to follow teaching that is false.

216. When Moses says the earth was corrupt before God, he clearly points out the contrast—the hypocrites and oppressors judged Noah's teaching and practise as wholly wrong, and their own as altogether holy. The reverse, Moses says, was true. Mankind was assuredly corrupt measured by the first table. They lacked the true Word and the true worship. This distinction between the first and the second tables commends itself strongly to my judgment and was doubtless suggested by the Holy Spirit.

217. The additional statement—"and the earth was filled with violence"— points to this unfailing sequence. With the Word lost, with faith extinct, with traditions and will-worship—to use St. Paul's phraseology (Col 2, 8)—having replaced the true cult, there results violence and shameful living.

218. The correct significance of the word *hamas* is violence force, wrong, with the suspension of all law and equity, a condition where pleasure is law and everything is done not by right, but by might. But if such was their life, you may

say, how could they maintain the appearance and reputation of holiness and righteousness? As if we did not really have similar instances before our eyes today. Has the world ever seen anything more cruel than the Turks? And they adorn all their fierceness with the name of God and religion.

219. The popes have not only seized for themselves the riches of the earth, but have filled the Church itself with stupendous errors and blasphemous doctrines. They live in shocking licentiousness. They alienate at pleasure the hearts of kings. Much is done by them to bring on bloodshed and war. And yet, with all such blasphemies and outrages, they arrogate to themselves the name and title of the greatest saints and boast of being vicars of Christ and successors of Peter.

220. Thus the greatest wrong is allied to the names of Church and true religion. Should any one offer objection, immediately is he put under the ban and condemned as a heretic and an enemy of God and man. Barring the Romans and their accomplices, there is no people which plumes itself more upon religion and righteousness than the Turks. The Christians they despise as idolaters; themselves they esteem as most holy and wise. Notwithstanding, what is their life and religion but incessant murder, robbery, rapine and other horrible outrages?

221. The present times, therefore, illustrate how those two incompatible things may be found in union—the greatest religiousness with abominations, the greatest wrong with a show of right. And this is the very cause for men becoming hardened and secure without apprehending the punishment they merit by their sins.

V. 12. *And God saw the earth, and, behold, it was corrupt; for all flesh had corrupted their way upon the earth.*

222. Inasmuch as the wrath of God is appalling and destruction is imminent for all flesh except eight souls, Moses is somewhat redundant in this passage, and uses repetitions, which are not superfluous but express an emphasis of their own. Above he said the earth was corrupt; now he says that God, as if following the customary judicial method, saw this and meditated punishment. In this manner he pictures, as it were, the order in which God proceeds.

223. The judgment of spiritual people concerning the pope at the present day is that he is the Antichrist, raging against the Word and the kingdom of Christ. But they who censure it are unable to correct this wickedness. Wickedness is growing daily and contempt for godliness is becoming greater every day. Now comes the thought: What is God doing? Why does he not punish his enemy? Does he sleep and care no longer for human affairs? The delay of judgment causes the righteous anguish. They themselves cannot come to the succor of a stricken religion and they see God who could help, connive at the fury of the popes, who securely sin against the first and the second tables of the Law.

224. Just so Noah sees the earth filled with wrongs. Therefore, he groans and sighs to heaven in order to arouse God from the highest heaven to judgment. Such voices occur here and there in the Psalms (10, 1): "Why standest thou afar off?"; (13, 1): "How long, O Jehovah?"; (9, 13): "Have mercy upon me, O Jehovah; consider my trouble"; (7, 6-9): "Arise, judge my cause, etc."

225. What Moses here describes comes at length to pass, that God also sees these things and hears the cry of the righteous who are able to judge the world; for they who are spiritual judge all things (1 Cor 2, 15), though they cannot alter anything. Wickedness is incorrigible when adorned with a show of piety, and so is oppression when it assumes the disguise of justice and foresight. It is nothing new that they who seize the wives, daughters, houses, lands and goods of others desire to be just and holy, as we showed above in respect of the papacy.

226. This is the second stage then: When the saints have seen and judged the wickedness of the world, God also sees it. He says of the Sodomites: "The cry of them is waxed great before Jehovah" (Gen 19, 13); and above (ch 4, 10): "The voice of thy brother's blood crieth unto me." But always before the Lord takes note, the sobs and groans of the righteous precede, arousing, as it were, the Lord from slumber.

What Moses desires to show in this passage through the word, "saw" is that God finally perceived the afflictions and heard the cries of the righteous, filling at last all heaven. He who hitherto had winked at everything and seemed to favor the success of the wicked, was awakened as from slumber. The fact is he saw everything much sooner than Noah; for he is the searcher of hearts and cannot be deceived by simulated piety as we can. But not until now, when he meditates punishment, does Noah perceive that he sees.

227. Thus we are afflicted today by extreme and unheard of wickedness, for our adversaries condemn from sheer caprice the truth they know and profess. They try to get at our throats and shed the blood of the righteous with a satanic fury. Such blasphemous, sacrilegious and parricidal doings against the kingdom and name of God, manifest as such beyond possibility of denial, they defend as the acme of justice. While contending for the maintenance of their tyrannical position they go so far as to arrogate to themselves the name of the Church. What else can we do here but cry to Jehovah to make his name sacred and not to permit the overthrow of his kingdom nor resistance to his paternal will?

228. But so far the Lord sleeps. He apparently does not observe such wickedness, because he gives no sign as yet of observing it. Rather he permits us to be tormented by such woeful sights. We are, therefore, thus far in the first stage and this verse, stating that the whole earth is corrupt, applies to our age. But at the proper time the second stage will be reached, when we can declare in certainty of faith that not only we but God also sees and hates such wickedness. Though God, in his long-suffering, has continued to wink at many things, he shall retain the name of One who in righteousness shall judge the earth.

229. How bitter and hard such delay is for the righteous, the lamentations of Jeremiah in Jeremiah 12, 1ff., and 20, 7ff, show. There the holy man almost verges on blasphemy until he is told that the Babylonian king should come and inflict punishment upon the unbelieving scoffers. Thereupon Jeremiah recognizes that God looks down on the earth and is Judge upon the earth.

230. The universal judgment which follows is terrible in the extreme, namely that all flesh upon the earth had corrupted its way and that God, when he had

begun to examine the sons of men, did not, from the oldest to the youngest of the fathers, find any he could save from destruction.

This strikes our ears as still more awful when we take into consideration the condition of the primitive world, not judging by the miserable fragments we have today. As the physical condition of the world at that time was infinitely ahead of this age, so we may conclude that the majesty and pomp of our rulers and the show of sanctity and wisdom on the part of the popes are not to be compared to the show of religion, righteousness and wisdom found among those renowned men of the primitive world.

And yet the text says that all flesh had corrupted its way, save Noah and his offspring. That means all men were wicked, lived in idolatry and false religion and hated the true worship of God. They despised the promise of the seed, and persecuted Noah, who proclaimed forgiveness through the seed and threatened to those, who should fail to believe his forgiveness, eternal doom.

**VI. GOD DECIDES TO PUNISH THE FIRST WORLD;
COMMANDS NOAH TO BUILD AN ARK; THE COVENANT.**

A. HOW GOD DECREED TO PUNISH THE OLD WORLD IN HIS WRATH.

1. How punishment finally comes when God has suffered sin long enough.
 * Luther's hope that God's judgment may soon break upon the last world.
2. Whether reason can grasp the wrath and punishment of God.
3. How God's promises stand in the midst of his wrath and punishment.
4. The first world thought itself secure against God's wrath.
 * The Papal security and boldness against the Evangelicals.
5. By what means God punished the first world.
 * The Holy Spirit must reveal that God's wrath and punishment do not violate his promises.
6. The causes of this wrath and punishment.
 * By what may it be known that God will visit Germany with punishment.
 * God complains more of the violence shown to the neighbor than to himself.
 * The damages of the deluge.
 * The ground of the earth was in a better state before the flood than now.
 * The colors in the rainbow signs of the punishment of the first and the last world.

**VI. GOD DECIDES TO PUNISH THE FIRST WORLD;
COMMANDS NOAH TO BUILD AN ARK; THE COVENANT.**

A. God Decides to Punish the Old World.

V. 13. *And God said unto Noah, The end of all flesh is come before me; for the earth is filled with violence through them; and, behold, I will destroy them with the earth.*

231. After Noah and his people had for a long time raised their accusing cry against the depravity of the world, the Lord gave evidence that he saw the depravity and intended to avenge it. This, the second stage, we also look for today, nor is there any doubt that men shall exist, to whom this coming destruction of the world is to be revealed, unless the destruction be the last day and the final judgment, which I truly wish. We have seen enough wickedness in these brief and evil days of ours. Godless men, as in Noah's time, adorn their vices with the name of holiness and righteousness. Hence, no penitence or reformation is to be hoped for. This stage having been reached in the times of Noah, sentence is finally passed, having been previously announced by the Lord when he gave command that striving should cease and issued the declaration that he regretted having made man.

232. Reason is incapable of believing and perfectly understanding such wrath. Just consider how different this is from what had been. Above we have read (ch 1, 31) that God saw everything he had made and behold, it was very good; that he gave man and beast the additional blessing of propagation; that he subjected to man's rule the earth and all the treasures of the earth; that as the highest blessing, he added the promise of the woman's seed and life eternal and instituted not only the home and the State, but also the Church. How, then, is it that the first world, called into being in this way through the Word, should, to use Peter's expression, perish by water?

233. There is no doubt that the sons of the world threw all this up to Noah as he preached the coming universal destruction, and publicly charged him with lying, on the ground that home, State and Church had been instituted by God; that God surely would not overturn his own establishment by a final destruction; that man had been created for propagation and dominion upon the earth, not for the rule of water over him to his destruction.

234. Just so the Papists press us with the one argument that Christ will be with the Church to the end of the world (Mt 28, 20); that the gates of hell will not prevail against it (Mt 16, 18). This they vaunt in a loud-voiced manner, believing their destruction to be an impossibility. Swept by the waves Peter's ship may be, they say, but the waters cannot overwhelm it.

235. Quite similar was the security and assurance before the flood; notwithstanding, we see that the whole earth perished. The scoffers boasted that God's regulations are perpetual, and that God had never completely abolished or altered his creation. But consider the outcome and you will see that they were wrong, while Noah alone was right.

236. Unless the additional light of the Holy Spirit is vouchsafed, man will surely be convinced by such argument; for is it not equivalent to making God inconstant and changeable, to maintain that he will completely destroy his creature? Yet God gives Noah the revelation that he will make an end of flesh and earth, not in part, but of all flesh and all the earth. Would it not be awful enough to partition the earth into three parts and to threaten destruction to one? But to rage against the whole earth and against all mankind seems to be in conflict with God's government and the declaration that everything is very good. These things are too

sublime to be understood or comprehended by human reason.

237. What is the cause of wrath so great? Surely, the fact that the earth is filled with violence, as he here says. Astonishing reason! He says nothing here concerning the first table; he mentions only the second. It is, as if he said: I shall say nothing of myself that they hate, blaspheme and persecute my Word. Among themselves how shamefully do they live! Neither home nor State are properly administered; everything is conducted by force, nothing by reason and law. Therefore, I shall destroy at the same time both mankind and the earth.

238. We see also in our age that God winks at the profanation of the mass, a horrible abomination that fills the whole earth, and at ungodly teachings and other offenses which have hitherto been in vogue in religion. But when men live so together that they disregard both State and home, when huge covetousness, graft of every description and manifold iniquity have waxed strong, does it not become clear to every man that God is compelled, as it were, to punish, yea to overturn Germany?

239. It is the fullness of his mercy and love that prompts God rather to make complaint concerning the wrongs inflicted upon his members than those inflicted upon himself. We observe he maintains silence respecting the latter, while he threatens punishment, not to man alone, but even to the very earth itself.

240. A twofold effect is traceable to the flood; a weakening of man's powers and an impairment of his wealth and that of the earth. The latter-day fruit of trees is in nowise to be compared with that in the days before the flood. The antediluvian turnips were better than afterward the melons, oranges or pomegranates. The pear was finer than the spices of today. So it is likely that a man's finger possessed more strength than today his whole arm. Likewise man's reason and understanding were far superior. But God, because of sin, has brought punishment to bear, not alone upon man, but also upon his property and domain, as witness to posterity also of his wrath.

But how is the destruction to be effected? Assuredly, by his seizing the watery element and blotting out everything. The force with which this element is wont to rage is common knowledge. Though the atmosphere be pestilential, it does not always infect trees and roots. But water not only overturns everything, not only does it tear out trees and roots, but it also lifts the very surface of the earth. It alters the soil, so that the most fertile fields are marred by the overflow of salty earth and sand (Ps 107, 34). This was therefore equal to the downfall of the primitive world.

241. The penalty of the present world, however, will be different, as the color of the rainbow shows. The lowest color the extent of which is well defined, is that of water. For the fury of the water in the deluge was so great that limits were set to its havoc, and the earth was restored to the remnant of the godly after the destruction of the evil-doers. But the other arch of the rainbow, the outer, which has no clearly defined bounds, is of the color of fire, the element which shall consume the whole world. This destruction shall be succeeded by a better world, which shall last forever and serve the righteous. This the Lord seems to have written in the color of the rainbow.

B. GOD COMMANDS NOAH TO BUILD AN ARK.

  * That Noah had only three children is a sign of God's mercy.

1. The kind of wood used in building the ark.

2. Its various rooms.

3. The pitch by which it was protected.

4. Why God instructed Noah so particularly how each part was to be constructed.

5. The form of the ark, and how teachers differ on this point.

6. The place Noah occupied in the ark, and that of the animals.

7. Whether the ark had the proportions of a human body.

8. How the ark was a type of the body of Christ—of the Church.

9. The windows of the ark:

    a. Whether it had more than one window.

    * The Latin version is not clear here.

    b. What kind of a window it was, and how it could stand the rain.

    c. Luther's opinion of the Jews' ideas about the window.

10. The door of the ark.

11. How to meet the various questions about the ark.

  * The deluge was a new method of punishment, hence the non incredible.

  * God was in earnest in the threatening of this flood.

B. God Commands Noah to Build an Ark.

V. 14. *Make thee an ark of gopher wood; rooms shalt thou make in the ark, and shalt pitch it within and without with pitch (bitumen).*

242. God's first thought was to save a remnant through that tiny seed, the three sons of Noah, for Noah ceased henceforth to beget children. This strongly attests the mercy of God toward those who walk in his ways.

243. *Gopher* some make out to be pine, others hemlock, still others cedar; hence, a guess is rather difficult. The choice appears to have been made owing to its lightness or its resinous quality, so that it might float more easily upon the water and be impervious to it.

244. *Kinnim* signifies "nests" or "chambers"; that is separate spaces for the various animals. Bears, sheep, deer and horses did not dwell in one and the same place, but the several species had their respective quarters.

245. But what is meant by *bitumen,* I do not know. With us vessels are made water tight with pitch and tow. Pitch, it is true, withstands water, but it also invites the flame. There is no bitumen with us which resists water, hence we raise no objection to "bitumen" being rendered "pitch."

246. You may ask: Why does God prescribe everything so accurately? The in-

junction to build the ark should have been sufficient. Reason could determine for itself the rules concerning dimensions and mode of construction. Why, then, does God give such careful instruction with reference to dimensions and materials? Certainly that Noah, after undertaking all things according to the Lord's direction (as Moses built the tabernacle according to the model received on the mount), should with the greater faith trust that he and his people were to be saved, nor entertain any doubt concerning a work ordered by the Lord himself, even how it should be made. This is the reason the Lord gives his directions with such attention to detail.

V. 15. *And this is how thou shalt make it: the length of the ark three hundred cubits, the breadth of it fifty cubits, and the height of it thirty cubits.*

247. A nice geometrical and mathematical exercise concerning the form and dimensions of the ark is here presented. The views of writers vary. Some claim it was four-cornered, others that it was gabled like nearly all our structures in Europe. As for myself, I hold it was four-cornered. Eastern people's were not acquainted with gabled buildings. Theirs were evidently of four-cornered form, as the Bible mentions people walking on roofs. Similar was the shape of the temple.

248. There is a difference of opinion also concerning the arrangement of the animals in their quarters, which occupied the upper, which the central and which the lower places, this being the distinction warranted by the text. No certainty, however, can be arrived at. It is likely that Noah himself and the birds occupied the upper part, the clean animals the central and the unclean animals the lower one. The rabbis assert the lower part served the purpose of storing dung. But I think the dung was thrown out of the window, for its removal was necessitated by such a multitude of beasts abiding in the ark for over a year.

249. Augustine quotes Philo against Faustus in stating that on geometrical principles, the ark had the proportions of the human body, for when a man lies on the ground his body is ten times as long as it is high and six times as long as broad. So three hundred cubits are six times fifty and ten times thirty.

250. An application is made of this to the body of Christ, the Church, which has baptism as the door, through which clean and unclean enter without distinction. Although the Church is small, she rules the earth notwithstanding, and it is due to her that the world is preserved, just as the unclean animals were preserved in the ark. Others stretch the application so far as to point to the wound in the side of Jesus' body as prefigured by the windows in the ark. These are allegories which are not exactly profound, but still harmless because they harbor no error and serve a purpose other than that of wrangling, namely, that of rhetorical ornamentation.

V. 16. *A light shalt thou make to the ark, and to a cubit shalt thou finish it upward; and the door of the ark shalt thou set in the side thereof; with lower, second, and third stories shalt thou make it.*

251. Behold, how diligent an architect God is! With what care he interests himself in all the parts of the structure and their arrangement. Furthermore, the word *Zohar* does not properly signify window, but southern light. The question may be raised here whether the ark had only one window or several. For the Hebrew

language permits the use of the singular for the plural, or of the collective for the distributive term, as for instance: "I will destroy man from the face of the ground." Here evidently not one man but many are spoken of. But to me it seems there was only one window that shed light upon man's domicile.

252. The Latin interpreter is so strangely obscure as to fail to make himself understood. My unqualified opinion is that he was unable to divest himself of the image of a modern ship, in which men are commonly carried in the lower part. Nor is it quite intelligible what he says about the door, inasmuch as it is certain that the ell-long window was in the upper part, and the door in the center of the side or in the navel of the ark. Thus, also, Eve was framed from the middle portion of man's body. The whole structure was divided into three partitions, a higher, a central and a lower one, and it was the upper one which, according to my view, was illuminated by the light of day through the window.

253. You may say, however: What kind of a window was it, or how could it exist in those frequent and violent rains? For rain did not fall then as it does ordinarily, since the water in forty days rose to such proportions as to submerge the highest mountains by fifteen arm-lengths. The Jews claim that the window was closed by a crystal which transmitted the light. But too curious a research into these matters appears to me useless, since neither godliness nor Christ's kingdom are put in jeopardy from the fact of our remaining in ignorance concerning some features of this structure of which God was the architect. It seems to me sufficiently satisfactory to assume that the window was on the side of the upper partition.

254. As to the door, it is certain that it was about thirteen or fourteen cubits from the earth. The ark, when it floated, sank about ten feet into the water with its great weight of animals of every kind and provender for more than a year. This may suffice as a crude conception of the ark; for, besides height and length, Moses merely indicates that it had three partitions, a door and a window.

255. We will dismiss innumerable other questions such as: What kind of air was used in the ark? for such a stupendous mass of water, particularly falling water, must have produced a violent and pestilential stench; whence did they draw their drinking-water? for water cannot be preserved a whole year, hence mariners often call at ports in their vicinity for the purpose of drawing water; again, how could the bilge-water with its obnoxious odor be drawn up?

256. Such questions and other subordinate points related to the experience of the mariner we may pass by. Otherwise there will be no end of questions. We will be content with the simple supposition that the lower part probably served the purpose of securing the bears, lions, tigers and other savage animals; the middle part, that of housing the gentle and tractable animals, together with the provender, which cannot be kept in a place devoid of all air-currents; the upper that of accommodating human beings themselves, together with the domestic animals and the birds. This should be enough for us.

V. 17. *And I, behold, I do bring the flood of waters upon the earth, to destroy all flesh, wherein is the breath of life, from under heaven; everything that is in the earth shall die.*

257. Above God has threatened in general the human race with destruction.

Here he points out the method; namely, that he intends to destroy everything by a new disaster, a flood. Such a punishment the world hitherto had not known. The customary punishments, as we see from the prophets, are pestilence, famine, the sword and fierce beasts. Men and beasts perish of pestilence. The earth is laid waste by war, for it is deprived of those who till it. The sufferings of famine, though they seem to be less cruel, are by far the most terrible. With the fourth class of penalties, our regions have almost no experience at all. Although these are severally sufficient for the chastisement of the human race, the Lord desired to employ a novel kind of punishment against the primeval world, through which all flesh having the breath of life was to perish.

258. Because this punishment was unheard of in former ages, the wicked were slower to believe it. They reasoned thus: If God is at all angry, can he not correct the disobedient by the sword, by pestilence? A flood would destroy also the other creatures which are without sin; surely God will not plan anything like this for the world.

259. But in order to remove such unbelief from the mind of Noah and the righteous, he repeats with stress the pronoun, "And I, behold, I do bring." Afterward he clearly adds that he will destroy all flesh that is under heaven and in the earth; for he excludes here the fishes whose realm is widened by the waters. This passage tends to show the magnitude of the wrath of God, through which men lose, not only body and life, but also universal dominion over the earth.

C. GOD'S COVENANT WITH NOAH.

  * The way God comforted Noah in announcing the flood, and why such comfort was needed.

1. The nature of this covenant.

    a. The views of Lyra, Burgensis and others.

    b. Luther's views.

2. Whether the giants or tyrants were embraced in this covenant and how received by them.

3. Why it was made only with Noah.

4. How this covenant was made clearer from time to time, and why it was needed at this time.

5. How a special call was added to this covenant.

  * God's judgment upon the first world terrible.

  * Why Ham was taken into the ark, who was later rejected.

  * Foreknowledge and election.

    a. Why we should avoid thinking and disputing on this subject.

    b. To what end should the examples of Scripture on this theme serve.

    c. How consideration of the same may help and harm us.

C. God's Covenant with Noah.

V. 18. *But I will establish my covenant with thee; and thou shalt come into the ark, thou, and thy sons, and thy wife, and thy sons' wives with thee.*

260. To this comfort Moses before pointed when he declared that Noah had found grace. Noah stood in need of it, not only to escape despair amid such wrath, but also for the strengthening of his faith in view of the raging retribution. For it was no easy matter to believe the whole human race was to perish. The world consequently judged Noah to be a dolt for believing such things, ridiculed him and, undoubtedly, made his ship an object of satire. In order to strengthen his mind amid such offenses, God speaks with him often, and now even reminds him of his covenant.

261. Interpreters discuss the question, what that covenant was. Lyra explains it as the promise to defend him against the evil men who had threatened to murder him. Burgensis claims this covenant refers to the perils amid the waters, which were to be warded off. Still others believe it was the covenant of the rainbow, which the Lord afterward made with Noah.

262. In my opinion, he speaks of a spiritual covenant, or of the promise of the seed, which was to bruise the serpent's head. The giants had this covenant, but when its abuse resulted in pride and wickedness, they fell from it. So it was afterward with the Jews, whose carnal presumption in reference to God, the Law, worship and temple led to their loss of these gifts and they perished. To Noah, however, God confirms this covenant by certainly declaring that Christ was to be born from his posterity and that God would leave, amid such great wrath, a nursery for the Church. This covenant includes not only protection of Noah's body, the view advocated by Lyra and Burgensis, but also eternal life.

263. The sentiment, therefore, of the promise is this: Those insolent despisers of my promises and threats will compel me to punish them. I shall first withdraw from them the protection and assurance which are theirs by reason of their covenant with me, that they may perish without covenant and without mercy. But that covenant I shall transfer to you so that you shall be saved, not alone from such power of the waters, but also from eternal death and condemnation.

264. The plain statement is, "With thee." Not the sons, not the wives, does he mention, whom he was also to save; but Noah alone he mentions, from whom the promise was transmitted to his son Shem. This is the second promise of Christ, which is taken from all other descendants of Adam and committed alone to Noah.

265. Afterward this promise is made clearer from time to time. It proceeded from the race to the family, and from the family to the individual. From the whole race of Abraham it was carried forward to David alone; from David to Nathan; from Nathan down to one virgin, Mary, who was the dead branch or root of Jesse, and in whom this covenant finds its termination and fulfilment. The establishment of such a covenant was most necessary in view of the imminence of the incredible and incalculable wrath of God.

266. You will observe here, however, a special call when he says: "Thou shalt

come into the ark, thou, and thy sons, etc." If Noah had not received this special call, he would not have ventured to enter the ark.

267. How terrible is it that from the whole human race only eight persons should be selected for salvation and yet from among them, Ham, the third son of Noah, be rejected! By the mouth of God he is numbered here among the elect and saints. Yea, with them he is protected and saved. Nor is he distinguished from Noah. If he had not believed and prayed for the same things, if he had not feared God, he would in nowise have been saved in the ark; and yet, afterward he is rejected!

268. The sophists wrangle here concerning an election that takes place according to the purpose of God. But often have I exhorted to beware of speculations about the unveiled majesty, for besides being anything but true, they are far from being profitable. Let us rather think of God as he offers himself to us in his Word and sacraments. Let us not trace these instances back to a hidden election, in which God arranged everything with himself from eternity. Such doctrine we cannot apprehend with our minds, and we see it conflicts with the revealed will of God.

269. What, then, you will ask, shall we declare with reference to these examples? Nothing but that they are pointed out to inspire us with the fear of God, so that we believe it is possible to fall from grace after once receiving grace. Paul warns, "Let him that thinketh he standeth take heed lest he fall." 1 Cor 10, 12. We should heed such examples to teach us humility, that we may not exalt ourselves with our gifts nor become slothful in our use of blessings received, but may reach forth to the things which are before, as Paul says in Philippians 3, 13. They teach us not to believe that we have apprehended everything.

270. Malignant and most bitter is our enemy, but we are feeble, bearing this great treasure in earthen vessels. 2 Cor 4, 7. Therefore, we must not glory as if we were secure, but seeing that men so holy fell from grace, which they had accepted and for a long time enjoyed, we should look anxiously to God as if in peril at this very moment. In this manner these examples are discussed to our profit; but those who give no attention to them and chase after complex high thoughts on an election according to the purpose of God, drive and thrust their souls into despair, to which they naturally incline.

VII. ANIMALS AND FOOD IN THE ARK; NOAH'S OBEDIENCE.
A. THE ANIMALS NOAH TOOK INTO THE ARK.

1. The number and kinds of animals.
2. The differences in the animals.
   a. What is understood by the "Behemoth".
   b. By the "Remes".
   c. Whether this difference is observed in all places.
3. Whether wild and ferocious animals were in paradise, and if created from the beginning.

4. How Noah could bring the animals, especially the wild ones, into the ark.

* The animals at the time felt danger was near.

5. The animals came of themselves to Noah in the ark.

B. THE FOOD NOAH TOOK INTO THE ARK.

1. Why necessary to take with them food.

* The kind of food man then had, and if he ate flesh.

2. God's foreknowledge shines forth here.

3. Why God did not maintain man and the animals in the ark by a miracle.

* The extraordinary ways and miracles of God.

    a. Why man should not seek miracles, where ordinary ways and means are at hand.

    b. The monks seek extraordinary ways and thus tempt God.

    * Whether we should use medicine, and if we should learn the arts and languages.

    c. Why God did not save Noah in the water without the ark, when he could have done so.

    d. When does God use extraordinary means with man.

C. NOAH'S OBEDIENCE.

1. In what respect it was especially praised.

* Obedience to God.

    a. How one is to keep the golden mean, and not turn to the right or left.

    b. How man can by obedience or disobedience mark out his own course.

    c. Why most people shun obedience.

    d. How we are here not to look to the thing commanded, but to the person commanding.

    e. How sadly they fail who look at the thing commanded.

    * How the Papists neither understand nor keep God's commandments.

    * What we are to think of the holiness of the Papists.

    f. All God commands is good, even if it seems different to reason.

    * How the Papists do harm by the works of their wisdom, and only provoke God to anger, as king Saul did.

    g. How in his obedience Noah held simply to God's Word and overcame all difficulties.

VII. THE ANIMALS AND THEIR FOOD, AND NOAH'S OBEDIENCE.

A. The Animals Noah took into the Ark.

Vs. 19-20. *And every living thing of all flesh, two of every sort shalt thou bring into the ark, to keep them alive with thee; they shall be male and female. Of the birds after their kind, and of the cattle after their kind, of every creeping thing of the ground after its kind, two of every sort shall come unto thee, to keep them alive.*

271. Here again a dispute arises, as is the case when in historical narratives one proceeds to the application and incidental features. Our text appears to vindicate the view that here two and two are spoken of; but in the beginning of the seventh chapter seven and seven. Hence, Lyra quarrels with one Andrea, who believed fourteen specimens were included in the ark, because it is written: "Of every clean beast thou shalt take to thee seven and seven." But I approve Lyra's interpretation, who says seven specimens of every class were inclosed in the ark, three male and three female, and the seventh also male, to be used by Noah for purposes of sacrifice.

272. When Moses says here that two and two of the several species were brought into the ark, we must necessarily understand the seventh chapter as speaking only of the unclean animals, for the number of clean animals was the greater. Of the unclean seven of every species were inclosed in the ark.

273. It is also necessary that we here discuss the signification of terms as "all life," "beasts," "cattle." Though these are often used without discrimination, still at various places the Scripture employs them discriminatingly; for instance, when it says, "Let the earth bring forth living creatures." Gen 1, 24. "Let the waters swarm with swarms of living creatures." Gen 1, 20. In those places the words of the genus stand for all living beings on the earth and in the waters. Here the constituent species are named—*chayah*, *remes*, and *behemah*—though frequently used without discrimination.

274. The cattle he calls here *behemoth*, though in Ezekiel, first chapter, those four animals are called by the common name, *hachayoth*, a word by which we commonly designate not so much animals as beasts, subsisting not on hay or anything else growing out of the earth, but flesh; as lion, bear, wolf and fox. *Behemoth* are cattle or brutes which live on hay and herbs growing from the earth; as sheep, cows, deer and roe.

275. *Remes* means reptile. The word is derived from *ramas*, which means to tread. When we compare ourselves with the birds, we are *remasian*, for we creep and tread upon the earth with our feet like the dogs and other beasts. But the proper meaning is, animals which do not walk with face erect. The animals which creep and which we term reptiles have a specific name, being called *sherazim*, as we see in Leviticus from the word *sharaz*, which means to move, hereafter used in the seventh chapter. The word *oph* is known, meaning bird.

276. Such are the differences among these terms, although, as I said before, they are not observed in some places. The interpretation must be confined, however, to the time after the flood; otherwise the inference would be drawn that such savage beasts existed also in paradise. Who will doubt that before sin, dominion having been given to man over all animals of earth, there was concord not only among men but also between animals and man?

277. Though the first chapter clearly proves that these wild beasts were creat-

ed with the others, on account of sin their nature was altered. Those created gentle and harmless, after the fall became wild and harmful. This is my view, though since our loss of that state of innocent existence it is easier to venture a guess than to reach a definition of that life.

278. But, you ask, if because of sin the nature of animals became completely altered, how could Noah control them, especially the savage and fierce ones? The lion surely could not be controlled, nor tigers, panthers and the like. The answer is: Such wild animals went into the ark miraculously. To me this appears reasonable. If they had not been forced by a divine injunction to go into the ark, Noah would not have had it within his power to control such fierce animals. Undoubtedly he had to exercise his own human power, but this alone was insufficient. And the text implies both conditions, for at first it says: "Thou shalt bring into the ark," and then adds: "Two of every sort shall come unto thee." If they had not been miraculously guided, they would not have come by twos and sevens.

279. That two by two and seven by seven came of their own accord is a miracle and a sign that they had a premonition of the wrath of God and the coming terrible disaster. Even brute natures have premonitions and forebodings of impending calamities, and often as if prompted by a certain sense of compassion, they will manifest distress for a man in evident peril. We see dogs and horses understand the perils of their masters and show themselves affected by such intelligence, the dogs by howling, the horses by trembling and the emission of copious sweat. As a matter of fact it is not rare that wild beasts in danger seek refuge with man.

280. When, therefore, there is elsewhere in brute natures such an intelligence, is it a wonder that, after having been divinely aroused to a sense of coming danger, they joined themselves voluntarily to Noah? For the text shows they came voluntarily. In the same manner history bears witness, and our experience confirms it, that, when a terrible pestilence rages or a great slaughter is imminent, wolves, the most ferocious of animals, flee not only into villages, but, on occasion, even into cities, taking refuge among men and humbly asking, as it were, their help.

B. The Food Noah took into the Ark.

V. 21. *And take thou unto thee of all food that is eaten, and gather it to thee; and it shall be for food for thee, and for them.*

281. Inasmuch as the flood was to last a whole year, it was necessary to remind Noah of the food to be collected from the herbs and the fruits of trees in order to preserve the life of man and of animals. Though the wrath of God was terrible, to the destruction of everything born on earth, the goodness of the Lord shines forth, notwithstanding, in this an awful calamity. He looks to the preservation of man and the animals, and through their preservation to that of the species. The animals chosen for preservation in the ark were sound and of unblemished body, and through divine foresight, they received food suitable to their nature.

282. As for man, it is established that, as yet, he did not use flesh for food. He ate only of the vegetation of the earth, which was far more desirable before the flood than at present, after the remarkable corruption of the earth through the

brackish waters.

283. We observe here the providence of God, by whose counsel the evil are punished and the good saved. By a miracle God preserves a portion of his creatures when he punishes the wicked and graciously makes provision for their posterity.

284. It would have been an easy matter for God to preserve Noah and the animals for the space of a full year without food, as he preserved Moses, Elijah and Christ, the latter for forty days, without food. He made everything out of nothing, which is even more marvelous. Yet God, in his government of the things created, as Augustine learnedly observes, allows them to perform their appropriate functions. In other words, to apply Augustine's view to the matter in hand, God performs his miracles along the lines of natural law.

285. God also requires that we do not discard the provisions of nature, which would mean to tempt God; but that we use with thanksgiving the things God has prepared for us. A hungry man who looks for bread from heaven rather than tries to obtain it by human means, commits sin. Christ gives the apostles command to eat what is set before them, Lk 10, 7. So Noah is here enjoined to employ the ordinary methods of gathering food. God did not command him to expect in the ark a miraculous supply of food from heaven.

286. The life of the monks is all a temptation of God. They cannot be continent and still they refrain from matrimony; likewise they abstain from certain meats, though God has created them to be received with thanksgiving by them that believe, and by those who know the truth, that every creature of God is good, and nothing to be rejected, if it be received with thanksgiving, 1 Tim 4, 3-4. The use of medicine is legitimate; yea, it has been created as a necessary means to conserve health. The study of the arts and of language is to be cultivated and, as Paul says, "Every creature of God is good, and nothing is to be rejected, if it be received with thanksgiving; for it is sanctified through prayer." 1 Tim 4, 4-5.

287. God was able to preserve Noah in the midst of the waters. They fable of Clement that he had a cell in the middle of the sea. Yea, the people of Israel were preserved in the midst of the Red Sea and Jonah in the belly of the whale. But this was not God's desire. He rather willed that Noah should use the aid of wood and trees, so that human skill might thereby have a sphere for its exercise.

288. When, however, human means fail, then it is for you either to suffer or to expect help from the Lord. No human effort could support the Jews when they stood by the sea and were surrounded in the rear by the enemy. Hence, a miraculous deliverance was to be hoped for, or a sure death to be suffered.

C. Noah's Obedience.

V. 22. *Thus did Noah; according to all that God commanded him, so did he.*

289. This phrase is very frequent in Scripture. This is the first passage in which praise for obedience to God is clothed in such a form of words. Later we find it stated repeatedly that Moses, the people, did according to all that God com-

manded them. But Noah received commendation as an example for us. His was not a dead faith, which is no faith at all, but a living and active faith. He renders obedience to God's commands, and because he believes both God's promises and threats, he carefully carries out what God commanded with reference to the ark and the gathering of animals and food. This is unique praise for Noah's faith, that he remains on the royal way—adds nothing, changes nothing and takes nothing from the divine command, but abides absolutely in the precept he has heard.

290. It is the most common and at the same time most noxious sin in the Church, that people either altogether change God's commands or render something else paramount to them. There is only one royal road to which we must keep. They sin who swerve too much to the left by failing to perform the divine commands. Those who swerve to the right and do more than God has commanded, like Saul when he spared the Amalekites, also sin even more grievously than those who turn to the left. They add a sham piety; for, while those who err on the left cannot excuse their error, these do not hesitate to ascribe to themselves remarkable merit.

291. And such error is exceedingly common. God is wont sometimes to command common, paltry, ridiculous and even offensive things, but reason takes delight in splendid things. From the common ones it either shrinks or undertakes them under protest. Thus the monks shrank from home duties and chose for themselves others apparently of greater glamour. Today the great throng, hearing that common tasks are preached in the Gospel, despises the Gospel as a vulgar teaching, lacking in elegance. What noteworthy thing is it to teach that servants should obey their master and children their parents? Such a common and oft-taught doctrine the learned papists not only neglect but even ridicule. They desire rather something unique, something remarkable either for its reputed wisdom or for its apparent difficult character. Such is the madness of man's wisdom.

292. In general it is wisdom to observe not so much the person that speaks as that which he says, because the teacher's faults are always in evidence. But when we consider precepts of God and true obedience, this axiom should be reversed. Then we should observe not so much that which is said, but the person of him who speaks. In respect to divine precepts, if you observe that which is said and not him who speaks, you will easily stumble. This is illustrated by the example of Eve, whose mind did not dwell upon the person who issued the command. She regarded only the command and concluded it to be a matter of small moment to taste the apple. But what injury was thereby wrought to the whole human race!

293. He who observes him that gives the command will conclude that what is very paltry in appearance is very great. The Papists estimate it a slight thing to govern the State, to be a spouse, to train children. But experience teaches that these are very important matters, for which the wisdom of men is incompetent. We see that at times the most spiritual men have here shamefully fallen. When we, therefore, remember him who gives the command, that which is paltry and common becomes a responsibility too great to discharge without divine aid.

294. The Papists, therefore, who look only at the outward mask, like the cow at the gate, can make light of duties toward home and State, and imagine they

perform others of greater excellence. In the very fact that they are shameless adulterers, blasphemers of God, defilers of the sanctuary and brazen squanderers of the Church's property, they powerfully testify against themselves that they can in no wise appreciate the paltry, common and vulgar domestic and public duties.

295. In what, therefore, consists the holiness they vaunt? Forsooth, in that on certain days they abstain from meat, that they bind themselves to certain vows, that they have a liking for certain kinds of work. But, I ask you, who has given command to do those things? No one. That which God has enjoined or commanded, they do not respect. They render paramount something else concerning which God has given no command.

296. Hence, the vital importance of this rule, that we observe not the contents of the command but its author. He who fails to do this will often be offended, as I said, by the insignificance or absurdity of a task. God should receive credit for wisdom and goodness. Assuredly that which he himself enjoins is well and wisely enjoined, though human reason judge differently.

297. From the wisdom of God the Papists detract when they consider divinely enjoined tasks as paltry and attempt to undertake something better or more difficult. God is not propitiated by such works, but rather provoked, as Saul's example shows. As if God were stupid, dastardly, and cruel in that he commanded to destroy the Amalekites and all their belongings, Saul conceived a kinder plan and reserved the cattle for the purpose of sacrifice. What else was such action but to deem himself wise and God foolish.

298. Hence Moses rightly commends in this passage Noah's obedience when he says that he did everything the Lord had enjoined. That means to give God credit for wisdom and goodness. He did not discuss the task, as Adam, Eve and Saul did to their great hurt. He kept his eye on the majesty of him who gave the command. That was enough for him, even though the command be absurd, impossible, inexpedient. All such objections he passes by with closed eyes, as it were, and takes his stand upon the one thing commanded by God. This text therefore is familiar as far as hearing it is concerned, but even as to the performance and practice of it, it is known to very few and is extremely difficult.

CHAPTER VII.

I. NOAH OBEYS COMMAND TO ENTER THE ARK.

1. Noah saw God's favor in his command.
 * Noah experienced severe temptations and needed comfort.
2. What God wished to teach Noah by calling him to enter the ark.
3. Whether God spoke this commandment directly to Noah.
 * When God speaks to us through men it is to be viewed as God's Word.
 * The thoughts of the Jews on the seven days.
 * The office of the ministry.
    a. Through it God deals with mankind.
    b. Why we should not despise the office and expect revelations direct from God.
 * God speaks with man in various ways.
 * Corruption and destruction of the first world.
    a. The ruin of the first compared with that of the last world.
     * The need of posterity to pray that they retain pure doctrine.
    b. Why so few righteous persons were found in Noah's day.
     * The efforts of the pope and bishops to crush the Gospel.
    c. First world severely punished, neither old nor young were spared.
    d. Punishment of first world greatly moved Peter when he wrote about it.
 * Peter's record of sermon Christ delivered to the spirits of the first world in prison.
    a. Who are to be understood here by the unbelieving world.
    b. Peter here shows the wrath and long suffering of God.
    c. Nature and manner of this sermon.
     * Apostles had special revelations we cannot grasp.
4. How Noah was righteous before God.
5. How the world laughed at him while executing God's command, God then comforted him.
6. Greatness of Noah's faith and steadfastness in executing this command.
 * Luther's confession he would have been too weak for such a work.

* The great firmness of John Huss and Jerome of Prague.

* We are to comfort ourselves when all the world forsakes and condemns us.

7. God commands Noah to take the animals he names along into the ark.

* Why God so often repeats the same thing.

    a. What is to be understood by Behemoth.

    b. How many of each kind entered the ark.

      * The rain at the flood was exceptional.

      * The flood is a token of God's righteousness and from it we conclude God will punish the sins of the last world.

8. By what may we learn Noah's faith and obedience to God.

* Why God did not save Noah in some other way.

I. NOAH OBEYS COMMAND TO ENTER THE ARK.

V. 2a. *And Jehovah said unto Noah, Come thou and all thy house into the ark.*

1. As soon as that extraordinary structure, the ark, was built, the Lord commanded Noah to enter it, because the time of the deluge, which the Lord announced one hundred and twenty years before, was now at hand. All this convinced Noah that God was taking care of him; and not only this, but also, as Peter says (2 Pet 1, 19), gave him an ample and abundant word to support and confirm his faith in such great straits. Having foretold the deluge for more than a century, he doubtless was bitterly mocked by the world in many ways.

2. As I have said repeatedly, God's wrath was incredible. It could not be grasped by the human mind, in that original age of superior men, that God was about to destroy the whole human race, except eight souls. Noah, being holy and just, a kindly and merciful man, often struggled with his own heart, hearing with the greatest agitation of mind the voice of the Lord, threatening certain destruction to all flesh. It was needful, then, that repeated declaration should confirm his agitated faith, lest he might doubt.

3. God's command to enter the ark amounted to this: "Doubt not, the time of punishment for the unbelieving world is close at hand. But tremble not, do not fear, for faith is at times very weak in the saints. I shall take care of you and your house." To us such promise would have been incredible, but we must admit that all things are possible with God.

4. Notice Moses' peculiar expression again: "Jehovah said." It gives me particular pleasure that these words of God did not sound from heaven, but were spoken to Noah through the ministry of man. Although I would not deny that these revelations may have been made by an angel, or by the Holy Spirit himself, yet where it can plausibly be said that God spoke through men, there the ministry must be honored. We have shown above that many of God's words according to Moses, were spoken through Adam; for the Word of God, even when spoken by man, is truly the Word of God.

5. Now, as Methuselah, Noah's grandfather, died in the very year of the deluge, it would not be inapt to infer that (since Lamech, Noah's father, had died five years before the flood,) this was, so to speak, Methuselah's last word and testament to his grandson, a dying farewell. Perhaps he added some remarks as these: My son, as thou hast obeyed the Lord heretofore, and hast awaited this wrath in faith, and hast experienced God's faithful protection from the wicked, henceforth firmly believe that God will take care of thee. The end is now at hand, not mine alone, which is one of grace, but the end of all mankind, which is one of wrath. For after seven days the flood will begin, concerning which thou hast long and vainly warned the world. After this manner, I think, spoke Methuselah, but the words are attributed to God, because the Spirit of God spoke through the man.

Thus I like to interpret these instances to the honor of the ministry wherever, as in this case, it can appropriately be done. Since it is certain that Methuselah died in the very year of the flood, the supposition is harmless that these were his last words to Noah, his grandson, who heard his words and accepted them as the Word of God.

6. The Jews' peculiar idea concerning these seven days is that they were added to the one hundred and twenty years in honor of Methuselah, that therein his posterity might bewail his death. This is a harmless interpretation, for the patriarch's descendants did not fail to do their duty, particularly his pious children.

7. But the first view concerning the ministry of the Word, is not only plausible, but also practical. God does not habitually speak miraculously and by revelation, particularly where, he has instituted the ministry for this very purpose of speaking to men, teaching, instructing, consoling and entreating them.

8. In the first place, God entrusts the Word to parents. Moses often says: "Thou shalt tell it to thy children." Then to the teachers of the Church is it entrusted. Abraham says (Lk 16, 29): "They have Moses and the prophets; let them hear them." We must expect no revelation, be it inward or outward, where the ministry is established; otherwise all ranks of human society would be disturbed. Let the pastor preach in Church; let the magistrate rule the State; let parents control the house or family. Such are the ministries of men instituted by God. We should make use of them and not look for new revelations.

9. Still I do not deny that Noah heard God speak after Methuselah's death. God speaks ordinarily through the public ministry—through parents and the teachers of the Church—and in rare cases by inward revelation, through the Holy Spirit. It is well that we remember not to overlook the Word in vain expectation of new revelations, as the fanatics do. Such a course gives rise to spirits of error, a source of disturbance to the whole world, as the example of the Anabaptists proves.

V. 1b. *For thee have I seen righteous before me in this generation.*

10. This is truly a picture of the primitive, ancient world, as Peter calls it. 2 Pet 2, 5. His appellation carries the thought of a peculiarity of that particular age, which is foreign to the people of our own. Could words be more appalling than these, that Noah alone was righteous before the Lord? The world is similarly pictured in Ps 14, 2-3, where we read that the Lord looked down from heaven to see

if there were any that did understand, that did seek God. But he says: "They are all gone aside; they are together become filthy; there is none that doeth good, no, not one."

11. Similar to this judgment upon the world was Christ's declaration as to the last days. He says: "When the Son of man cometh, shall he find faith on the earth?" Lk 18, 8. It is a fearful thing to live in such an evil and godless world. By the goodness of God, since we have the light of his Word, we are still in the golden age. The sacraments are rightfully administered in our Churches, pious teachers proclaim the Word purely, and, though magistrates be weak, wickedness is not desperately rampant. But Christ's prophecy shows that there will be evil times when the Lord's day approaches. Wholesome teaching nowhere will be found, the Church being dominated by the wicked, as today the plans of our adversaries are a menace. The pope and the wicked princes zealously strive totally to destroy the ministry of the Word, oppressing or corrupting the true ministries, that everyone may believe whatever pleases him.

12. So much the more diligently should we pray for our posterity, and take earnest heed that a more wholesome doctrine be transmitted to them. If there had been more godly teachers in the days of Noah, there might have been more righteous people. The fact that Noah alone was proclaimed a righteous man makes it evident that the godly teachers had been either destroyed or corrupted, leaving Noah the sole preacher of righteousness, as Peter calls him, 2 Pet 2, 5. Since government had been turned into tyranny and the home vitiated by adultery and whoredom, how could punishment be delayed any longer?

13. Such danger awaits us also if the last days are to be like the days of Noah. Truly, the popes and bishops strenuously endeavor to suppress the Gospel and to ruin the Churches which have been rightfully established. Thus does the world assiduously press onward to a period similar to the age of Noah, when, with the light of the Word extinguished, all shall go astray in the darkness of wickedness. For without the preaching of the Word, faith cannot endure nor prayer, nor the purity of the sacraments.

14. Such, according to Moses, was the condition of the ancient world in Noah's day, when the world was young and at its best. The greatest geniuses flourished everywhere and people were well educated by experience because they lived so long. What will be our fate in the frenzy, so to speak, that shall befall the world in its dotage? We should remember to care for our posterity and continually pray for it.

15. As the first world was most corrupt, it was thus subject to terrible punishment. Adults perished who provoked God to anger by their wicked deeds, also those of an innocent age, who had knowledge and were unable to distinguish between their right hand and their left. Many, doubtless, were deceived by their own guilelessness; but God's wrath does not discriminate, it falls upon and destroys alike adults and infants, the crafty and the guileless.

16. This awful punishment appears to have moved even the Apostle Peter. Like one besides himself, he uses words which we today are not able to understand. He

says: Christ, having been made alive in the Spirit, also "went and preached unto the spirits in prison, that aforetime were disobedient, when the long suffering of God waited in the days of Noah, while the ark was a preparing, wherein few, that is, eight souls, were saved through water," etc. (1 Pet 3, 19-20).

17. A strange declaration, and an almost fanatical saying, by which the Apostle describes this event! By these words, Peter assures us that there was a certain unbelieving world to whom the dead Christ preached after their death. If this is true, who would doubt that Christ took Moses and the prophets with him to those who were fettered in prison, in order to change the unbelieving world into a new and believing one? This seems to be intimated by Peter's words, though I should not like to make this assertion authoritatively.

18. But doubtless those whom he calls an unbelieving world were not the wicked despisers of his Word nor the tyrants. If they were overwhelmed in their sins, these were certainly condemned. The unbelieving world of which he speaks seems rather to be the children and those whose lack of judgment precluded belief. These were at that time, seized and carried away headlong to their destruction, by the offenses of the world, as if in the power of a rapid stream, only eight souls being saved.

19. In this way does Peter magnify the awful intensity of God's wrath. At the same time he praises his long-suffering in that he did not deprive those of the Word of salvation who at the time did not or could not believe because they hoped in the patience of God and would not be convinced that he would visit such fearful and universal punishment upon the world.

20. How this came to pass is beyond our understanding. We know and believe that God is wonderful in all his works and has all power. Therefore he who in life preached to the living, could also in death preach to the dead. All things hear, feel and touch him, though our human minds can not understand the process. Nor is it to our discredit when we are ignorant of some of the mysteries of Holy Writ. The apostles had each his own revelation, and contention concerning them would be presumptuous and foolish.

21. Such was the revelation of Christ given to the spirits that evidently perished in the flood, and we may perhaps, not inappropriately connect it with that article of our creed which speaks of the descent of Christ into hell. Such was also Paul's revelation concerning paradise, the third heaven (2 Cor 12, 2-4), and certain other matters of which we may be ignorant without shame. It is false pride to profess to understand these things. St. Augustine and other teachers give their fancy loose rein when they discuss these passages. May it not be that the apostles had revelations which St. Augustine and others did not have? But let us return to Moses.

22. A truly fearful description of the world is vouchsafed in this declaration of God that he saw Noah alone to be righteous before him, in spite of the small children and those others who had innocently been misled. Let us particularly note the term, "Before me." It signifies that Noah was blameless not only as regards the second table of the Law, but also as regards the first. He believed in God, and hal-

lowed, preached and called upon his name; he gave thanks to God; he condemned godless teachings. For, to be righteous before God means to believe God and to fear him, and not, as they taught in popedom, to read masses, to free souls from purgatory, to become a monk, and like things.

23. This term "Before me" has reference also to the condemnation of the ancient world. Having neglected the worship demanded by the first table, they criminally transgressed also the second. Not only did they mock Noah as a fool, but they went so far as to condemn his teaching as heresy. Meanwhile they ate, drank, and celebrated festivals in security. Before the world, accordingly, Noah was not righteous; measured by her code he was a sinner.

24. Hence God, or the grandfather, Methuselah, consoles Noah with the Word of counsel to disregard the blind and wicked verdict of the world, neither to care for her views and utterances, but to close eyes and ears while heeding alone the Word and verdict of God, believing himself to be righteous before God, or approved and acceptable to him.

25. And Noah's faith was truly great; he could rely upon God's utterance. I, forsooth, should not have believed. I realize what weight the whole world's hostile and condemnatory judgment must carry. We are condemned in the judgment of the Pope, the Sacramentarians, and the Anabaptists, but this is mere play and pleasure, compared to what the righteous Noah had to bear, who found not a single person in the whole world to approve of his religion or life, except his own sons and his pious grandfather. We have, the endorsement of many Churches, by God's grace, and our princes fear no danger in defense of their doctrine and religion. Noah had no such protectors, and he saw his enemies living in peaceful leisure and enjoyment. If I had been he, I surely should have said: Lord, if I am righteous, if I am well pleasing to thee and if those people are wicked and displeasing to thee, why, then, dost thou enrich them? Why dost thou heap upon them all manner of favors, while I, with my family, am greatly harassed and almost without assistance? In short, I should have despaired in such great afflictions unless the Lord had given me that spirit which Noah had.

26. Therefore, Noah is a brilliant and admirable example of faith, who opposed the judgments of the world with an heroic steadfastness of mind in the assurance that he was righteous while all the rest of the world was wicked.

27. Often when I think of those most holy men, John Huss and Jerome of Prague, I view with astonishment the courage of their souls, as they, only two in number, set themselves against the judgment of the whole world, of pope, emperor, bishops, princes, universities and all the schools throughout the empire.

28. It is helpful often to reflect upon such examples. Since the prince of the world battles against us, endeavoring to kindle despair in us with his fiery darts, it behooves us to be well armed, lest we succumb to the enemy. Let us say with Noah: I know that I am righteous before God, even though the whole world condemn me as heretical and wicked, yea, even desert me. Thus did the apostles desert Christ, leaving him alone; but he said (Jn 16, 32): "I am not alone." Thus did the false brethren desert Paul. Hence, this is no uncommon danger, and it is not for

us to despair; but with courage to uphold the true doctrine, in spite of the world's condemnation and curse.

Vs. 2-3. *Of every clean beast thou shalt take to thee seven and seven, the male and his female; and of the beasts that are not clean two, the male and his female. Of the birds also of the heavens, seven and seven, male and female; to keep seed alive upon the face of all the earth.*

29. It is evident that God takes pleasure in speaking to Noah. Hence, he does not confine himself to a single command, but repeats the same things in the same words. To human reason such repetition appears to be absurd talkativeness, but to a soul struggling against despair the will of God cannot be repeated too often, nor can too exhaustive instruction be given relative to the will of God. God recognizes the state of a soul that is tempted, and hence makes the same statements again and again, so that Noah may learn from frequent conversations and conferences that he is not only not forsaken though the whole world forsake him, but that he has a friend and protector in God who so loves him that he never seems to weary of conversing with him. This is the cause of the statements being repeated. However, as has been explained, God spoke with Noah not from heaven but through men.

30. In respect to the language, this passage shows that *ha-behemah* signifies not only cattle, the larger animals, but also the smaller ones which were commonly used for sacrifice, as sheep, goats and the like. The custom of offering sacrifices was not first instituted by Moses, but was in the world from the beginning, being handed down, as it were, by the patriarchs to their posterity; as shown by the example of Abel, who brought of his first fruits an offering to God.

31. As to the remainder of the passage, we explained at the end of the sixth chapter how to harmonize the discrepancies apparent in the fact that here seven beasts of each kind are ordered to be taken into the ark while only two of each kind are mentioned there. To repeat is not necessary. Since Noah was saved by a miracle, he thought that a seventh animal should be added to the three pairs of clean beasts as a thank-offering to God, after the flood, for his deliverance.

V. 4. *For yet seven days, and I will cause it to rain upon the earth forty days and forty nights; and every living thing that I have made will I destroy from off the face of the ground.*

32. Here you see God's care to give Noah complete assurance. He sets a limit of seven days, after which will follow a rain of forty days and forty nights. God speaks with peculiar significance when he says that it shall rain. It was not a common rain, but fountains of the deep as well as the windows of heaven were opened; that is, not only did a great mass of rain fall from heaven, but also an immense amount of water streamed forth from the earth itself. And an immense amount of water was necessary to cover the highest mountain tops to a depth of fifteen cubits. It was no ordinary rain, but the rain of God's wrath, by which he set out to destroy all life upon the face of the earth. Because the earth was depraved, God despoiled it, and because the godless people raged against the first and second tables of the commandments, therefore God also raged against them, using heaven and earth as his weapons.

33. This story is certain proof that God, though long-suffering and patient, will not allow the wicked to go unpunished. As Peter says (2 Pet 2, 5), if he "spared not the ancient world," how much less will he spare the popes or the emperors who rage against his Word? How much less will he spare us who blaspheme his name when our life is unworthy of our calling and profession, when we freely and daily sin against our consciences? Let us, then, learn to fear the Lord, humbly to accept his Word and obey it; otherwise punishment will overtake also us, as Peter threatens.

Vs. 5-10. *And Noah did according unto all that Jehovah commanded him. And Noah was six hundred years old when the flood of waters was upon the earth. And Noah went in, and his sons and his wife, and his sons' wives with him, into the ark, because of the waters of the flood. Of clean beasts, and of beasts that are not clean, and of birds, and of everything that creepeth upon the ground, there went in two and two unto Noah into the ark, male and female, as God commanded Noah. And it came to pass after the seven days, that the waters of the flood were upon the earth.*

34. This is clear from what precedes. Noah's faith is praiseworthy in that he obeyed the Lord's command and unwaveringly entered the ark with his sons and their wives. God truly could have saved him in innumerable other ways; he did not employ this seemingly absurd method because he knew no other. To him who kept Jonah for three days in the midst of the sea and in the belly of the whale, what do you think is impossible? But Noah's faith and obedience are to be commended because he took no offense at this plan of salvation divinely shown to him, but embraced it in simple faith.

II. COMPLETE DESTRUCTION BY FLOOD.

* Why Moses so often repeats and expresses in few words what other writers describe at length.
* Noah's grief because of the approaching calamity.
* The way of coarse and satiated spirits.
1. When did the flood commence.
   a. Some think it began in the spring.
   b. Others think it began in the autumn.
   c. Which is the more probable.
   * What to think of the Jews reckoning the year has two beginnings.
2. How the flood continued.
   a. Must distinguish the fountains of the earth, the windows of heaven and the rain.
   * Of the earth and the water.
      (1) Why the water does not overflow the earth since the earth floats in the water.
      (2) Why the water above the earth does not fall and overflow the earth.

(3) How the prophets wondered at this as a miracle, but we in our day give it little thought.

b. How were the fountains broken up, how can such a work be ascribed to God.

* Overflowing of the German fountains at Halle.

c. How were the windows of heaven opened.

(1) What is meant by the windows of heaven.

(2) Why such words used here.

3. Flood covered and destroyed the whole earth.

4. Why God sent the deluge.

* Why God so often repeats the same thing.

* What is meant by Zippor.

* How God's wrath as seen in the deluge was very great.

5. The deluge was a terrible spectacle; Noah and his sons took courage from it.

* Noah's glorious faith at the sight of the deluge.

* Noah's long ship voyage; how he was comforted.

6. How the world's destruction harmonizes with God's promises: how the promises to the Church agree with his threatenings.

* God's threatenings and man's unbelief.

a. Why the first world believed not the threatenings about the deluge.

b. Why the Jews believe not the threatenings of the prophets.

c. Why the Papists believed not the threats against them.

* God's Church and her maintenance.

a. The world understands not how the church is maintained.

b. What is the true form of the true Church.

c. God's promises not rescinded when rejected; who bear the name of the Church.

7. Whether God fully rescinded through the flood the rule over the earth he once gave man.

* How God preserved his Church through the deluge.

8. The deluge was apparently against God's promise.

* God allows nothing to hinder the punishment of the impenitent.

* By what means Papists adorn themselves and how it is all in vain.

* Why we should not rely on present, temporal things, but upon God's Word.

* The marks of a true Church.

a. What they are not and what they are.

b. Papists have characteristics Holy Scriptures give as marks of Antichrist.

c. Church born of God's Word and is to be known by that Word.

d. Rule to be observed in the marks of the true Church.

e. How far one may consider the Papists the true church, and how far not.

f. The true church is where the Word is, although few belong to it and it has no temporal power.

g. Whether the Evangelicals can justly be accused of falling from the old church.

h. How and why the Evangelical or Gospel Church is really the true Church.

* How Noah retained all and remained lord of the world although the deluge destroyed everything.

II. COMPLETE DESTRUCTION.

Vs. 11-12. *In the six hundredth year of Noah's life, in the second month, on the seventeenth day of the month, on the same day were all the fountains of the great deep broken up, and the windows of heaven were opened. And the rain was upon the earth forty days and forty nights.*

35. We see that Moses uses a great many words, which results in tiresome repetition. How often he mentions the animals! how often the entrance into the ark! how often the sons of Noah who entered at the same time! The reason for this must be left to the spiritually minded; they alone know and see that the Holy Spirit does not repeat in vain.

36. Others, however, who are more materially minded may think that Moses, being moved, when he wrote the passage, by the greatness of God's wrath, desired to enforce its truths by repetition; for reiteration of statements is soothing to troubled minds. Thus did David repeat his lament over his son Absalom, 2 Sam 18, 33. So viewed, this narrative shows depth of feeling and extreme agitation of mind. This example of wrath so impresses the narrator that for emphasis he mentions the same thing again and again, and in the same words.

37. This is not the custom of poets and historians. Their emotions are factitious; they are diffuse in their descriptions; they pile up words for mere effect. Moses husbands his words, but is emphatic by repetition that he may arouse the reader's attention to the importance of the message and compel him to feel his own emotions instead of reading those of another.

38. Evidently Moses did not only wish to convey by persistent repetition the extreme agitation of his own mind, but also of that of Noah himself, who, being filled with the Holy Spirit, and burning with love, necessarily deplored the calamity when he saw that he could not avert it. He foresaw the doom of the wisest and most distinguished and eminent men. Thus did David mourn when he could not

call back Absalom to life. So Samuel mourned when he despaired of saving Saul.

39. The text is not a mere tautology or repetition. The Holy Spirit does not idly repeat words, as those superficial minds believe, which, having read through the Bible once, throw it aside as if they had gathered all its contents. Yet these very repetitions of Moses contain a statement more startling than any to be found in heathen records—that Noah entered the ark in the six hundredth year, the second month and the second day of his life.

40. Opinions differ as to the beginning of the year. One is, that the year begins at the conjunction of the sun and the moon which occurs nearest to the vernal equinox. Thus this month is called the first by Moses in Exodus. If the flood set in on the seventeenth day of the second month, it must have continued almost to the end of April, the most beautiful season of the year, when the earth seemingly gathers new strength, when the birds sing and the beasts rejoice, when the world puts on a new face, as it were, after the dreary season of winter. Death and destruction must have come with added terror at that season which was looked forward to as a harbinger of joy and the apparent beginning of a new life. This view is substantiated by the words of Christ in Matthew 24, 38, where he compares the last days of the world to the days of Noah and speaks of feasting, marriage and other signs of gladness.

41. A second opinion makes the year begin with that new moon which is nearest to the autumnal equinox, when all the harvest has been gathered from the fields. Its advocates declare this to be the beginning of the year, because Moses calls that month in which such new moon occurs, the end of the year. They call this autumnal equinox the beginning of the civil year, and the vernal equinox the beginning of the holy year. The Mosaic ceremonies and festivals extend from the latter season up to the autumnal equinox.

42. If Moses in this passage is speaking of the civil year, then the flood occurred in September or October, an opinion I find Lyra held. It is true that fall and winter are more liable to rains, the signs of the zodiac pointing to humidity. Again, as Moses writes further on, a dove was sent forth in the tenth month and brought back a green olive branch. This fact seems to harmonize with the view that the deluge began in October.

43. But I cannot endorse this argument of the Jews, assuming two beginnings of the year. Why not make four beginnings, since there are four distinct seasons according to the equinoxes and solstices? It is safer to follow the divine order, making April the first month, starting with the new moon which is nearest to vernal equinox. The Jews betray their ignorance in speaking of an autumnal beginning of the year: the autumnal equinox is necessarily the end of the year. Moses so calls it for the reason that all field labors had then ceased and all products had been gathered and brought home.

44. Hence, it is my belief that the flood began in the spring, when all minds were filled with hope of the new year. Such is the death of the wicked that when they shall say, "Peace and safety," they perish. 1 Thes 5, 3. Nor is any inconsistence shown in the fact that the green olive branch is afterward mentioned, for certain

trees are evergreen, as the boxwood, fir, pine, cedar, laurel, olive, palm and others.

45. But what does Moses mean by saying that the fountains of the great deep burst, and that the windows of heaven were opened? No such record is found in all pagan literature, although the heathen searched with zeal the mysteries of nature. One discrimination should be made as regards the abysses of the earth, the floodgates or windows of heaven, and the rain. Rain, as we know it, is a common phenomenon, while that of bursting floodgates and abysses is both unfamiliar and amazing.

46. Almost all interpreters are silent on this point. We know from Holy Writ that God, by his Word, established a dwelling-place for man and other living beings on dry land, above the water, contrary to nature; for it is opposed to natural law that the earth, being placed in water, should rise up out of it. If you cast a clod into the water, it sinks at once. But the dry land stands up out of the water by virtue of the Word, which has set bounds for the sea, as Solomon (Prov 8, 27) and Job (ch 38, 11) declare. Unless the water were restrained by the power of the Word, with a bound, as it were, they would overflow and lay waste everything. Thus is our life guarded every single moment, and wonderfully preserved by the Word. We have an illustration in partial deluges, when at times entire states or regions are flooded, proving that we should daily suffer such unpleasant things if God did not take care of us.

47. But just as there are waters below us, and beneath the earth, so, too, are there waters above us, and beyond the sky. If they should descend, obeying natural law, destruction would result. The clouds float as if suspended in space. When at times they descend, how great the terror they cause! But imagine the result of a universal collapse! How they would burst, in obedience to the law of their nature, did they not remain in place above us, suspended, as it were, by the Word!

48. Thus we are girt about on all sides by water, shielded only by a frail ceiling of unsubstantial material—the air that we breathe—which bears up the clouds and carries that weight of water, not in obedience to the laws of nature, but by the command of God, or by the power of the Word.

49. When the prophets think of these things they are lost in admiration. It is contrary to nature that such a weight should remain in suspension above the earth. But we, blinded by daily witnessing of such wonders, neither observe nor admire them. That we are not at any moment overwhelmed by waters from above or from below, we owe to the divine majesty which orders all things and preserves all creatures so wonderfully, and he ought to be the object of our praise.

50. Startling and significant are the words Moses uses—the fountains of the great deep were broken up. The conception he would convey is that they had been closed by God's power and sealed, as it were, with God's seal, as today; and that God did not open them with a key, but rent them with violence, so that the ocean, in a sudden upheaval, covered everything with water. It is not to be supposed that God moved his hand, because the fountains of the deep are said to have been broken up. It is the custom of Scripture to adapt itself to our understanding in the phraseology employed, and that under consideration here denotes that God gives

leave to the waters in that he no longer restrains or coerces them but suffers them to rage and break forth unchecked according to their nature. That is the reason the ocean seemed to swell and boil. In the salt works in our neighborhood there is a spring named after the Germans, which, if it is not pumped out at certain times, swells and overflows with terrific force.

51. They say that in olden times the town of Halle was once destroyed by a violent overflow of a spring of the kind described. If a single spring could work such destruction what would be the result of the uncurbed power of ocean and seas? Thus mankind was destroyed before they even knew their danger. Whither should they flee when the waters poured in upon them with such force?

52. But this is not all: the windows of heaven also were opened. Moses' word implies that to that time the windows were closed as they are closed today. Indeed, the world thought such opening impossible; their sins, however, made it possible.

53. Moses' use here of the word "windows" signifies the literal opening of heaven. With rain as we know it, the water appears to fall by drops from the pores of the rain-clouds, but at the time of the flood it came down with great force, not through pores, but through windows, like water poured from a vessel with one movement, or as when water-skins burst in the middle. Moses uses this figure of speech for the sake of effect, so that those occurrences are brought to our vision.

54. A volume of water, therefore, swept over the earth, from the sky as well as from the innermost parts of the earth, until at last the whole earth was covered with water, and the fertile soil, or the entire face of the earth was destroyed by the briny flood. A like instance occurs nowhere in any book. The Holy Scriptures alone teach us that these things were visited upon the world sinning in imagined security, and that to this day the waters suspended in the clouds are restrained only by the kindness of God. Otherwise they would descend in vast volume, as in the flood, according to the law of their nature.

Vs. 13-16. *In the selfsame day entered Noah, and Shem, and Ham, and Japheth, the sons of Noah, and Noah's wife, and three wives of his sons with them, into the ark; they, and every beast after its kind, and all the cattle after their kind, and every creeping thing that creepeth upon the earth after its kind, and every bird after its kind, every bird of every sort. And, they went in unto Noah and the ark, two and two of all flesh wherein is the breath of life. And they that went in, went in male and female of all flesh, as God commanded him.*

55. Here Moses begins to be remarkably verbose. His wordiness hurts tender ears when he so often and apparently without any use repeats the same things. It is not sufficient to say "all birds," but he names three kinds of birds. Of these, the term *zippor* is usually said to mean "a sparrow," but this passage shows clearly that it is a generic term, doubtless so called from the sound, *zi, zi.* He also names three kinds of beasts. Also, when speaking of the flood itself, he is very wordy, saying that the waters prevailed, that they increased, that they flooded and covered the face of the earth. Finally, when he tells of the effect of this flood, he makes similar repetition: "All flesh expired, died, was destroyed," etc.

56. But I said above (§37) that Moses repeats these things contrary to his style, in order to force the reader to pause and more diligently learn and meditate upon

this great event. We cannot fully comprehend the wrath which destroys, not man alone, but all his possessions. Moses wishes to arouse hardened and heedless sinners by such a consideration of God's wrath.

57. Hence, these words are not idle, as a shallow and unspiritual reader might judge. They rather challenge us to fear God, and call attention to the present so that, sobered by the thought of such wrath, we may make an earnest beginning in the fear of God, and cease from sin. For not without many tears does Moses appear to have written this account! So utterly is he with eyes and mind absorbed in this horrible spectacle of wrath that he cannot but repeat the same statements again and again. Doubtless he does this with the purpose to thrust such darts of divine fear, so to speak, into the souls of pious readers.

58. It may be well to transport ourselves in thought into the time of the event. What do you think would be our state of mind if we had been put into the ark, if we had seen the waters spreading everywhere with overwhelming force and the wretched human beings perishing without possibility of help? Let us remember that Noah and his sons were also flesh and blood; that is, they were men who, as that person in the comedy (Terence, Heaut. 1: 1, 25) says, thought nothing human was foreign to themselves. They were in the ark for forty days before it was lifted off the earth. In those days were destroyed all the human beings and animals living upon the earth. This calamity they saw with their own eyes; who would doubt that they were violently stirred by the sight?

59. Furthermore, the ark floated upon the waters for one hundred and fifty days, buffeted on all sides by the waves and winds. There was no hope for any harbor, or for any meeting with men. As exiles, therefore, as vanished from the earth, as it were, they were driven here and there by currents and winds. Is it not a miracle that those eight human beings did not die from grief and fear? Truly, we are made of stone if we can read this story with dry eyes.

60. What outcry, sorrow and wailing if from the shore we see a small boat overturned, and human beings miserably perishing! Here, however, not one boatload, but the entire world of men perish in the waters; a world composed not only of grown persons, but also babes; not only of criminal and wicked ones, but also simple-hearted matrons and virgins. They all perished. Let us believe that Moses told the tale of this calamity with such redundancy of words in order that we might be impelled to give earnest attention to this important event. Noah's faith was truly of a rare kind, since he consoled himself and his family with the hope of promised seed and dwelt more upon this promise than the destruction of all the rest of the world.

Vs. 16-24. *And Jehovah shut him in. And the flood was forty days upon the earth; and the waters increased, and bare up the ark, and it was lifted up above the earth. And the waters prevailed, and increased greatly upon the earth; and the ark went upon the face of the waters. And the waters prevailed exceedingly upon the earth; and all the high mountains that were under the whole heaven were covered. Fifteen cubits upward did the waters prevail; and the mountains were covered. And all flesh died that moved upon the earth, both birds, and cattle, and beasts, and every creeping thing that creepeth upon the earth, and every man: all, in whose nostrils was the breath of the spirit of life, of all that was on the dry land, died. And every living thing was destroyed that was upon the face of the ground, both man, and cattle, and creeping things, and birds of the heavens; and they were destroyed from the earth: and Noah only was left, and they that were with him in the ark. And the waters prevailed upon the earth a hundred and fifty days.*

61. For forty days the ark stood in some plain. By that time the waters had risen to such an extent that they lifted the ark, which then floated for one hundred and fifty days. A long sea voyage indeed, and one of great mourning and tears. Yet the occupants upheld themselves by faith, not doubting the kindness of God toward them. They had experienced his goodness when building the ark, when preparing the food, when getting ready other things needful for this occasion, and finally when the Lord closed the ark after the flood came in its power.

62. The question arises, how can God be truthful here? He had set man as master over the earth to cultivate and rule it. God did not create the earth to lie waste, but to be inhabited and give its fruits to men. How can we reconcile such purpose of the creator with the fact that he destroyed all mankind except eight souls? I have no doubt that this argument influenced the descendants of Cain as well as the wicked posterity of the righteous generation not to believe Noah when he proclaimed the flood. How can we harmonize God's promise to Adam and Eve, "You shall rule the earth," and his words here to Noah, "The water shall overpower all men, and destroy them all." So the unbelievers decided that Noah's preaching was wicked and heretical.

63. In like manner the books of the prophets bear witness that the threats of the Assyrian and Babylonish captivity were not believed by the priests and kings, who knew this grand promise: "This is my resting-place forever: here will I dwell; for I have desired it," Ps 132, 14; and that other, by Isaiah: "Here is my fire, and my hearth-stone," Is 31, 9. To them it was incredible that either the State or the temple should be overthrown by the gentiles. And the Jews, miserable outcast though they be, even to this day hold fast the promise that they are God's people and heirs of the promises given Abraham and the fathers.

64. Thus is the pope puffed up with the promises given to the Church: "I am with you unto the end of the world," Mt 28, 20; "I will not leave you desolate," Jn 14, 18; "I made supplication for thee, that thy faith fail not," Lk 22, 32; and others. Though he sees and feels the wrath of God, yet, caught in these promises, he dreams, and likewise his followers, that his throne and power are secure. Hence the Papists blatantly use the name of the Church to overwhelm us, promising themselves the utmost success, as if they could force God to establish the Church according to their dreams and desires.

65. Fitly, then, do we here raise the question how the flood, by which all mankind perished, agrees with the will of God, who created human nature and gave it the promise and endowment of dominion. The answer to this question will likewise settle the one concerning the Church. It is this: God remains truthful, preserving, ruling and governing his Church though in a manner transcending the observation and understanding of the world. He permits the Roman pontiff and

his adherents to think that the pope is the Church. He suffers him to feel secure and to enjoy his dignity and title. But in fact God has excommunicated the pontiff, because he rejects the Word and establishes idolatrous worship.

66. On the other hand, God has chosen for himself another Church, which embraces the Word and flees idolatry, a Church so oppressed and shamefully afflicted that it is not considered a Church but a band of heretics and the devil's school. Thus Paul writes to the Romans (ch 2, 17) that the Jews do not fear God yet they glory in the Law and in God, at the same time denying, blaspheming and offending God. And while the Jews, who take pride in being God's people, are doing this, God prepares for himself a Church from the gentiles, who truly glory in God and embrace his Word.

67. But who should dare to accuse God of untruthfulness because he preserves the Church in a manner unknown and undesired by man? Of similar nature were the promises concerning the preservation of Jerusalem and the temple. These promises were not violated when that city and temple were laid waste by the Babylonians. For God established another Jerusalem and another temple in the Spirit and by the Word; Jeremiah promised (Jer 29, 10-11) that the people should return after seventy years and that then both the temple and the nation should be re-established.

68. As regards the Jews, these were destroyed at that time, but not as regards God who had promised in his Word that they should be rebuilt. The Jews argue correctly that God will not desert the nation and temple; but God keeps his promise in a way foreign to the thought of the Jews, who believed that the nation would not be destroyed because the promise said: "This is my resting-place forever." God permitted destruction in order to punish the sins of his people, and yet he preserved and protected the Church when the pious were brought back by Cyrus and built the temple.

69. In like manner, dominion over the world was given to man in the beginning of creation. This is taken away in the flood, not forever, but for a time, and that not altogether. Though the greater part of the world perishes, yet man retains his mastery; and this mastery is preserved to mankind, not as represented by a multitude, as the world desired and believed, but by a few persons—eight souls—a thing which seemed incredible to the world.

70. Hence God did not lie; he kept his promise, but not as the world would have had it. He destroyed the sinners and saved the righteous few, which, like a seed, he thereafter multiplied in many ways.

71. The Papists should keep before their eyes this judgment of God. It teaches that neither numbers nor power nor his own promise is allowed to prevent him from punishing the impenitent. Otherwise he would have spared the first world and the offspring of the patriarchs to whom he had granted dominion over the earth. Now he destroys all and saves only eight.

72. Is it wonderful, then, that he deals with the Papists in the same way? Though they boast of rank, dignity, numbers, and power, yet, because they trample the Word of God under foot and rage against it, God will cast them away,

choosing for himself another Church, which will humbly obey the Word and accept with open arms the gifts of Christ which the pope's Church, trusting in its own merits, haughtily spurns.

73. Therefore none should trust in the good things of present possession, though they be promised by the divine Word. We must look to the Word itself and trust in it alone. Those who set the Word aside and put their trust in present things, will not go unscathed in their fall from faith, however much they may boast of power and numbers. This truth is shown by the flood, by the captivity of the Jews and their present misfortune, and by the seven thousand men in the kingdom of Israel.

74. The proof is sufficiently strong, that great numbers do not make a Church. Nor must we trust in holiness of origin, in forefathers, or in the gifts of God which we enjoy. We must look to the Word alone and judge thereby. Those alone who truly embrace the Word will be as immovable forever as Mount Zion. They may be few in number and thoroughly despised by the world, as were Noah and his children. But God, through these few, preserved to man the truth of that promised mastery when he had not even room to set his foot upon the earth.

75. Our enemies, setting aside the Word, make much of number, outward appearance, and persons. But the apostles foretold that the Antichrist will be a respecter of persons, that will rely upon numbers and ancient origin, that he will hate the Word and corrupt God's promises and that he will kill those who cling to the Word. Shall we, then, consider such people to be the Church?

76. The Church is a daughter born from the Word, not the mother of the Word. Therefore, whoever loses the Word and looks to men instead, ceases to be the Church and lapses into utter blindness; nor will either great numbers or power avail. They who keep the word, as did Noah and his family, are the Church, though they be few in number, even but eight souls. The Papists at this time surpass us in numbers and rank; we not only are cursed, but suffer many things. But we must endure until the judgment, when God will reveal that we are his Church, and the Papists the church of Satan.

77. So, then, we must observe that rule in 1 Sam 16, 7, where the Lord says to Samuel: "Look not on his countenance, or on the height of his stature; because I have rejected him: for Jehovah seeth not as man seeth; for man looketh on the outward appearance, but Jehovah looketh on the heart."

78. Let us not, therefore, give heed to the greatness and might of the pope, who boasts that he is the Church, proclaiming the apostolic succession and the majesty of his person. Let us look to the Word. If the pope embraces it, let us judge him to be the Church; but if he does violence to it, let us judge him to be the slave of Satan.

79. Paul says (1 Cor 2, 15) that the spiritual person judgeth all things. If I were the only one on the face of the earth to keep the Word, I should be the Church, and rightfully pass judgment upon all the rest of the world that they were not the Church. Our enemies have the office without the Word, and really have nothing. We, on the other hand, have the Word, though we have nothing; yet we have everything through the Word. Therefore, either let the pope, the cardinals and the

bishops come over to our side, or let them cease to boast that they are the Church, which they cannot be without the Word, since it is begotten only by the Word.

80. We bear a great load of hatred, being accused of having deserted the ancient Church. The Papists, on the other hand, boast that they have remained true to the Church, and they want to leave everything to the judgment of the Church. But we are accused falsely. To speak the truth, we must say that we departed from the Word when we were still in their Church and now we have returned to the Word and have ceased to be apostates from the Word.

81. Therefore though in their judgment they rob us of the title of the Church, still we retain the Word, and through the Word we have all ornaments of the true Church. For whoever has the Creator of all, must needs also possess the creatures themselves. In this sense Noah remained master of the world, though the waters prevailed, and the earth perished. Though he lost his property, yet, because he retained the Word by which everything was created, it may truly be said he retained everything.

CHAPTER VIII.

I. NOAH'S CONDITION IN THE ARK; THE WATERS ABATE.
A. NOAH'S CONDITION IN THE ARK.

1. How Noah and his family anxiously waited for God's promise, and lived in faith, which is a hard life.

2. He had a hard time in the ark. What sustained him.

3. How he suffered in two ways.

  * Whether God can forget his saints.

  * Severest temptations are when man thinks he is forsaken by God.

4. Noah's condition became more miserable because of his family's distress.

5. Noah and family with difficulty overcame their temptation.

  * Christians need steadfastness.

  * Why God for a time conceals himself from his faithful ones.

  * Temptations severe when saints imagine God has forsaken them.

B. THE WATERS ABATE.

1. The time the waters abated.

2. How the wind blew upon the earth and dried it..

3. The abating of the waters was a sign by which God comforted Noah.

  * Noah's Ark.

    a. When it began to float, how long it floated and when it rested.

    b. On what mountain did it rest.

    c. What to think of Josephus' testimony.

4. When the mountain tops first seen.

5. How Noah learned the deluge had ceased.

    a. Why Noah sent forth the raven, and how the error arose the raven never returned.

      * The Jews' unclean thoughts of the raven.

    b. Noah sent forth a dove, and if at the same time with the raven.

    c. Noah sent out a second dove, which assured him that the flood had ceased.

      (1) Dove returned with an olive leaf.

(2) Whether it did this of its own impulse, and what God thereby wished to indicate.

(3) The Jews' ideas on where the dove got the olive leaf.

(4) Why an olive leaf.

6. How long Noah and family were in the ark.

I. NOAH IN ARK—FLOOD ABATES.

A. Noah's Condition in the Ark.

V. 1a. *And God remembered Noah, and all the beasts, and all the cattle that were with him in the ark.*

1. When that horrible wrath had exhausted itself, and all flesh with the earth had been destroyed, the promise made by God to Noah and his sons, that they were to be the seed of the human race, began to be realized. No doubt this promise was to them an object of eager expectation. No life is so hedged about with difficulties as that of faith. This was the life lived by Noah and his sons, whom we see absolutely depending upon the heavens for support. The earth was covered with water. Bottom on which to stand there was none. It was the word of promise that upheld them, as they drifted in this welter of waters.

2. When the flesh is free from danger, it holds faith in contempt, as the claims of the Papists show. It loves showy and toilsome tasks; in these it sweats. But behold Noah, on all sides surrounded by waters, yet not overwhelmed! Surely it is not works that sustain him but faith in God's mercy extended through the word of promise.

3. The difficulty besetting Noah is hinted at in the words: "God remembered." Moses thus intimates that Noah had been tossed on the water so long that God seemed to have forgotten him altogether. They who pass through such a mental strain, when the rays of divine grace are gone and they sit in darkness or are forgotten by God, find by experience that it is far more difficult to live in the Word or by faith alone than to be a hermit or a Carthusian monk.

4. Hence, it is not a meaningless expression when the Holy Spirit says that "God remembered Noah." He means that from the day Noah entered the ark, no word was spoken, nothing was revealed to him; that he saw no ray of divine grace shining, but merely clung to the promise which he had accepted, while in the meantime the waters and waves raged as if God had certainly forgotten. The same danger beset his children and also the cattle and all the other animals throughout the one hundred and fifty days they were in the ark. And though the holy seed by the aid of the conquering Spirit overcame those difficulties, the victory was not won without vexation of the flesh, tears and stupendous fear, felt, in my opinion, even by the brutes.

5. Thus a twofold danger beset them. The universal flood which swallowed up all mankind could not vanish without stupendous grief to the righteous, particularly as they saw themselves reduced to so small a number. Further, it was

a serious matter to be buffeted by the waters for almost half a year without any consolation from God.

6. The expression used by Moses, "God remembered Noah," must not be short of its meaning by calling it a rhetorical figure, signifying that God acted after the manner of one who had forgotten Noah, whereas God cannot in truth forget his saints. A mere master of rhetoric, indeed, does not know what it means to live in such a state as to feel that God has forgotten him. Only the most perfect saints understand that, and can in faith bear, so to speak, a God who forgets. Therefore the Psalms and all the Scriptures are filled with complaints of this nature, in which God is called upon to arise, to open his eyes, to hear, to awaken.

7. Monks possessed of a higher degree of experience, at times underwent this temptation and called it a suspension of grace. The latter may be experienced also in temptations of a slighter nature. The flame of lust found in young people is altogether unbearable unless it is held in check by the Word of God and the Holy Spirit. Similarly, at a more mature age, impatience and the desire for revenge can nowise be overcome unless God tears them from the soul. How much more liable is the soul to fall into the darkness of despair, or into ensnaring predestinarian tenets, when more severe temptations beset us and the suspension of grace is felt.

8. Hence this expression is not to be passed by as a mere rhetorical ornament, according to the interpretation of the rabbis. It is intended rather to portray the state of soul which feels despair coming on amid unutterable groanings of heart, with just a spark of faith left to wrest victory from the flesh. In the same way that Paul suffered from Satan's messenger, we may believe that Noah felt himself stabbed in the heart, and that he often argued thus within himself: Dost thou believe that thou alone art so beloved of God? Dost thou believe that thou will be kept safe to the end, when waters are boundless, and those immense clouds seem to be inexhaustible?

9. When, then, such broodings found their way also into the weak souls of the women, what cries, wails and tears may we surmise to have been the result? Almost overcome by sadness and grief, he was forced to lift up and comfort those with the cheer his own heart did not feel.

10. It was, therefore, no jest or frolic for them to live so long locked up within the ark, to see the endless downpour of rain and to be carried to and fro floating upon the waves. This was the experience of having been forgotten by God which Moses implies when he says that God at last remembered Noah and his sons.

11. Though the occupants of the ark overcame this feeling by faith, they did not do so without great vexation of the flesh; just as a young man who leads a chaste life overcomes lust, but surely not without the greatest vexation and trouble. In this instance, where the trial was greater, where all evidence was at variance with the fact that God was gracious and mindful of them, they indeed triumphed, but not without fearful tribulation. For the flesh, weak in itself, can bear nothing less patiently than the thought of a God who has forgotten. Human nature is prone to be puffed up and haughty when God remembers it, when he vouchsafes success and favor. Is it a wonder, then, that we become broken in spirit and desperate

when God seems to have cast us away and everything goes against us?

12. Let us remember that this story sets before us an example of faith, of endurance, and of patience, to the end that, having the divine promise, we should not only learn to believe it, but should also consider that we are in need of endurance. Endurance is not maintained without a great struggle, and Christ calls upon us, in the New Testament, to acquire it when he says: "He that endureth to the end, the same shall be saved," Mt 24, 13.

13. This is the reason why God hides for a time, as it were, seeming to have forgotten us, suspending his grace, as they say in the schools. As in this temptation not only the spirit but also the flesh is afflicted, so afterward, when he again begins to remember us, the perception of grace which during the trial was evident only to the spirit and most faintly at that, is extended to the flesh also.

14. Hence, the word "remembered" indicates that great sadness beset both man and beast during the entire time of the flood. It must have been by dint of great patience and extraordinary courage that Noah and the others bore this lapse from God's memory, which is simply unbearable to the flesh without the spirit even in slight trials. True, God always remembers his own, even when he seems to have forsaken them; but Moses indicates that he remembered his people here in a visible way, by a sign, and by openly fulfilling what he had previously promised through the Word and the Spirit. This is the most important passage in this chapter.

B. Waters Abate.

Vs. 1b-3. *And God made a wind to pass over the earth, and the waters assuaged; the fountains also of the deep and the windows of heaven were stopped, and the rain from heaven was restrained; and the waters returned from off the earth continually; and after the end of a hundred and fifty days the waters decreased.*

15. Moses said above (ch 7, 11-12) that the deluge raged in three different ways; for not only were the fountains of the great deep broken up and the windows of heaven opened, but also the rain descended. When these forces ceased on the one hundred and fiftieth day, quiet was once more in evidence and the fact that God remembered, and Noah with his sons and their wives, as also the animals, was refreshed after terror so great and continuous. If a storm of two days duration causes seafarers to despair, how much more distressing was that tossing about for half a year!

16. The question here arises, how the wind was made to pass over the earth, which as yet was entirely covered with water. It is nothing new that winds have the power to dry, especially those from the east, called by our countrymen "hohle winde," and by Virgil "parching winds," from the drouth which they bring upon the earth. These are mentioned also by Hosea 13, 15. The explanation, accordingly, is simple. Moses says that the wind was made to pass over the earth, that is, over the surface of the waters, for such a length of time that at last, the waters being dried up, the earth again appeared. So, in Exodus, a burning wind is said to have dried up the Red Sea. Now, God might have accomplished this without any wind,

yet he habitually employs a natural means to attain his purposes.

17. Up to this time Noah had lived in darkness, seeing nothing but the waters rolling and raging in a terrifying volume. Now the delicious light of the sun bursts forth once more, and the winds cease to roar from all points of the compass. Only the east wind, calculated to reduce the waters, is blowing, and gradually it takes away the stagnant flood. Other means also are effective; the ocean no longer hurls its waves upon the land, but takes back the waters which it had spewed forth, and the floodgates of heaven are closed up.

18. These are outward and tangible signs by which God consoles Noah, showing him that he had not forgotten, but remembered him. This is a practical and needed lesson also for us. When in the midst of dangers we may with certainty look for God's help, who does not desert us if we continue in faith, looking forward to the fulfilment of God's promises.

V. 4. *And the ark rested in the seventh month, on the seventeenth day of the month, upon the mountains of Ararat.*

19. The waters increased for forty days, until the ark was lifted from the earth. Then for one hundred and fifty days it floated upon the waters, driven by the winds and the waves, without a sign of God's remembrance. At length the waters began to decrease, and the ark rested.

20. The point of dispute among the Jews here is the number of months. But why waste any more time upon immaterial matters, particularly as we see that the suggestions of the rabbis are not at all wise? It is more to the purpose for us to inquire where the mountains of Ararat are to be found. It is generally believed that they are mountains of Armenia, close by the highest ranges of Asia Minor, the Caucasus and the Taurus. But it appears to me that more likely the highest of all mountains is meant, the Imaus (Himalaya), which divides India. Compared to this range, other mountains are no more than warts. That the ark rested upon the highest mountain is substantiated by the fact that the waters continued to fall for three whole months before such smaller ranges as Lebanon, Taurus, and Caucasus were uncovered, which are, as it were, the feet or roots of the Himalaya, just as the mountains of Greece may be called branches of the Alps extending up to our Hercinian Forest (Harz). To anyone who surveys them with care the mountains seem to be wonderfully related and united.

21. Josephus has wonderful things to tell about the mountains of Armenia, and he records that during his time remains of the ark were discovered there. But I suppose nobody will judge me to be a heretic if I occasionally doubt the reliability of his statements.

V. 5. *And the waters decreased continually until the tenth month: in the tenth month, on the first day of the month, were the tops of the mountains seen.*

22. Moses said before that by the seventh month the waters had fallen so far that the ark rested upon Ararat. In the third month thereafter, the tops of the lower mountains began to appear, so that Noah, looking down from the mountains of Ararat as if from a watchtower, saw also the peaks of the other mountains, of the

Taurus in Asia, the Lebanon in Syria, and the like. All these were signs of God's remembrance.

Vs. 6-7. *And it came to pass at the end of forty days, that Noah opened the window of the ark which he had made: and he sent forth a raven, and it went forth to and fro, until the waters were dried up from off the earth.*

23. So far the history; the allegorical significance we shall discuss at its proper place. The carelessness of a translator has caused a dispute upon this part of the story. The Hebrew text does not say that the raven did not return, as Jerome translated; hence there was no need to invent a reason why he did not return—because he found dead bodies lying about everywhere. They claim that abundance of food prevented him.

24. On the contrary, Moses says that the raven which had been sent forth, returned; although he did not permit himself to be again imprisoned in the ark as the dove did. Moses implies that Noah sent forth the raven to find out whether animals could, by that time find dry land and food. The raven, however, did not faithfully carry out his mission, but rejoicing to be set free from his prison, he flew to and fro, and paying no attention to Noah, he enjoyed the free sky. The swinish Jews, however, show the impurity of their minds everywhere. For they suppose that the raven had fears concerning his mate, and that he even suspected Noah concerning her. Shame upon those impure minds!

Vs. 8-9. *And he sent forth a dove from him, to see if the waters were abated from off the face of the ground; but the dove found no rest for the sole of her foot, and she returned unto him to the ark; for the waters were on the face of the whole earth: and he put forth his hand, and took her, and brought her unto him into the ark.*

25. When Noah's hopes had been set at naught by the raven, which flew about wantonly but brought no tidings concerning the condition of the earth, he took a dove, thinking that she would more truly perform the mission. The text almost authorizes us to say that those two birds were sent forth at the same time, so that Noah might have two witnesses from whom to gain desired knowledge. The raven enjoying the free sky, flew round about the ark, but did not want to return into it. The dove, however, fleeing from the corpses and corruption, comes back and permits itself to be caught. This story, as we shall hear, offers a fine allegory concerning the Church.

Vs. 10-12. *And he stayed yet other seven days; and again he sent forth the dove out of the ark; and the dove came in to him at eventide; and, lo, in her mouth an olive-leaf plucked off: so Noah knew that the waters were abated from off the earth. And he stayed yet other seven days, and sent forth the dove; and she returned not again unto him any more.*

26. The dove, being a faithful messenger, is sent forth once more. Moses carefully describes how the waters decreased gradually, until at last the surface of the earth, together with the trees, was laid bare. We do not believe that the dove brought the olive leaf intentionally, but by the command of God, who wanted to show Noah, little by little, that he had not altogether forgotten but remembered him. This olive leaf was an impressive sign to Noah and his fellow-prisoners in the ark, bringing them courage and hope of impending liberation.

27. The Jews dispute sharply in respect to this matter of where the dove found the olive leaf, and some, in order to secure special glory for their homeland, make the ludicrous assertion that she took it from the Mount of Olives in the land of Israel, which God had spared from the flood that destroyed the remainder of the earth. But the saner Jews rightly refute this nonsense by arguing that if this were true, the olive leaf could not have been a sign for Noah that the waters had fallen. Others have invented the fable that the dove was admitted to paradise and brought the leaf from there.

28. But I have (ch 2, §39-42) set forth at length my views concerning paradise, and this nonsense is not worthy the effort of a refutation. It serves a better purpose to remind you that all these things happened miraculously and supernaturally. A dove is not so intelligent as to pluck a bough and bring it to the ark in order that Noah might form a judgment with reference to the decrease of waters. God ordained these events. Other trees had leaves at that time, particularly the taller ones which rose sooner from the waters. The olive tree is comparatively short, hence it was calculated to furnish information concerning the decrease of the waters and to serve as an object lesson of the cessation of the wrath of God and the return of the earth to its former state. Of this he had more certain proof however, when the dove, having been sent out the third time, did not return: for not only did it find food on earth, but was able to build nests and to flit to and fro.

Vs. 13-14. *And it came to pass in the six hundred and first year, in the first month, the first day of the month, the waters were dried up from off the earth: and Noah removed the covering of the ark, and looked, and, behold, the face of the ground was dried. And in the second month, on the seven and twentieth day of the month, was the earth dry.*

29. Here we see that Noah was in the ark an entire year and ten days; for he entered the ark on the seventeenth day of the second month, and came out again, after a year had passed, in the same month, but on the twenty-seventh day. Poor Noah, with his sons and the women, lived in the ark more than half a year in sore grief, without a sign of being remembered by God. Afterward God gave him gradual proof, through various signs, that he had not forgotten him, until at last, after the lapse of a year and ten days, he was again given dominion over the earth and sea. On this day of the second month, the flood had not only disappeared, but the earth was dry. This is the story of the flood and its abatement. After this fearful wrath, there ensues an immeasurable light of grace, as is shown in the following sermon addressed to Noah by God himself.

II. NOAH COMMANDED TO LEAVE THE ARK; HIS OFFERING TO GOD; GOD'S RESOLVE NOT TO CURSE THE EARTH AGAIN.

A. NOAH COMMANDED TO LEAVE THE ARK, AND HE OBEYED.

* Man should do nothing but what God commands.
* Is it right to start a new worship without God's command to do so.
* The examples of saints and special works.
    1. Should we imitate the works of the holy patriarchs.

2. The result among the Jews of a reckless imitation of the saints.

3. Should have regard here, not to works but to faith.

II. NOAH LEAVES ARK,
HIS SACRIFICE AND GOD'S PROMISE.

A. Noah Obeys Command to Leave the Ark.

Vs. 15-17. *And God spake unto Noah, saying, Go forth from the ark, thou, and thy wife, and thy sons, and thy sons' wives with thee. Bring forth with thee every living thing that is with thee of all flesh, both birds, and cattle, and every creeping thing that creepeth upon the earth; that they may breed abundantly in the earth.*

30. Up to this point the narrative is only a record of facts, or the description of a divine work. Though the works of God are not mute but eloquent witnesses, and present to our vision the will of God, a still greater comfort is vouchsafed when God links to the works the Word, which is not manifest to the eye but perceptible to the ear and intelligible to the heart through the promptings of the Holy Spirit. So far God had given proof by his work that he was appeased, that the God of wrath had turned into a God of mercy, who turns back the waters and dries up the earth. Such comfort he now amplifies by his Word in that he lovingly accosts and enjoins him to leave the ark with the other creatures, both men and animals.

31. In the light of this passage the frequent and emphatic application of the principle is justified that we should neither design nor do anything, especially in respect to God's service and worship, without the initiative and command of the Word. As above narrated, Noah enters the ark upon God's command; and he leaves the ark upon God's command to leave it. He does not follow superstitious notions, as we see the Jews do, who, when they establish anything temporary by command, endeavor to retain it forever, as if it were essential to salvation.

32. Noah might have argued thus: Behold, I built the ark by the command of God; I was saved in it while all other men perished: therefore I will remain in it, or keep it for a place of divine worship, since it has been sanctified by the Word of God and the presence of the saints, the Church. But the godly man did nothing of the kind. The Word had commanded him to go forth, therefore he obeyed. The ark had done its service during the flood and he left it, assured that he and his children were to live on the earth. So must we undertake nothing without the Word of God. In a holy calling, which has the Word and command of God, let us walk! For whosoever attempts anything without the command of God, will labor in vain.

33. To deny this, some one might cite as example the act of Noah, described below, when he built an altar without God's command, and offered a burnt-offering thereon to God from the clean animals. If this was permitted to Noah, why should we not be permitted to choose certain forms of worship? And, in truth, the Papacy has heaped up works and forms of worship in the Church without measure, just as it pleased. But we must hold fast to the principle, which is a theorem of general application, that whatsoever is not of faith, is sin, (Rom 14, 23). But faith cannot be separated from the Word; hence, whatsoever is done without the Word, is sin.

34. Furthermore, it is plainly dangerous to take the acts of the fathers as models. As individuals differ, so also do their duties differ, and God requires diverse works according to the diversity of our calling. Accordingly the epistle to the Hebrews fitly refers the various acts of the fathers to the one faith, in order to show that each of us must imitate, in his calling, not the works, but the faith of the fathers. Heb 11.

35. Hence works peculiar to the holy fathers must by no means be considered as models for us each to imitate as the monks imitate the fasting of Benedict, the gown of Francis, the shoes of Dominic and the like. Men become apes who imitate without judgment. The monks try to ape the works, but know nothing of the faith of the fathers.

36. Abraham was commanded to slay his son. Afterward his descendants most wickedly believed they should follow his example, and they filled the earth with innocent blood. In a similar manner the people worshiped the brazen serpent and offered sacrifices before it. In both instances the people wanted to justify themselves by the example of their forefathers; but since they established these forms of worship without the Word, they were righteously condemned.

37. Let us, therefore, remember not to establish anything without the Word of God. Duties differ, and so must the works of individuals. How foolish it would be for me to proclaim that I must follow Caesar's example, and that others must obey my laws! How wicked it would be for me to assert that I must follow the example of a judge, condemning some to the cross, others to the sword! Then, we must look, not upon the works, but upon the faith of individuals; for the faith of all saints is one, though their works are most diverse.

38. Think not that because Noah built an altar, you may do likewise; but follow the faith of Noah, who thought it right to show his merciful Savior that he understood his beneficent gifts, and was grateful for them. Follow Abraham, not in slaying your son, but in believing the promises of God, and in obeying his commandments. The epistle to the Hebrews fitly refers the deeds and acts of the fathers to their faith, setting forth that we should follow their faith.

B. NOAH'S SACRIFICE.

1. Whether Noah was commanded to offer a sacrifice and in what way sacrificing is justified.

 * Have monks divine command to support their order.

 * Shall we find fault with the works of saints, for which they apparently had no command.

 * How in all works we should have respect for God's command.

 * Lyra's unfounded thoughts on the words, "Be fruitful" etc..

 * Why Moses said so much about their leaving the ark.

2. Noah's sacrifice proves Moses did not originate the idea of sacrifice.

3. Why Noah's sacrifice was pleasing to God.

*   The meaning of "sweet savor".

4.   How it can be said God "smelled the sweet savor", and why this form of speech used.

B. Noah's Sacrifice.

39. The objection under consideration can be invalidated by the rejoinder that Noah did have a command to erect an altar and offer sacrifices. God approved the rite of sacrifice by ordering that more of the clean animals—suitable for sacrifice—should be taken into the ark. Nor was Noah permitted to cast aside the office of the priesthood, which had been established by the Word before the flood and had come down to him by the right of primogeniture. Adam, Seth, Enoch and others had been priests. From them Noah possessed the office of the priesthood as an inheritance.

40. Therefore Noah, as priest and prophet, was not only at liberty to offer sacrifice, but he was under obligation to do so by virtue of his calling. Since his calling was founded on God's Word, in harmony with that Word and by God's command he built an altar and offered sacrifices. Therefore let a monk prove it is his office and calling to wear a cowl, to worship the blessed Virgin, to pray the rosary and do like things, and we will commend his life. But since the call is lacking, the Word is not the authority and the office does not exist, the life and works of the monks in their entirety stand justly condemned.

41. Finally, even if all other arguments should fail, this argument, according to which man judges the cause by the effect, remains; namely, that God expresses approval of Noah's deed. Although such reasoning from effect to cause may not be unassailable, it yet is not without value in respect to such heroic and uncommon men, who meet not with rejection but approval on the part of God, although they appear to do what they have not been expressly commanded. They possess the inward conviction that they are guilty of no transgression, though the disclosure of this fact is delayed until later God expresses his approval. Such examples are numerous and it is noteworthy that God has expressed approval even of the acts of some heathen.

42. Let this maxim, then, stand, that everything must be done by the command of God in order to obtain the assurance of conscience that we have acted in obedience to God. Hence they who abide in their divinely assigned calling, will not run uncertainly nor will they beat the air as those who have no course in which they have been commanded to run, and in consequence may not look forward to a prize. 1 Cor 9, 24.

But I return to the text. Noah, with his sons and the women, is commanded to leave the ark, and to lead forth upon the earth every species of animals, that all his works may be sanctified and found in keeping with the Word. Concerning the animals Moses now expressly states:

Vs. 17-19. *Be fruitful, and multiply upon the earth. And Noah went forth, and his sons, and his wife, and his sons' wives with him: every beast, every creeping thing, and every bird, whatsoever moveth upon the earth, after their families, went forth out of the ark.*

43. The Lord speaks of the propagation of Noah and his sons in the ninth chapter and that, I believe, is the reason why he speaks here only of the propagation of the animals. From the expression here used, Lyra foolishly concludes that cohabitation had been forbidden during the flood and was now again permitted after the departure from the ark, since God says, "Go forth, ... thou and thy wife." Such thoughts belong to monks not to God, who plans not sinful lust, but propagation; the latter is God's ordination, but lust is Satan's poison infused into nature through sin.

44. Moses here uses many words to illustrate the overflowing joy of the captives' souls, when they were commanded to leave their prison, the ark, and to return upon the earth now everywhere open before them. In recounting the kinds of animals, however, he arranges them in a different order, distinguishing them by families, as it were, to let us see that only propagation was God's aim. It must have been a glad sight when each one of the many beasts, after leaving the ark, found its own mate, and then sought its accustomed haunt: the wolves, the bears, the lions, returning to the woods and groves; the sheep, the goats, the swine, to the fields; the dogs, the chickens, the cats, to man.

V. 20. *And Noah builded an altar unto Jehovah, and took of every clean beast, and of every clean bird, and offered burnt-offerings on the altar.*

45. This text shows conclusively that Moses was not the first person to introduce sacrifices but that, like a bard who gathers chants, he arranged and classified them as they had been in vogue among the fathers and transmitted from the one to the other. Thus also the law of circumcision was not first written by Moses but received from the fathers.

46. Above (ch 4, 4-5), where Moses mentioned the sacrifice of Abel and Cain, he called it *minchah*, an offering; here, however, we find the first record of a burnt-offering, one entirely consumed by fire. This, I say, is a clear proof that the law of sacrifices had been established before the time of Moses. His work, then, consisted in arranging the rites of the forefathers in definite order.

V. 21. *And Jehovah smelled the sweet savor.*

47. It is set forth here that Jehovah approved Noah's sacrifice which he offered by virtue of his office as a priest, according to the example of the fathers. However, the differences of phraseology is to receive due attention. Of the former sacrifice he said that Jehovah "had respect" to it; here he says that "Jehovah smelled the sweet savor." Moses subsequently makes frequent use of this expression. The heathen also adopted it; Lucian, for example, makes fun of Jove who was conciliated by the odor of meats.

48. The word in the original, however, does not properly signify the "savor of sweetness," but "the savor of rest", for *nichoach* meaning "rest", is derived from the verb *nuach*, which Moses used before, when he said that the ark rested upon the mountains of Ararat. Therefore it is the "savor of rest," because God then rested from his wrath, dismissing his wrath, becoming appeased, and, as we common-

ly say, well content.

49. Here the question might be raised why does he not say, Jehovah had respect to Noah and his burnt offering, rather than, Jehovah smelled the savor of rest, which latter certainly sounds shocking, as though he were not commending the man for his faith, but merely for his work. This objection is usually answered by saying that the Scriptures speak of God in human fashion. Men are pleased by a sweet savor. But it seems to me there is still another reason for this expression, namely, that God was so close at hand that he noticed the savor; for Moses desires to show that this holy rite was well-pleasing to God: Solomon says (Prov 27, 9) that perfume rejoiceth the heart. Physicians sometimes restore consciousness by sweet odors. On the other hand, a violent stench is extremely offensive to our nature, and often overpowers it.

50. In this sense, one may say that God, having been annoyed by the stench of wickedness, was now refreshed, so to speak, when he saw this one priest girded himself to perform holy rites in order to give proof of his gratitude, and to manifest by some public act he did not belong to the ungodly, but that he had a God whom he feared. This is the real meaning of a sacrifice. As it had pleased God to destroy mankind, he is now delighted to increase it. Moses uses this expression for our sake, that we, through the experience of God's grace, may learn that God delights to do us good.

C. GOD'S RESOLVE NOT TO CURSE THE EARTH AGAIN.

1. God solemnly and earnestly means it.
   * How understood "it repented God that he had made man".
   * Experiences in spiritual temptations and how God helps us to bear them.
2. The meaning of "God will not again smite the earth".

C. God's Resolve not to Curse the Earth Again.

V. 21b. *And Jehovah said in his heart.*

51. Moses points out that these words were not spoken by God without heart and feeling, but from his very vitals. This is the meaning of the Hebrew text which has it that God spoke to his own heart.

V. 21c. *I will not again curse the ground any more for man's sake.*

52. God speaks as if he were sorry for the punishment inflicted upon the earth on account of man, just as formerly he expressed regret for his creation, reproving himself, as it were, for his fury against man. This must not, of course, be understood as implying that God could possibly change his mind; it is written only for our consolation. He accuses and blames himself in order to rouse the little flock to the certain faith that God will be merciful hereafter.

53. And their souls stood in real need of such consolation. They had been terrified as they witnessed God's raging wrath, and their faith could not but be shaken. So now God is impelled to so order his acts and words that these people might expect only grace and mercy. Accordingly he now speaks with them, is present

at their sacrifice, shows that he is pleased with them, blames his own counsel, and promises that he will never do anything like it in the future. In brief, he is a different God from what he had been before. While God, indeed, does not change, he wants to change men, who have become altogether habituated to thoughts of wrath.

54. They who have experienced trials of the spirit, know full well how much the soul then stands in need of sure and strong consolation to induce it once more to hope for grace and to forget the wrath. One day, a whole month, perhaps is not enough for this change. Just as it takes a long time to recover from bodily disorders, so such wounds of the soul cannot be healed at once, or by one word. God sees this, and tries by various means to recall the terrified souls to a certain hope of grace; he even chides himself, speaking to his own heart, as in Jeremiah 18, 8, where he promises to repent of the evil he thought of doing, if the offenders also repent.

55. It should furthermore be noted that he says, "I will not again curse the ground." He speaks of a general destruction of the earth, not of a partial one, as when he destroys fields, cities, or kingdoms. The latter instances are for a warning; as Mary says, "He hath put down princes from their thrones." Lk 1, 52.

III. MAN'S NATURAL DEPRAVITY AND HIS NATURAL POWERS.

1. Natural depravity crops out in infancy.
2. It is seen as the years advance.
3. Whether those who would drown it have reason for doing so.
4. There is none untainted by it.
5. The godless yield to it, believers resist it.
 * Can God be charged with being changeable.
6. The knowledge of natural depravity is very necessary.
7. What moves sophists to ignore natural depravity.
8. How to view those who lightly regard natural depravity, and how to refute them.
 * Meaning of "the imagination of the heart".
 * True theological definition of man.
9. The proof of natural depravity and that the natural is not perfect.
10. Consequence of false teaching on natural depravity and the natural.
 * What sophists understand by Merito congrui and condigni.
11. How Scotus tried to prove that man's natural powers were all he had, and how to refute his opinion.
 * Value of the Scholastics and their theology.
12. How teachers in these things lead astray.
 * The virtues of the heathen.

   a. Estimate of them.

   b. How they differ from the good works of the saints.

   c. What they lack.

13. Natural depravity may sleep in youth, but it will awake as the years advance.

14. Those who ignore natural depravity may be refuted by experience.

15. Philosophy manifests its vanity and blindness in its attitude to this doctrine.

16. Experience confirms natural depravity.

17. Whether natural depravity can be completely eradicated: how to check it.

   * How to understand "God will not smite the earth again".

   * Nature thrown into great disorder by the deluge.

   * Seasons of the year again put in their order.

   * The people's talk about the signs of the last times.

   * The days of earth to be followed by the days of heaven, and we should prepare for them.

III. MAN'S NATURAL DEPRAVITY AND HIS NATURAL POWERS.

V. 21d. *For that the imagination of man's heart is evil from his youth.*

56. This is a powerful passage, relating to original sin. Whoever weakens its force, goes straying like the blind man in the sunlight, failing to see his own acts and experiences. Look at the days of our swaddling clothes; in how many ways sin manifests itself in our earlier years. What an amount of switching it requires until we are taught order, as it were, and attention to duty!

57. Then youth succeeds. There a stronger rebellion becomes noticeable, and in addition that untamable evil, the rage of lust and desire. If one take a wife, the result is weariness of his own and a passion for others. If the government of a State is entrusted to him, an exceptionally fruitful harvest of vice will follow—as jealousy, rivalry, haughtiness, hope of gain, avarice, wrath, anger, and other evils.

58. It is true, as the German proverb has it, that sins grow with the years: Je laenger, je aerger; je aelter, je kaerger (worse with time, stingier with age). All such vices are so blatant and gross as to become objects of observation and intelligence. What, then shall we say of the inward vices when unbelief, presumption, neglect of the Word, and wicked views grow up?

59. There are those who are and desire to be considered powerful theologians, though they extenuate original sin by sophistry. But vices so numerous and great cannot be extenuated. Original sin is not a slight disorder or infirmity, but complete lawlessness, the like of which is not found in other creatures, except in evil spirits.

60. But do those extenuators have any Scriptural proof to rest upon? Let us see

what Moses says. As I pointed out in explaining the sixth chapter, he does not call such things evil, as lust, tyranny, and other sins, but the imagination of the human heart; that is, human energy, wisdom and reason, with all the faculties the mind employs even in our best works. Although we do not condemn acts which belong to the social or civil sphere, yet the human heart vitiates these works in themselves proper, by doing them for glory, for profit, or for oppression, and either from opposition to the neighbor or to God.

61. Nor can we escape the force of this passage by saying that those are meant who perished by the flood. God uses a generic term which denotes that the heart of man, as such, is meant. At the time this was spoken there were no other people than those saved in the ark, and yet the declaration is: the imagination of man's heart is evil.

62. Therefore, not even the saints are excepted. In Ham, the third son, this imagination of the heart betrayed its nature. And the other brothers were no better by nature. There was only this difference, that they, believing in the promised seed, retained the hope of forgiveness of sin, and did not give way to the evil imagination of their hearts, rather resisting it through the Holy Spirit, who is given for the very purpose of contending against, and overcoming, the malignity of man's nature. Because Ham gives way to his nature, he is wholly evil, and totally perishes. Shem and Japheth, who contend against it in their spirit, though being evil, are not altogether so. They have the Holy Spirit, through whom they contend against the evil, and hence are holy.

63. It would seem here that God might be accused of fickleness. Before, when he was about to punish man, he assigned as a reason for his purpose the fact that the imagination of man's heart is evil; here, when he is about to give unto man the gracious promise that he will not thereafter show such anger, he puts forward the same reason. To human wisdom this appears foolish and inconsistent with divine wisdom.

64. But I gladly pass by such sublime themes, and leave them to minds possessed of leisure. For me it is enough that these works are spoken to suit our spiritual condition, inasmuch as God points out that he is now appeased and no longer angry. So parents, having chastised their disobedient children as they deserve, win again their affections by kindness. This change of mood is not deserving of criticism but rather of commendation. It profits the children; otherwise they, while fearing the rod, might also begin to hate their parents. This explanation is good enough for me, for it appeals to our faith. Others may explain differently.

65. We should give diligent attention to this passage because it plainly shows that man's nature is corrupt, a truth above all others to be apprehended, because without it God's mercy and grace cannot be rightly understood. Hence, the quibblers previously mentioned are to be despised and we have good reason to take to task the translator who gave occasion for this error by rendering the words so as to say, not that the imagination of man's heart is evil, but that it is inclined to evil. Upon this authority the quibblers distort or set aside those passages of Paul where he says that all are children of wrath (Eph 2, 3) that all have sinned (Rom 5, 12)

and are under sin (Rom 3, 9). They argue from our passage as follows: Moses does not say that human nature is evil, but that it is prone to evil; this condition, call it inclination or proclivity, is under the control of free will, nor does it force man toward the evil, or (to use their own words) it imposes no constraint upon man.

66. Then they proceed to find a reason for this statement and declare that even after the fall of man, there remains in him a good will and a right understanding. For the natural powers, say they, are unimpaired, not only in man but even in the devil. And finally they so twist Aristotle's teachings as to make him say that reason tends toward that which is best. Some traces of these views are found also in the writings of the Church fathers. Using Psalms 4, 6 as a basis, where the prophet says, "Jehovah, lift thou up the light of thy countenance upon us," they distinguish between a higher part of reason which inquires concerning God, and a lower part employed in temporal and civil affairs. Even Augustine is pleased with this distinction, as we stated above when discussing the fall of man.

67. But if only a spark of the knowledge of God had remained unimpaired in man, we should be different beings by far from what we now are. Hence, those quibblers who pick flaws in the plain statements of Paul are infinitely blind. If they would carefully and devoutly consider that very passage as they read it in their Latin Bible, they would certainly cease to father so bad a cause. For it is not an insignificant truth which Moses utters when he says the senses and the thoughts of the heart of man are prone to evil from his youth. This is the case especially in the sixth chapter (vs 5) where he says that the whole thought of his heart was bent on evil continually, meaning thereby that he purposes what is evil, and that in inclination, purpose and effort he inclines to evil. For example; an adulterer, whose desires are inflamed, may lack the opportunity, the place, the person, the time, and nevertheless be stirred by the fire of lust, unable to dwell upon anything else. In this manner, says Moses, does human nature always incline toward evil. Can, then, the natural powers of man be said to have remained unimpaired, seeing that man's thoughts are always set upon evil things?

68. If the minds of the sophists were as open toward the holy doctrine contained in the prophetical and apostolical writings as toward their own teachers who teach the freedom of the will and the merit of works, they surely would not have permitted themselves by so small an inducement as one little word to be led away from the truth so as to teach, contrary to Scripture, that man's natural powers are uninjured, and that man, by nature, is not under wrath or condemnation. Notwithstanding, it appears that they turn against their own absurdity. Although the natural powers of man are uninjured, yet they maintain that, to become acceptable, grace is required; in other words, they teach that God is not satisfied with man's natural goodness, unless it be improved by love.

69. But what is the need to argue longer against the madness of the sophists, since we know the true meaning of the Hebrew text to be, not that man's mind and thoughts are inclined to evil, but that the imagination of the human heart is evil from youth?

70. By imagination, as I stated several times before (ch 6, §148), he means

reason itself, together with the will and the understanding, even when it dwells upon God, or occupies itself with most honorable pursuits, be they those of State or Home. It is always contrary to God's law, always in sin, always under God's wrath, and it cannot be freed from this evil state by its own strength, as witness Christ's words: "If therefore the Son shall make you free, ye shall be free indeed," Jn 8, 36.

71. If you wish a definition of the word "man" take it from this text teaching that he is a rational being, with a heart given to imagination. But what does he imagine? Moses answers, "Evil"; that is, evil against God or God's Law, and against his fellow man. Thus holy Scriptures ascribe to man a reason that is not idle but always imagines something. This imagination it calls evil, wicked, sacrilegious, while the philosophers call it good, and the quibblers say that the natural gifts are unimpaired.

72. Therefore this text should be carefully noted and urged against the caviling quibblers: Moses declares the imagination of the human heart to be evil. And if it be evil, the conclusion is natural that the natural gifts are not unimpaired, but corrupted: Inasmuch as God did not create man evil, but perfect, sound, holy, knowing God, his reason right and his will toward God good.

73. Seeing we have clear testimony to the fact that man is evil and turned away from God, who would be mad enough to say that the natural gifts in man remain unimpaired? That would be practically saying that man's nature is unimpaired and good even now, whereas we have overwhelming evidence in our knowledge and experience that it is debased to the utmost.

74. From that wicked theory there have sprung many dangerous and some palpably wicked utterances, for instance, that when man does the best in his power, God will unfailingly give his grace. By such teaching they have driven man, as by a trumpet, to prayer, fasting, self-torture, pilgrimages and similar performances. Thus the world was taught to believe that if men did the best that nature permitted, they would earn grace, if not the grace "de merito," at least that "de congruo." A "meritum congrui" (title to reward based upon equity) they attribute to a work which has been performed not against but in accordance to the divine law, inasmuch as an evil work is subject not to a reward but a penalty. The "meritum condigni" (a title to reward based upon desert) they attribute not to the work itself but to its quality as being performed in a state of grace.

75. Another saying of this kind is the declaration of Scotus that man by mere natural powers may love God above all things. This declaration is based upon the principle that the natural powers are unimpaired. He argues as follows: A man loves a woman, who is a creature, and he loves her so immoderately that he will imperil his very life for her sake. Similarly, a merchant loves his wares, and so eagerly that he will risk death a thousand times if only he can gain something. If therefore, the love of created things is so great, though they rank far below God, how much more will a man love God who is the highest good! Hence, God can be loved with the natural powers alone.

76. A fine argument, indeed, and worthy of a Franciscan monk! For he shows

that, though he is a great teacher, he does not know what it means to love God. Nature is so corrupt that it can no longer know God unless it be enlightened by the Word and Spirit of God; how then can it love God without the Holy Spirit? For it is true that we have no desire for what we do not know. Therefore, nature cannot love God whom it does not know, but it loves an idol, and a dream of its own heart. Furthermore, it is so entirely fettered by the love of created things that even after it has learned to know God from his Word, it disregards him and despises his Word. Of this the people of our own times are an example.

77. Such foolish and blasphemous deliverances are certain proof that scholastic theology has degenerated into a species of philosophy that has no knowledge of God, and walks in darkness because it disregards his Word. Also Aristotle and Cicero, who have the greatest influence with this tribe, give broad instructions concerning moral excellences. They magnify these exceedingly as social forces since they recognize them as useful for private and public ends. In nowise, however, do they teach that God's will and command is to be regarded far more than private or public advantage (and those who do not possess the Word are ignorant of the will of God). Quite plainly the scholastics have fallen victims to philosophical fancies to such an extent as to retain true knowledge neither of themselves nor of God. This is the cause of their lapse into such disastrous errors.

78. And, indeed, it is easy to fall after you have departed from the Word; for the glitter of civil virtues is wonderfully enticing to the mind. Erasmus makes of Socrates almost a perfect Christian, and Augustine has unbounded praise for Marcus Attilius Regulus, because he kept faith with his enemy. Truthfulness indeed is the most beautiful of all virtues, and in this case another high commendation is added in that there was combined with it love of country, which in itself is a peculiar and most praiseworthy virtue.

79. You may find men of renown not famous for truthfulness. Themistocles, for instance, did not have this virtue though he was a heroic man and did his country great service. That is the reason why Augustine admires Attilius, finding his reason and will to be utterly righteous, that is as far as it is possible for human nature to be. Where, then, is vice in this case? Where is wickedness? The hero's work surely cannot be censured.

80. First, Regulus knew not God, and, although his conduct was right, it is still to be seen whether a theologian should not censure his motive. For to his zeal in behalf of his country is added the thirst for glory. He evinces contempt for his life so as to achieve immortal glory among those to live after him. Contemplating, therefore, merely his life's dream, as it were, and the outward mask, it is a most beautiful deed. But before God it is shameful idolatry; because he claims for himself the glory of his deed. And who would doubt that he had other failings besides this thirst for glory? Attilius cannot claim the great virtues of truthfulness and love of country without tending violently and insanely toward wickedness. For it is wicked for him to rob God of the glory and to claim it for himself. But human reason cannot recognize this spoliation of the Deity.

81. A distinction must be made between the virtues of the heathen and the

virtues of Christians. It is true that in both instances hearts are divinely prompted, but in the former ambition and love of glory afterward defile the divine impulse.

82. If now, an orator should come forth, who would dilate upon the efficient cause, but disguise the ultimate and vicious one, would it not be apparent to every one that with the two most potent causes, the formal (that which gives moral value to an act) and the ultimate one, disguised, an eloquent man could extol such a wretched shadow of a virtue? But a man apt in logic will readily discover the deception; he will observe the absence of the formal cause, namely the right principle, there being no true knowledge of God nor of the proper attitude toward him. He sees, furthermore, that the final cause is vicious, because the true end and aim, obedience to God and love of neighbor, is not taken into consideration. But what kind of virtue is that where nearly every cause is lacking except the natural cause, which is a passion, an impetus or impulse, by which the soul is moved to show loyalty to an enemy? These impulses, as I said, are found also in the ungodly. If exercised for the good of the country, they become virtues; if for its injury, they become vices. This Aristotle sets forth very skillfully.

83. I refer to these things that students of sacred literature may make special note of this passage, which advisedly declares human nature to be corrupt. For those make-believe virtues, found among the heathen, seem to prove the contrary—that some part of nature has remained as it was originally. Hence there is need of careful judgment in order to distinguish in this matter.

84. Moses adds, "from his youth," because this evil is concealed during the first period of life and sleeps, as it were. Our early childhood so passes that reason and will are dormant and we are carried along by animal impulses, which pass away like a dream. Hardly have we passed our fifth year when we affect idleness, play, unchastity, and evil lust. But we try to escape discipline, we endeavor to get away from obedience, and hate all virtues, especially of a higher order as truth and justice. Then reason awakes out of a deep sleep, as it were, and sees certain kinds of pleasure, but not yet the true ones, and certain kinds of evils, but not yet the most powerful ones, by which it is held captive.

85. Where, then, the understanding has attained to maturity, not only the other vices are found to have grown strong, but there are joined to them now sexual desire and unclean passion, gluttony, gambling, strife, rape, murder, theft, and what not? And as the parents had to apply the rod, so now the government must needs use prison and chains in order to restrain man's evil nature.

86. And who does not know the vices of a more advanced age? They march along in unbroken file—love of money, ambition, pride, perfidy, envy, and others. These vices are so much the more harmful as at this age we are more crafty in concealing and masking them. Hence, the sword of government is not sufficient in this respect; there is need of hell fire for the punishment of crimes so manifold and great. Justly, then, did Moses say above (ch 6) that the human heart, or the imagination of the heart, is only evil each day—or at all times—and here again, that it is evil from youth.

87. The Latin version, it is true, makes use of a weaker term; yet it says enough

by stating that it is inclined toward evil, just as the comic dramatist says that the minds of all men are inclined to turn from labor to lust, Ter Andr 1, 1, 51. But those who try to misuse this expression for the purpose of making light of original sin, are shown to be in the wrong by the common experience of mankind; chiefly, however, that of the heathen, or ungodly men. For if spiritual men, who surely enjoy divine help from heaven, can hardly hold their ground against vices and be kept within the bounds of discipline, what can any man do without this help? If divine aid contends against the captivity of the law of the flesh only with fierce struggles (Rom 7, 22-23), how insane is it to dream that, without this divine help, human nature can withstand corruption?

88. Hence reason of itself does not decide upon the right, nor does the will, of itself, strive after the same, as a blind philosophy declares which does not know whence these fearful impulses to sin arise in children, youths, and old men. Therefore it defends them, calls them emotions or passions only, and does not call them natural corruption.

89. Furthermore, in noble men, who check and control these impulses, it calls them virtues; in others who give the reins to their desires, it calls them vices. This is nothing less than ignorance of the fact that human nature is evil. The Scriptures, on the contrary agree with our experience and declare that the human heart is evil from youth. For we learn by experience that even holy men can scarcely stand firm; yea that even they are often entangled by gross sins, being overwhelmed by such natural corruptions.

90. The term *ne-urim* denotes the age when man begins to use his reason; this usually occurs in the sixth year. Similarly, the term *ne-arim* is used to denote boys and youths who need the guidance of parents and teachers up to the age of manhood. It will be profitable for each of us to glance backward to that period of life and consider how willingly we obeyed the commands of our parents and teachers, how diligent we were in studying, how persevering we were, how often our parents punished our sauciness. Who can say for himself that he was not much more pleased to go out for a walk, to play games, and to gossip, than to go to Church in obedience to his parents?

91. Although these impulses can be corrected or bridled to a certain extent by discipline, they cannot be rooted out of the heart altogether, as the traces of these impulses show when we are grown. There is truth in that unpolished lie: "The angelic youth becomes satanic in his older years." God, indeed, causes some persons to experience emotions which are naturally good; but they are induced by supernatural power. Thus Cyrus was impelled to restore the worship of God, and to preserve the Church. But such is not the tendency of human nature. Where God is present with his Holy Spirit, there only, the imagination of the human heart gives place to the thoughts of God. God dwells there through the Word and the Spirit. Of such, Moses does not speak here, but only of those who are without the Holy Spirit; they are wicked, even when at their best.

V. 21e. *Neither will I again smite any more everything living, as I have done.*

92. Moses clearly speaks of a general destruction, like that which was caused

by the flood. From this it does not follow that God will also abstain from partial destruction, and that he will take no heed of anybody's sin. There will also be an exception in the case of the last day, when not only all living things will be smitten, but all creation will be destroyed by fire.

V. 22. *While the earth reigneth, seedtime and harvest, and cold and heat, and summer and winter, and day and night shall not cease.*

93. Following this text, the Jews divide the year into six parts, each comprising two months, a fact which Lyra also records in this connection. But it seems to me that Moses simply speaks of the promise that we need not fear another general flood. During the time of the flood such confusion reigned that there was no season, either of seedtime or harvest, and by reason of the great darkness caused by the clouds and the rain, day could not readily be distinguished from night. We know how heavy clouds obscure the light. How much greater, then, was the darkness when the waters, lying under the clouds like a mirror, reflected the darkness of the clouds into the faces and eyes of the beholders!

94. The meaning, accordingly, is simply that God here promises Noah the imminent restoration of the earth, so that the fields might again be sowed; that the desolation caused by the flood should be no more; that the seasons might run their course in accordance with regular law: harvest following seedtime, winter following summer, cold following heat in due order.

95. This text should be carefully remembered in view of the common notions concerning the signs before the last day. Then, some declare, there will be eclipses of I know not how many days duration. They say foolishly that for seven years not a single woman will bring forth a child, and the like. But this text declares that neither day nor night, neither summer nor winter, shall cease; therefore these natural changes will go on, and there will never be an eclipse which will rob human eyes of an entire day.

96. Nor is it a phrase devoid of meaning when he says, "While the earth remaineth," for he gives us to understand that the days of this earth shall sometime be numbered, and other days, days of heaven, shall follow. As long, therefore, as the days of the earth endure, so long shall the earth abide, and with it the rotation of seasons. But when these days of the earth shall pass, then all these things shall cease, and there shall follow days of heaven, that is, eternal days. There shall be one Sabbath after the other, when we shall not be engrossed with bodily labor for the purpose of gaining a livelihood; for we shall be as the angels of God, Mk 12, 25. Our life will be to know God, to delight in God's wisdom and to enjoy the presence of God. This life we attain through faith in Christ, in which the eternal Father may mercifully keep us, through the merit of his son, our Savior, Jesus Christ, by the ruling and guidance of the Holy Spirit. Amen. Amen.

CHAPTER IX.

I. GOD BLESSES NOAH AND THE RACE.
A. MARRIAGE STATE BLESSED.

1. Why this blessing necessary.
2. Wedlock established twice.
3. Evidence of God's love to the human race.
4. Did this blessing pertain to Noah.
* Bearing of children a special blessing of God unknown to the heathen.

I. GOD BLESSES NOAH AND THE RACE.
A. Marriage State Blessed.

V. 1. *And God blessed Noah and his sons, and said unto them, Be fruitful, and multiply, and replenish the earth.*

1. This consolation was indeed needed after the whole human race had been destroyed by the flood and only eight souls were saved. Now Noah knew that God was truly merciful, since, not content with that first blessing which he had bestowed upon mankind in the creation of the world, he added this new blessing, that Noah might have no misgivings whatever in regard to the future increase of his posterity. And the joy brought by this promise was all the greater for God's emphatic promise on a previous occasion, that he would never again visit mankind with such severe punishment.

2. In the first place, then, this chapter renews the establishment of marriage. God, by his Word and command, joins male and female for the purpose of repopulating the earth. Inasmuch as God had been roused to anger before the flood by the sin of lust, it was now needful, by reason of that fearful proof of wrath, to show that God does not abhor the lawful cohabitation of man and woman, but that it is his will to increase mankind by this means.

3. The fact that God had expressed it as his will that the human race should be propagated through a union between man and woman, an end which could have been attained from stones had he failed to approve such union as lawful, after the manner of Deucalion of whom the poets fable—this fact tended to furnish Noah sure evidence that God loved man, and desired his welfare, and that now all anger was at an end. Therefore this passage illustrates the dignity of wedlock, which is the foundation of the family and State, and the nursery of the Church.

4. The objection is here raised that Noah had already reached an age no longer fit for procreation in view of the fact that the Bible records no instance of children being born to him afterwards, and therefore this promise was valueless. To this I reply that this promise was given, not to Noah alone, but also to his sons, even to all mankind; so that the expectation of offspring was entertained even by the grandsire Noah.

5. This passage, furthermore, tends to convince us that children are a gift of God and a result of his blessing, as is shown in Psalms 127, 3. The heathen, who know nothing of God's Word, ascribe the increase of mankind partly to nature and partly to chance, in view of the fact that those who are evidently most fit for procreation often remain without offspring. Hence, they do not thank God for this gift, nor do they receive their children as a blessing from God.

B. MAN'S USE OF AND DOMINION OVER ANIMALS.

1. Whether animals feared man before the flood.
2. Relation between this use and dominion and of what they give evidence.
3. This use and rule a special blessing of God.
 * Whether the custom of slaying cattle dates from the beginning of the world.
4. Whether Adam knew of this use and dominion.
5. This use of animals is evidence of God's love to the human race.
 * God's blessings greater than his wrath.
6. Whether this use extends to unclean animals.
7. How man's fear of animals and their wildness and cruelty can exist with this dominion.
 * New sins accompanied by new punishments.
 * Sodom before and after its destruction.
 * God's punishment of Wittenberg, Bruges and Venice, and the cause.
 * God's command not to eat blood.
    a. Why given.
    b. How to treat this text, which contains God's Word.
     * Meaning of Nephesch and Basar.
    c. Right understanding of the command.
 * The words, "Surely your blood will I require" etc.
    a. Lyra's and the Rabbis' explanation.
    b. Their true meaning.

B. Man's Use of and Dominion Over Animals.

V. 2. *And the fear of you and the dread of you shall be upon every beast of the earth, and upon every bird of the heavens; with all wherewith the ground teemeth, and all the fishes of the sea, into your hand are they delivered.*

6. It would seem that the dominion of man is here increased for his greater consolation. For though after the creation man was given dominion over all animals, yet we do not read that the beasts feared and fled from him according to the description of Moses. The reason is found in the fact that heretofore the animals were not destined to be man's food; man had been a kind ruler of the beasts, not a killer and eater.

7. Here, however, they are subjected to man as a tyrant with unlimited power of life and death. Since the servitude of the beasts is increased and the power of man over them extended, the animals are harassed by terror and fear of man. We see even the tamed ones do not readily allow themselves to be handled; they feel the mastery of man and have a constant instinct of danger. I do not believe that such was the case before this Word of God was spoken. Before that time, men used suitable animals for their work and for sacrifice, but not for food. This increase of power also is a token of God's favor; he confers a privilege unknown to the patriarchs, as a token of his love and interest in man.

8. We must not undervalue this boon authority over the beasts; for it is a special gift of God, of which the heathen knew nothing, because they lack the Word. We are the ones who derive the greatest benefit from this gift. When this revelation was given to Noah, and such a privilege granted, there was really no need of it. A few men possessed the whole earth, so that its fruits were to be enjoyed by them in abundance and it was not necessary to add the flesh of beasts. But we today could not live altogether on the fruits of the earth; it is a great boon to us that we are permitted to eat the flesh of beasts, of birds and of fish.

9. This word, therefore, establishes the butcher's trade; it puts hares, chickens, and geese upon the spit and fills our tables with all manner of dishes. Necessity makes men industrious. Not only do they hunt the animals of the forests, but carefully fatten others at home for food. God in this passage establishes himself a slaughterer, as it were, for by his word he consigns to slaughter and death those animals which are suitable for food, as recompence to God-fearing Noah for his tribulations during the flood. For that reason would God feed Noah with lavish hand.

10. We must not think that this privilege was not divinely ordered. The heathen believe that this custom of slaughtering animals always existed. Such things are established, or rather permitted, by the Word of God; beasts could not have been killed without sin if God had not expressly permitted it by his Word. It is a great liberty for man to slaughter all kinds of beasts fit for food and eat them without wrong-doing. Had but a single kind of beasts been reserved for food, it would still have been a great boon; how much more should we value this lavish blessing, that all beasts suitable for sustenance are given into the power of man!

11. The godless and the gentiles do not recognize this; nor do the philosophers. They believe that this privilege has always been man's. As for us, however, we should have full light on the subject, in order that our consciences may enjoy both rest and freedom in the use of what God has created and allowed, there being absolutely no law against such food. There can be no sin in their use, though the

wicked priests have criminally burdened the Church on this subject.

12. In this passage, then, the power of man is increased and the brute beasts are committed to him, even unto death. They fear man and flee him under the new order, running counter to the experience of the past. Adam would have been averse to killing even a small bird for food. But now, since the promulgation of this Word, we know that, as a special blessing, God has furnished our kitchens with all kinds of meat. Later on he will also take care of the cellar by showing man how to cultivate the vine.

13. These are sure proofs that God no longer hates man, but favors him. This story bears witness that, as God's wrath, once aroused, is unbearable, so his mercy is likewise endless and without measure when it again begins to glow. But his mercy is the more abundantly exercised because it is the very nature of God, while wrath really is foreign to God; he takes it upon himself contrary to his nature and forced thereto by the wickedness of men.

V. 3. *Every moving thing that liveth shall be food for you; as the green herb have I given you all.*

14. Here a question arises. In chapter 7, 2, Moses showed the difference between clean and unclean beasts; here, however, he speaks of all animals, without any distinction. Did God, then, permit man to use also the unclean animals for food?

15. The statement as such is general: every moving thing that moveth upon the earth. There are some who believe that men at the time of Noah made no distinction between clean and unclean animals as regards food. But I hold a different opinion. For since such difference had been established before that time and was carefully observed in the Law afterward, I believe that men used only clean beasts for food; that is, such as were offered in sacrifice. Hence the general declaration must be understood with a modification: Everything that liveth and moveth, of clean beasts, is to be food for you. For, in general, human nature loathes serpents, wolves, ravens, mice, and dormice, though certain tribes may be found who relish even these animals. The fear and terror of man is upon all beasts of the earth, because he is allowed to kill them; but it does not follow that man uses them all for food. It is probable that Noah ate clean beasts only; and only clean beasts, he knew, were acceptable to Jehovah in sacrifice.

16. But there is another thing hard to understand. How can it be that the terror and fear of man is upon all animals when wolves, lions, bears, wild boars, and tigers devour men, and are rather a terror to men? So with the entire family of serpents, from which we flee at a glance. What shall we say here? Is the Word of God untruthful? I answer: Though we, being aware of our danger, flee from such beasts and are afraid of them, yet they, likewise, fear man. Even the fiercest beasts become terrified and flee at the first sight of man; but when they become enraged they overcome man by reason of their bodily strength.

17. But, you say, why do they fear when they are stronger? I answer: They know that man is endowed with reason, which is more powerful than any beast. The skill of man masters even elephants, lions, and tigers. Whatever man's bodily

strength is unable to do, that he accomplishes by his skill and his reasoning powers. How would it otherwise be possible for a boy of ten years to control an entire herd of cattle? Or for man to guide a horse, an animal of singular fierceness and strength, to go in whatever direction he desires, now urging it forward and then compelling it to a more moderate gait? All these things are done by man's skill, not by his strength. Hence, we do not lack clear proofs that the fear of man remains upon the beasts, which harm man when they become enraged, and for that reason are feared by him.

18. I have no doubt, however, that at the time of Noah and the patriarchs immediately succeeding, this fear in the beasts was greater, because righteousness then flourished and there was less of sin. Afterward, when holiness of life declined and sin increased, man began to lose this blessing, and the wild beasts became a punishment for sin. Moses threatens in Deut 32, 34 that God would send upon them the teeth of beasts. How fearful, also, was the plague of the fiery serpents in the desert! Num 21, 6. Bears tore to pieces the lads who mocked the prophet, 2 Kings 2, 24. Why did the beasts here lose their fear of man? Why did they rage against man? Was not sin the cause?

19. Therefore, as stated before, when new sins arise, new punishments will also arise. So we see that in our day disease and misfortunes heretofore rare become general, like the English sweat, the locusts which in the year 1542 devastated great stretches of land in Poland and Silesia, and other examples.

20. In like manner, God promised seasons of seeding and of harvest, of heat and cold, and yet he does not so close his eyes to our sins that the seasons, both of seeding and of harvest, are not subject to climatic disturbances, such as the fearful drouth of the year 1504 and the almost unending rains of the two following years. Considering the wickedness of our age, why should we wonder that the blessing gives place to a curse, so that the beasts, which would fear us were we not wicked, are now a terror unto us and harmful?

21. The country of the Sodomites was like a paradise; but by reason of sin it was turned into a sea of asphalt; and those who have seen that country tell us that most beautiful apples grow there, but when they are cut open they are found to be filled with ashes and offensive odor. The reason for this is that the Sodomites did not acknowledge the gifts of God who blessed them, but misused them according to their own will. Furthermore, they blasphemed God, and persecuted his saints, being haughty by reason of those good gifts. Therefore the blessing was taken away, and everything became curse-ridden. This is the true explanation of the fact that, though there are signs of terror in wild animals, we are nevertheless afraid of them, and they inflict harm upon us.

22. I am quite certain that very wicked men once lived in this country of ours; how could we otherwise explain the parched soil and barren sands? Names also show that the Jews at one time peopled this country. Where bad people live, there the land gradually grows bad by the curse of God.

23. The city of Bruges in Flanders used to be a renowned port; but from the time when they held King Maximilian captive, the sea retreated, and the port

ceased to exist. Of Venice they say the same thing today. Nor is this very astonishing, since to the numberless sins of rulers of the State, defence of idol worship and persecution of the Gospel was added.

V. 4. *But flesh with the life thereof, which is the blood thereof, shall ye not eat.*

24. What we have heard so far, referred to domestic matters; now God adds a commandment pertaining to civil government. Since it was no more a sin to kill an ox or a sheep for food than it was to pluck a flower or an herb, growing in the field, there was some danger that men might misuse this God-given power over the beasts and go beyond it even to the shedding of human blood. Hence, he now adds a new law, that human blood must not be shed, and at the same time he curtails the liberty of eating flesh; he forbids them to eat flesh which has not first been drained of blood.

25. The Hebrew text presents many difficulties, and, for this reason, interpreters are at variance. It is needless to recite all renderings of this verse. I steadily follow the rule that the words must explain the things, not the things the words. Hence, I spend no time upon the ideas of those who explain the words according to their own inclinations, making them serve the preconceived notions which they bring to their literature.

26. Let us first look at the meaning of the words. *Rephesh* properly denotes a body with a soul, or a living animal, such as the ox, the sheep, man, etc. It denotes not merely the body, but a living body, as when Christ says: I lay down my life for the sheep, Jn 10, 15. Here the word "life" means nothing else than the life animating the body. *Basar*, however, means flesh, which is a part of the material element, and yet has its breath and its energy, not from the body, but from the soul. For the flesh or the body, of itself and without the soul, is an inanimate thing, like a log or a stone; but when it is filled with the breath of the soul, then its fluids and all bodily forces assume activity.

27. God here forbids the eating of a body which still contains the stirring, moving, living soul, as the hawk devours chickens, and the wolf sheep, without killing them, but while still alive. Such cruelty is here forbidden by Jehovah, who sets bounds to the privilege of slaughtering, lest it be done in so beastly a manner that living bodies or portions thereof be devoured. The lawful manner of slaughtering is to be observed, such as was followed at the altar and in religious rites, where the beast, having been slain without cruelty and duly cleansed from blood, was finally offered to God. I hold that the simple and true meaning of the text, which is also given by some Jewish teachers, is that we must not eat raw flesh and members still palpitating, as did the Laestrygones and the Cyclopes.

V. 5. *And surely your blood, the blood of your lives, will I require; at the hand of every beast will I require it: and at the hand of man, even at the hand of every man's brother, will I require the life of man.*

28. Here the Hebrew text is even more difficult than in the foregoing verse. Lyra, quoting the Rabbins, finds four kinds of manslaughter indicated here; he divides the statement into two parts, and finds a twofold explanation for each. He understands the first part to mean those who lay murderous hands upon them-

selves. If this is correct, then this passage is a witness for immortality; for how could God call to account a person who, being dead, no longer exists? Hence, punishment of sin after this life could be indicated here. But it seems to me that philology militates against this explanation. Though I do not lay claim to a perfect knowledge of the Hebrew tongue, yet I am certain that such a meaning is not here apparent.

29. The second kind of murder, he illustrates by the custom of throwing human beings before wild beasts, as was done aforetime in the theatres, truly a barbaric spectacle, repulsive to all human feeling; the third kind is murder at the instigation of another; the fourth, murder of a relative.

30. This distinction would be quite satisfactory if it could be proven from the words of the text; but it is a Jewish invention born of their hatred of the Roman laws. It is much simpler to understand this passage as a general prohibition of murder, according to the fifth commandment, which says, "Thou shalt not kill." God desires not even a beast to be killed, except for a sacred purpose or for the benefit of man. Much less does he permit taking the life of man, except by divine authority, as will be explained hereafter.

31. In the first place, then, wilful and wicked slaughter is forbidden. Culture is opposed to the wanton killing of animals and to the eating of raw meat. In the second place God forbids homicide of any description; for if God will require the blood of a murdered human being from the beast that slew him, how much more relentlessly will he require it at the hand of man? Thus this passage voices the sentiment of the fifth commandment, that no one shall spill human blood.

II. LAW CONCERNING MAN'S SLAUGHTER; GOD'S COVENANT WITH NOAH; THE RAINBOW.

A. LAW CONCERNING SLAYERS OF LIFE.

1. If it existed before the flood.
2. Relation of the flood to this law.
3. This the source of all human laws.
4. When and how this law can be executed.
 * Why is it well to observe that government was instituted by God.
5. In what respect is it a great blessing from God.
6. How is government a proof of God's love to man.
7. Why God gave this command, and why he punishes man-slaughter.
8. Hereby a new police and a new order are instituted.
 * Verdict of philosophy and of reason on civil authority.
 * Verdict of God's Word.
9. This law applies to all men.
10. Why God is such an enemy of man-slaughter, and so earnestly forbids it.
11. The conclusion that God loves life.

II. THE LAW AGAINST TAKING LIFE;
GOD'S COVENANT WITH NOAH; THE RAINBOW.

A. The Law Against Taking Life.

V. 6a. *Who sheddeth man's blood, by man shall his blood be shed.*

32. Here the carelessness of the Latin translator deserves reproof; for he omitted the very necessary expression "by man." The difference between the time before and that after the flood is thus brought out. When Cain had murdered his brother Abel, God revered human blood so highly that he threatened to visit sevenfold punishment upon anyone who should kill Cain. He would not have the slayer of man put to death even by due process of law; and though Adam punished the sin of his son severely by casting him out, he did not dare to pronounce sentence of death upon him.

33. But here Jehovah establishes a new law, requiring the murderer be put to death by man—a law unprecedented, because heretofore God had reserved all judgment to himself. When he saw that the world was growing worse and worse, he finally enforced punishment against a wicked world by the flood. Here, however, God bestows a share of his authority upon man, giving him the power of life and death, that thus he may be the avenger of bloodshed. Whosoever takes man's life without due warrant, him God subjects not only to his own judgment, but also to the sword of man. Though God may use man as his instrument in punishing, he is himself still the avenger. Were it not for the divine command, then, it would be no more lawful now to slay a murderer than it was before the flood.

34. This is the source from which spring all civil laws and the laws of nations. If God grants man the power of life and death, he certainly also grants power in matters of lesser importance—power over property, family, wife, children, servants and fields. God wills that these things shall be under the control of certain men, who are to punish the guilty.

35. We must remember well that between the power of God and of men there is this difference: God has the power to slay us when the world cannot even accuse us—when before it we are innocent. Sin is born with us; we are all guilty before God. Men have no authority to slay except where guilt is apparent and crime is proven. Hence courts have been established and a definite method of proceeding instituted for the purpose of investigating and proving the crime before the sentence of death is passed.

36. Heed, then, this passage. It establishes civil authority as God's institution, with power, not only of life and death, but jurisdiction in matters where life is not involved. Magistrates are to punish the disobedience of children, theft, adultery, perjury—all sins which are forbidden in the second table. He who grants jurisdiction over the life of man, at the same time grants judgment over lesser matters.

37. The importance of this text and its claim to attention consists in the fact that it records the establishment of civil authority by God with the sword as insignia of power, for the purpose that license may be curbed and anger and other sins inhibited from growing beyond all bounds. Had God not granted this power to

man, what kind of lives, I ask you, would we lead? He foresaw that wickedness would ever flourish, and established this external remedy to prevent the indefinite spread of license. By this safeguard God protects life and property as by a fence and a wall.

38. We find here no less a proof of God's great love toward man than his promise that the flood shall never again rage, and his promise that flesh may be eaten for the sustenance of human life.

V. 6b. *For in the image of God made he man.*

39. This is the powerful reason why God does not wish men to be killed by private arbitrament. Man is a noble creature, who, unlike other living beings, has been fashioned according to the image of God. While it is true that he has lost this image through sin, as we have seen above, it is capable of being restored through the Word and the Holy Spirit. This image God desires us to revere in each other; he forbids us to shed blood by the exercise of sheer force. But he who refuses to respect the image of God in man, and gives way to anger and provocation, those worst counselors of all, as some one has called them, his life is surrendered to civil authority in forfeit, by God, in that God commands that also his blood shall be shed.

40. Thus the subject under consideration teaches the establishment of civil authority in the world, which did not exist before the flood. Cain and Lamech—and this is a case in point—were not slain, though the holy patriarchs were the arbiters, judges, of public action. But in this Scripture they who have the sword, are commanded to use it against those who have shed blood.

41. Thus the problem is here solved that worried Plato and all sages. They concluded that it is impossible to administer government without injustice, because all men occupy the same level of dignity and position. Why did Caesar rule the world? Why did others obey him, since he was only human like themselves—no better, no stronger and liable to die as soon as themselves? He was subject to the same conditions as all men. Hence it seems to be tyranny for him, who was quite similar to other men, to usurp rulership among men. If he is like other men it is the highest wrong and injustice to ignore this similarity, and to foist his rule by force upon others.

42. This is the conclusion at which reason arrives and it cannot entertain any view to the contrary. But we, having the Word, can see that we must oppose to such reasoning the command of God, the author of this order of things. Accordingly, it is for us to render obedience to the divine order and to endure it, so that to our other sins this may not be added, that we are disobedient to the will of God at the very point where we derive benefit in so many ways.

43. To sum up, this passage permits the slaughter of animals for religious and personal use, but it emphatically forbids the taking of man's life, because man is made in the image of God. Those who violate his command he gives into the hands of the authorities to be slain.

V. 7. *And you, be ye fruitful, and multiply; bring forth abundantly in the earth, and multiply therein.*

44. The slaughter of animals having been granted, not only for sacrifice, but also for food, and the killing of human beings having been forbidden, we are given the reason why God regards the shedding of human blood with so much aversion. He desires mankind to multiply on the earth; but the slaughter of men lays the earth waste and produces a wilderness. We see this in case of war. God did not create the earth without purpose. He intended it to be inhabited, Is 45, 18. He makes it fruitful by rain and sunshine for man's benefit. Therefore he is displeased with those who remove from the earth its inhabitants. His will is life, and not death, Ps 30, 5.

45. These and similar sayings of the prophets are based upon promises like we find here, that God commands man to multiply. Plainly he is more inclined to give life and to do good than to be angry and to kill. If it were otherwise, why should he forbid the taking of human life? Why should pestilence be of rare occurrence? Pestilence and general epidemics occur scarce once in ten years. Men are born, animals grow, and crops without end are growing continually.

46. All these facts go to show that God loves, not death, but life. He created man, not that he should die, but that he should live; "but through the envy of the devil did death enter the world," Sap 2, 24. But even after the fall, the blessings which remain are so guarded as to render the conclusion inevitable that God loves life rather than death.

It is well for us to ponder these matters very often; thus, as Solomon has truly said, Jehovah shall be to us a fountain of blessings. Prov 18, 22.

B. GOD'S COVENANT WITH NOAH.

  * Why the same thing is repeated.

1. Whether this covenant applies to man alone or also to the animals.

2. Whether this covenant applies to the men and animals of that day only.

  * God always connected signs with his promises.

  * The significance of these to our first parents.

3. Nature of this covenant.

  * Characteristics of a humble heart and God's dealings with it.

4. This covenant given for man's comfort and as a proof of God's love.

5. It is a comfort to us at present.

B. God's Covenant with Noah.

Vs. 8-11. *And God spake unto Noah, and his sons with him, saying, And I, behold, I establish my covenant with you, and with your seed after you; and with every living creature that is with you, the birds, the cattle, and every beast of the earth with you; of all that go out of the ark, even every beast of the earth. And I will establish my covenant with you; neither shall all flesh be cut off any more by the waters of the flood; neither shall there any more be a flood to destroy the earth.*

47. Previously we at various times explained this massing of words. When the Holy Spirit is prolix, there is a cause for it. Let us therefore, consider what fear, dread and peril Noah and his family endured and it will be easily understood why it was necessary for God to say and to emphasize the same things with such frequency.

48. When, in addition it is remembered that the covenant here spoken of does not pertain to man alone but embraces every living soul, we recognize that the promise does not relate to the seed but merely, to this bodily life, enjoyed by man in common with the beasts; this God will not destroy by another flood.

Vs. 12-16. *And God said, This is the token of the covenant which I make between me and you and every living creature that is with you, for the perpetual generations: I do set my bow in the cloud, and it shall be for a token of a covenant between me and the earth. And it shall come to pass, when I bring a cloud over the earth, that the bow shall be seen in the cloud, and I will remember my covenant, which is between me and you and every living creature of all flesh; and the waters shall no more become a flood to destroy all flesh. And the bow shall be in the cloud; and I will look upon it, that I may remember the everlasting covenant between God and every living creature of all flesh that is upon the earth.*

49. The term "perpetual generations" deserves particular notice; it embraces not only man and beast at that time, but all their offspring down to the end of the world. We learn another thing from this passage. God usually confirms his promise with an outward sign. In the third chapter above we read of the coats of skin with which he covered the nakedness of the first parents as token of his protection and guardianship.

50. Some offer the following apt allegorical explanation. As the skin of the dead sheep keeps warm our body, so Christ, having died, keeps us warm by his Spirit, and will, on the last day, raise us up and give us life. Others say that the skins were selected as a sign of mortality. But this seems unnecessary; all our life reminds us of mortality. More expedient was a token of life, suggesting the blessing and favor of God. The office of such tokens is to console, not to terrify. So was the sign of the rainbow given, a supplement of the promise.

51. In chapter 8, 21-22, God says in his heart that he repents of that terrible punishment, and promises that he will not repeat it, because the imagination of man's heart is evil from his youth. If he should desire to so punish evil, there would be need of a flood every day. Here he again sends forth his Word to mankind, through an angel, or possibly through the mouth of Noah, promising that no flood shall hereafter come upon the earth. That the promise is repeated so often is evidence of God's endeavor, in loving kindness, to remove man's fear of punishment and to set before him a hope of blessing and utmost mercy.

52. Such consolation Noah and his loved ones required. One who has been humbled by God cannot forget the wound and the pain. Chastening is longer remembered than blessing. Boys are a case in point. The tender mother, having chastised her child with the rod, endeavors to calm him with toys and other allurements, yet the memory of pain lingers, and the child cannot restrain frequent sighs and bitter sobs. How much more difficult for the conscience to accept solace

after having felt the wrath of God and the fear of death! So firmly fixed are these in the mind that the soul trembles and fears in spite of gifts and consolations offered.

53. So God here shows his good will in manifold ways and feels singular joy in pouring forth mercy. He is like a mother who pets and caresses her boy until he at last begins to forget his tears and to smile into his mother's face.

54. Hence figures are employed, and words are massed and the subject is presented in a clearer and clearer light, in order to adapt the consolation to the needs of the wretched people who, for an entire year, had been witnesses of the immeasurable wrath of God. They could not be delivered from fear and terror by an occasional word. There was need of repeating the promise with much exposition to dry their tears and to soften their grief. For, though they were saints, they were flesh, even as we are.

55. Likewise we in our day need this consolation. At all times when the elements rage, we may be secure in the thought that the fountains of heaven and the wells of the deep are closed up by the word of God. The rainbow shows itself to this day for the purpose of symbolizing that, henceforth, there shall never be another general flood. And this promise requires, on our part, the faith that we trust God, in his mercy, will never bring another great flood upon us.

C. THE RAINBOW.

1. Can it be assigned to natural causes.
* What to think of the fiery meteors.
2. Can it be caused by the position of the clouds.
3. The rainbow witnesses of God's wrath and of his goodness.
4. Did it exist before the flood?
    a. Opinion of those believing it did, and their reasons.
    b. Luther's opinion that it was a new creation.
    c. Solomon's words, "There is nothing new", do not apply here.
5. Rainbow to be viewed as a new creature and as God's sign-board.
6. Colors of the rainbow.
    a. What are they and their number.
    b. What do they signify.
7. To what end should the rainbow serve us.

C. The Rainbow.

56. They further dispute whether the natural causes in the rainbow signify this. It is well known that philosophers, especially Aristotle in his book on Meteors, use all sorts of arguments on the color of the rainbow, on the character of the clouds where it is produced, and on its curvature. Quite appropriately the resemblance is noted between a mirror, which reflects an image, and the moist and arched cloud, which catches the rays of the sun, and by reflection produces the

rainbow. Reason sees in such phenomena what appears to it most probable, but it does not discover the truth everywhere. That is not in the power of the creature but of the Creator alone. As for me, I have never given to any book less credence than to that on meteors, the basic principle of which is the assumption that natural causes explain everything.

57. Some declare the rainbow to be a forerunner of a storm lasting three days, which I am ready to admit, but this much is certain, that it signifies that there will never be another flood. However, it derives this signification, not from any natural causes but only from the Word of God. Its meaning is such, only because God orders and declares it to be so through his Word. Circumcision was a token that the seed of Abraham were the people of God; yet circumcision did not have this meaning in itself, but only through the Word which was joined with it. Again, the clothing of skin signified life and safety, not because they contained this guarantee by nature, but because God had promised it. So, the significance of the rainbow that the flood shall not return, is not based upon the Word of God.

58. I do not altogether ignore theories along the lines of natural law concerning these matters; but since they are not substantiated, I place little trust in them. The reasoning of Aristotle regarding the humid and hollow cloud as the cause of the rainbow is not reliable, such clouds may exist without producing a rainbow. Again, according to the greater or lesser density of the medium, the bow may appear wider or narrower. I have seen here at Wittenberg a circular rainbow, forming a complete ring, not simply an arch terminating on the surface of the earth, as rainbows generally appear. Why, then, do rainbows assume different forms at different times? A philosopher, I suppose, will think of some reason; for he will consider it a disgrace not to be able to assign a reason for all things. But indeed, he will never persuade me to believe that he speaks the truth.

59. The only consistent and incontrovertable view to take is that all these phenomena are either works of God or of evil spirits. I have no doubt that the dancing goats (stars), the flying serpents, fiery lances, and the like, are produced by evil spirits, which thus gambol in the air, either to terrify or to deceive men. The flames which appear on board of ships were thought by the heathen to be Castor and Pollux. Sometimes the image of a moon appears above the ears of horses. It is certain that all these things are due to the antics of evil spirits in the air, though Aristotle believes them to be luminous air, just as he also declares that a comet is shining vapor.

60. To me it appears that we shall move with greater security and certainty, when, arguing from cause to effect, we conclude that the comet blazes, when it pleases God, as a sign of calamity, just as the rainbow glows, when it pleases God as a sign of mercy. Who can compute all the causes which produce the appearance of the rainbow in such diversity of beautiful color, and in the form of an arch of perfect curvature? The arrangement of the clouds alone surely does not produce this perfection. Hence it is by the will and the promise of God, and fulfilling his pleasure, that the rainbow is a sign to man and beast that there will nevermore at any time be a flood.

61. In recognition of this token we ought to give thanks to God. As often as the rainbow appears, it proclaims to the world with a loud voice, as it were, the story of the wrath of God, which once destroyed the world by a flood. And it proclaims solace for us, so that we may conclude that God is propitious to us henceforth and will never again visit upon us so fearful a punishment. It teaches both the love and the fear of God, the highest virtues, of which philosophy knows nothing. Philosophy only disputes about material and formal causes. It does not know the final cause of this most beautiful creation. But theology does explain it.

62. In this connection also the question has received much attention whether the rainbow existed from the beginning. And in this controversy much force has been displayed. Since it is written above (ch 2, 23) that God created heaven and earth in six days, and then rested from all his works, some conclude that the rainbow existed from the beginning. Otherwise it would follow that creation extended beyond those six days. What, however, occurred in Noah's time is this, that the rainbow, created in the beginning, was selected by God and made, through a new word, a fixed symbol, having existed hitherto without special significance. To support this view, they even quote the word of Solomon that "there is no new thing under the sun," Ec 1, 9. On this they base their argument that after those six days no new thing has been created.

63. My opinion is quite the contrary—that the rainbow never had existed before; it was then and there created. Thus, the coats of skin with which God clothed the first parents certainly were not created in those six days, but after man's fall; hence, they were a new creation. The statement that God rested, must not be interpreted to mean that he created nothing thereafter; for Christ says, "My Father worketh even until now, and I work," Jn 5, 17.

64. Solomon's statement that there is no new thing under the sun, has given much trouble to the learned. But is it not apparent that it refers not to the works of God, but to original sin, meaning that the same reasoning powers Adam had after the fall are found in man today—the same debates concerning morals, vices, virtues, the nurture of the body and the transaction of business? As the comic poet has it, speaking of another matter, "Nothing is said that has not been said before." Really, within the sphere of man's activity and effort there is nothing new; the same words, thoughts, designs, the same emotions, griefs, affections and incidents exist now which always existed. Consequently it is quite inappropriate, in consequence to apply this aphorism to God and his works.

65. Therefore, I believe that the rainbow was a new creation, not seen in the world before that time. It was established to remind the world of the bygone wrath, traces of which are still seen in the rainbow, and to give assurance of the mercy of God. It is a record, or picture in which both the bygone wrath and the present mercy are revealed.

66. There is also a difference of opinion as to the colors of the rainbow. Some say there are four colors: the fiery, the bright yellow, the green and the color of water, or blue. But I think there are only two, those of fire and water. The fiery color is above, unless the rainbow is seen reversed; then, as in a mirror, that which is above

is seen below. Where the hues of fire and water meet, or blend, yellow results.

67. The colors have been thus arranged by God for a definite purpose. The blue should be a reminder of bygone wrath; the fiery color, a picture to us of the future judgment. While the interior or blue portion is restricted, the outer and fiery color is without bounds. Thus, the first world perished by the flood, but an end was set to God's wrath. A remnant was preserved and a second world arose, but bounds are set to it. When God shall destroy the world by fire, this bodily life will never be restored. The wicked will suffer the everlasting punishment of death in the fire, while the saints will be raised up unto a new and everlasting life, which, though in the body, shall not be of the body, but of the spirit.

68. Let this sign teach us to fear God and to trust in him. So may we escape the punishment of fire, even as we have escaped the punishment of the flood. It will be more practical to think of these things than to consider those philosophical arguments concerning the material cause.

III. ALLEGORIES.
A. ALLEGORIES IN GENERAL.

1. Luther at first given to allegories.
2. How and why monks and Anabaptists esteem them so highly.
3. How we should regard them.
4. Are they to be entirely rejected.
5. Some are, and others not.
6. How to regard Origen's, Augustine's and Jerome's allegories.
7. Pope's allegories of the sun, moon and ark.
8. What to think of the doctrine of these allegories.

III. CONCERNING ALLEGORIES.
A. Allegories in General.

69. At last we have finished the story of the flood, which Moses satisfactorily describes at great length. It is a fearful example of the immeasurable and all but boundless wrath of God, which is beyond the power of human utterance. There remains to be said a word or two concerning its allegorical meaning. I have often declared that I take no great pleasure in allegories, although in my younger days they had such a fascination for me that I thought everything ought to be shown to have an allegorical meaning. I was influenced in this respect by the example of Origen and Jerome, whom I admired as the greatest of all theologians. I may add that Augustine also uses the allegory quite frequently.

70. But while I followed the example of these men, I discovered at last that, to my great loss, I had followed a shadow, and had overlooked the very sap and marrow of the Scriptures. Thereupon I began to hate allegories. They are pleasing, to be sure, especially when they contain happy allusions. They may be compared to choice pictures. But as much as real objects with their native hues surpass a pic-

ture, even though it should glow, as the poet has it (stat silo V. 1, 5), with Apelles-like colors, closely copied from nature, so much the historical narrative itself is superior to the allegory.

71. In our day the ignorant mob of the Anabaptists is as much filled with immoderate craving for allegory as are the monks. They love to delve in the more mysterious books, such as the Revelation of John, and that worthless fabrication passing under the title of the second and third books of Esdras. For, there you are at liberty to follow your fancy as you please. We recall that Muntzer, the seditious spirit, turned everything into allegory. But true it is, that he who, without judgment, makes allegories or follows those made by others, will not only be deceived but sustain deplorable injury, as there are examples to prove.

72. Allegories must either be avoided altogether or be worked out with the best judgment. They must conform to the rule followed by the apostles, of which we shall soon have occasion to speak. Let us avoid falling into those ugly and baneful absurdities, not only of those who are misnamed theologians, but also of the Canonists, or rather Assinists, of which the decretals and decisions of that most detestable master, the pope, are an example.

73. This statement, however, must not be taken for a general condemnation of all allegory. Christ and the apostles made use of allegories at times. These, however, were in keeping with the faith according to the injunction of Paul (Rom 12, 6) that prophecy, or doctrine, should be according to the proportion of faith.

74. When we put the allegory under the ban, we confine ourselves to that species which, with the setting aside of scriptural warrant, is altogether the product of man's mind and fancy. Those which are tested by the analogy of faith, serve not only as ornaments of the doctrine but also as consolation for the soul.

75. Peter turns this very story of the flood into a most beautiful allegory, saying that baptism is symbolized by the flood, and saves us. For, in it not only the filth of the flesh is washed away, but conscience makes good answer toward God through the resurrection of Jesus Christ, who is enthroned at the right hand of God and has destroyed death in order to make us heirs of eternal life; who, moreover, is gone into heaven; angels and authorities and powers being made subject unto him, 1 Pet 3, 21-22. This is, indeed, a theological allegory, in accordance with faith, and full of solace.

76. Such is also the allegory of Christ in John 3, 14, concerning the serpent lifted up in the wilderness and the healing of those bitten by the serpent's tooth who gazed upon it. Again, there is that one by Paul (1 Cor 10, 1), All our fathers did drink from the same spiritual rock, etc. Such allegories as these not only agree with the matter itself, but also instruct the heart in faith and are a help to the conscience.

77. But take a look at the ordinary allegory of Jerome, Origen and Augustine. These men, when they create an allegory, leave faith altogether out of consideration, and merely air philosophical opinions, foreign alike to the sphere of faith and to that of morals; not to speak of the fact that they are quite silly and a mass of absurdities.

78. In a former chapter (ch 3. §§61, 298, 304), we heard of Augustine's allegory concerning the creation of man and woman, by which he illustrates the higher and the lower attributes of man, that is, reason and the emotions. But, I ask you, what is the value of this figment?

79. The pope, however, carries away the real honors for piety and learning when he thunders from his high seat as follows: God made two great lights, the sun and the moon; the sun represents the authority of the pope, from which his imperial majesty borrows its light as the moon does from the sun. Away with such rash impudence and vicious ambition!

80. In a similar style the ark, of Noah's story, is compared to the Roman Catholic Church, in which is found the pope with his cardinals, bishops, and prelates, while the laymen are swimming in the sea. That is, the laymen are altogether given to earthly business and would not be saved did not those helmsmen of the ark, or Church, cast boards and ropes to the swimmers, drawing them into the ark by these means. Pictures of this nature were frequently painted by monks to represent the Church.

81. Origen shows more sanity than the papists, in that his allegories conform to moral standards, as a rule. Yet, he ought to have kept in view the rule laid down by Paul, who demands that prophesy is to be the guardian of faith; for faith is edifying and the proper sphere of the Church. Rules governing morals can be laid by even heathen philosophers who know nothing whatever concerning faith.

B. ALLEGORIES IN DETAIL.

1. Allegory of the baptism of the Israelites under Moses; the ark and the flood.
 * Points of likeness and unlikeness in the death of believers and unbelievers.
 * In what way is death to be conquered.
 * How all temptations are to be overcome and believers be preserved.
2. Allegories of the ark's proportions.
3. Allegories of the sun and moon.
 * To what all allegories should point.
4. Allegory of the cup.
5. Allegory of the dove Noah sent out of the ark.
6. Allegory of the raven Noah sent forth.
    a. Thoughts of the fathers on this point.
    b. The correct allegory of the raven.
    *   The law and the teachings of the law.
        (1) How illustrated by the raven.
         * Luther's opponents falsely accuse him of forbidding good works.
        (2) They are no better than the intelligent moralists among the heathen.

        (3)   They cannot quiet the conscience.

        *   The raven a perfect representative of the Papists.

        (4)   How the Papists make the unrighteous righteous and condemn the righteous.

   7.   Allegories of the doves in detail.

    *   Characteristics of the dove.

      a.   First dove sent forth.

        (1)   A figure of the office of grace.

        (2)   A figure of the Old Testament prophets.

      b.   Second dove returned with the olive leaf.

        (1)   A figure of New Testament preachers.

        *   The fanatics and Anabaptists wait in vain for new revelations.

        *   Nature of true Gospel preachers.

        (2)   A figure of the New Testament.

      c.   Third dove did not return.

   8.   Allegory of the seven days Noah waited after he sent forth the first dove.

   9.   Allegory of the evening the dove returned.

      *   Several things to be remembered in this connection.

        (1)   Allegories are not to have a world-wide treatment like the articles of faith.

        (2)   Defects in the allegories of the fathers.

        *   Lyra is to be preferred to all commentators.

        (3)   Right use of allegories.

B. Allegories in Detail.

82. Writing to the Corinthians, Paul says (1 Cor 10, 2) that the Israelites "were all baptized unto Moses in the cloud and in the sea." If you regard only the outward circumstance and the words, even Pharaoh was baptized, but he perished with his men, while Israel passed through safe and unharmed. Noah and his sons were saved in this baptism of the flood, while all the rest of the world, being outside of the ark, perished thereby. Such a way of speaking is appropriate and forcible. "Baptism" and "death" are interchangeable in Scripture. Paul says (Rom 6, 3): "All we who were baptized into Christ Jesus were baptized into his death," and Jesus says, "I have a baptism to be baptized with; and how am I straitened till it be accomplished!" (Lk 12, 50). And to his disciples he said, "Ye shall ... be baptized with the baptism that I am baptized with" (Mt 20, 23).

83. In this sense the Red Sea was a baptism indeed. It represented to Pharaoh death and God's anger. Yet though Israel was baptized with the same baptism, they passed through it unharmed. So the flood is truly death and the wrath of God, and yet, the faithful are saved in the midst of the flood. Death engulfs and

swallows all mankind; for, the wrath of God smites both the good and the bad, the pious and the wicked, without distinction. The flood was sent upon Noah the same as upon the rest of the world. The Red Sea that engulfed Pharaoh was the same as that through which Israel passed unharmed. But in both cases the believers are saved while the wicked perish. That is the point of difference. The ark was Noah's salvation, and it was but an expression of the promise and Word of God. In these he had life, but the wicked, who believed not the Word, were left to perish.

84. This is the difference which the Holy Spirit desired to bring out, so that the righteous, warned by this example, might believe and hope for salvation through the mercy of God in the very midst of death. They consider baptism as bound together with the promise of life, as Noah did the ark. Therefore, though the wise man and the fool must suffer the same death—for Peter and Paul die, not otherwise than Nero and other wicked persons die—yet the righteous believe that in death they will be saved unto eternal life. And this hope is not vain, for they have Christ, who receives their souls, and will, on the last day, raise up also the bodies of his believers unto eternal life.

85. This class of allegory is of great service, and tends to comfort the heart when you consider the contrast in the ultimate outcome. The testimony of the material eye would seem to confirm the statement of Solomon (Ec 2, 16) that the wise man dieth as the fool, that the righteous man dieth as though he were not the beloved of God. But the eyes of the soul must view this point of difference, that Israel enters into the Red Sea and is saved, while Pharaoh, pressing upon the heels of Israel, is overwhelmed by the waves and perishes. It is the same death, then, which takes away the righteous and the wicked, and almost always the end of the former is ignominious, while that of the latter is attended by elements of splendor and power; but in the eyes of God, while the death of sinners is deplorable, that of his saints is precious, for it is consecrated by Christ, through whom it becomes the beginning of eternal life.

86. As the flood and the Red Sea were instruments to save Noah and Israel from death, so to us, death is but the instrument to give us life, if we remain in faith. When the children of Israel were in utmost peril, suddenly the sea parted and rose on the right side and on the left, like an iron wall, so that Israel passed through without danger. Why was it? In order that so death might be made to serve life. Divine power overcomes the assaults of Satan. Thus it was in Paradise. Satan purposed to slay all mankind by his venom. But what happens? By reason of the truly happy guilt of our first parents, as the Church sings, it comes to pass that the Son of God became incarnate to free us from evil.

87. This allegory, then, beautifully teaches, strengthens and consoles us, enabling us to fear neither death nor sin, but to despise all perils, giving thanks to God that he has so called and dealt with us that even death, the universal destroyer, is compelled to be a servant of life, just as the flood, an occasion of destruction to the rest of the world, was one of salvation for Noah; and the Red Sea, when Pharaoh met his doom, served to save the children of Israel.

88. What has been here expressed, finds application to the subject of tempta-

tion in general, so that we learn to despise dangers and be hopeful even where no hope seems to remain. When death or any other danger is imminent, we should rise to meet it, saying: Behold, here is my Red Sea; here is my flood, my baptism and my death. Here my life—as the philosopher said of the sea-farers—is removed from death barely by a hand's breadth. But fear not; this danger is as a handful of water opposed to the flood of grace which is mine through the Word. Therefore death will not destroy me, but will lift me and bear me to life. Death is so utterly incapable of destroying the Christian, that it constitutes the very escape from death. For bodily death ushers in the emancipation of the spirit and the resurrection of the flesh. Thus, Noah in the flood was not borne by the earth, nor by trees, nor by mountains, but by the very flood which destroyed the total remainder of the human race.

89. Well may the prophets often extol those wonderful works of God—the passage through the Red Sea, the exodus from Egypt, and the like. For the sea, which by its nature can only devour and destroy, is forced to part and rise and protect the Israelites, lest they be overwhelmed by its tides. That which in its very nature is wrath, becomes grace to the believer; that which in reality is death, becomes life. Therefore, whatever calamity comes—and this life has it in infinite measure—to threaten our property and our lives, it will all become salvation and joy if we only are in the ark; that is, if by faith we lay hold of the promise made in Christ. Then even death, by which we are removed, must be turned into life, and the hell, which swallows us, into a way to heaven.

90. Therefore Peter says (1 Pet 3, 21) that we are saved by the water in baptism, which was prefigured by the flood. The water which streams about us, or the plunge into it, is death, and yet from this death or plunge, life results by virtue of the ark of safety—the Word of promise to which we cling. The inspired Scriptures set forth this allegory, which is not only free from weaknesses but of service in every way, and worthy of our careful attention, since it offers wonderful consolation even in the utmost perils.

91. The fathers have added another allegory taken from the form and dimensions of the ark. The human body, measured from the top of the head to the sole of the foot, is six times as long as it is wide. Now, the ark, which was fifty cubits wide, measured six times as much in length, namely 300 cubits. Hence, they say, the ark typifies Christ the man, in whom all promises center. Therefore, those who believe in him are saved even in the midst of the flood, that is, in death itself.

92. This conception is both appropriate and beautiful; above all, it agrees with faith. Though there may be a mistake in the application, the groundwork is strong and secure. There is no doubt that the Holy Spirit found various ways to illustrate the promises to be fulfilled in Christ, and the wonderful counsel of salvation for mankind through faith in Christ. Hence, allegories of this nature, though lacking in aptness, are not necessarily wicked and a source of offense.

93. If one were to say the sun represents Christ, while the moon represents the Church, which receives its light by the grace of Christ, he might possibly be mistaken in his choice of illustration, yet his error is based, not upon an errone-

ous, but upon a sure foundation. But when the pope declares the sun represents the papal authority, while the moon represents the emperor's, then not only the application is inapt and foolish, but the very foundation is evil. Such allegories are not conceived and invented by the Holy Spirit, but by the devil, the spirit of lies.

94. Allegories must have some application to the promises and the doctrine of faith if they are to comfort and strengthen the soul. Peter's allegory teaches us this. Because Peter saw that Noah was set free in the midst of death and that the ark was an instrument of life, the ark was rightly applied to typify Christ. Only divine power can save in the midst of death and lead unto life. The Scriptures declare that to God belong the issues from death, (Ps 68, 21), and he makes death the occasion, yea, even an aid to life.

95. This has given rise to expressions used in Scripture, where afflictions and perils are likened to a cup that intoxicates. This is an apt and vivid figure of speech. So the passion of Christ is called a draught from a brook (Ps 110, 7), meaning that it is a medicinal draught or mixture, which, though bitter, is healing in its bitterness and gives life by causing death. Such soothing words serve to console us that we may learn to despise death and other perils and meet them with greater readiness.

96. Satan, also, has his cup; but it is sweet, and inebriates unto nausea. He who, attracted by its sweetness, drinks it, loses his life and dies the eternal death. Such was the cup the Babylonians drained, as the prophet has it (Jer 25, 15-27). Let us, therefore, accept the cup of salvation with thanksgiving, and, as Paul declares of believers, rejoice in tribulation (Rom 5, 3).

97. Having explained this figure of the ark and the meaning of the flood according to the canonical Scriptures, we will say something also about the other features of this story—about the raven which did not return, and the doves, the first of which returned because she found no resting-place for her foot, while the second brought back with her a twig from an olive tree, and the third did not return because the earth was no more covered by water.

98. In our treatise on the narrative proper, we stated that these things occurred to be a consolation for Noah and his sons; to assure them that God's wrath had passed and that he was now pacified. The dove did not bring the olive branch of her own volition. She miraculously obeyed divine power. So the serpent in paradise spoke, not of its own volition, but through the inspiration of the devil, who had taken possession of it. As, on that occasion, the serpent, by the devil's prompting, spoke, with the result that man was led into sin, so, on this occasion, it was not its own volition or instinct which moved the dove to bring the olive branch, but the prompting of God, in order that Noah might gain comfort from the pleasant sight. For the olive does not supply the dove with food; she prefers the several species of wheat or pease.

99. The incident of the dove, then, is a miraculous occurrence with a definite meaning. The prophets in their messages concerning the kingdom of Christ, frequently make mention of doves (Ps 68, 13) and (Is 60, 8). Solomon also in his Song seems to mention the dove with particular pleasure. Therefore, we should not despise the picture this allegory holds before us, but treat its truth skillfully

and aptly.

100. The allegory of the raven, invented by the doctors, is well known. Because ravens delight in eating dead bodies, they have been taken as a likeness of carnal men, who delight in carnal pleasures and indulge in them. The Epicureans were an example. A very fair explanation but inadequate, because it is merely of that moral and philosophical sort which Erasmus was in the habit of giving after the example of Origen.

101. We must look for a theological explanation. In the first place, those moralists fail to observe that Scripture commends the raven for not leaving the ark of his own will. He went out at the bidding of Noah, to ascertain if the waters had ceased and if God's wrath was ended. The raven, however, did not return, neither did he become a messenger of happy omen. He remained without the ark, and, though he came and went, yet he did not suffer himself to be taken by Noah.

102. In all these points the allegory fittingly typifies the ministry of the Law. Black, the color of the bird, is a token of sadness, and the sound of his voice is unpleasant. This is true of the teachers of the Law, who teach justification by works. They are the ministers of death and sin, Paul calling the ministry of the Law a ministry of death, (2 Cor 3, 6). The Law is unto death (Rom 7, 10). The Law worketh wrath. (Rom 4, 15.) The Law entered that trespass might abound. (Rom 5, 20).

103. And yet, Moses was sent forth by God with the Law, just as the raven was sent out by Noah. It is God's will that mankind be taught morality and holiness of life, and that wrath and sure punishments be announced to all who transgress the Law. Nevertheless, such teachers are naught but ravens wandering aimlessly about the ark; nor do they have the certain assurance that God is pacified.

104. For, the Law is a teaching of such character that it cannot assure, strengthen and console an uneasy conscience, but rather terrifies it, since it only teaches what God requires of us, what he wishes to be performed by us. Our consciences bear witness against us that we not only have failed to carry out the will of God as set forth in the Law, but that we have done the very contrary.

105. With all justice, therefore, we may say of the teachers of the Law, in the words of Psalms 5, 9: "There is no certainty in their mouth." Our translation has it "There is no faithfulness in their mouth." Their teaching at its best can only say: If you do this, if you do that, you will be saved. Christ speaks ironically when he answers the scribe who had grandly set forth the doctrine of the Law, by saying, "This do, and thou shalt live" (Lk 10, 28). He shows the scribe that the doctrine is holy and good, but since we are corrupt, it follows that we are guilty, since we do not, and cannot, fulfil the Law.

106. Hence, we declare rightly that we are not justified by the works of the Law. By the works of the Law we mean, not the ceremonial commandments, but those highest commandments of all, to love God and our neighbor. The reason we are not justified is that we cannot keep the commandments. We have reason, however, to challenge the impudence of our opponents who set up the cry that we forbid good works and condemn the Law of God because we deny that justification is by works. This would be true if we did not admit that the raven was sent

forth from the ark by Noah. But we do say that the raven was sent out from the ark. And this we deny, that it was not a raven, or that it was a dove. All the clamor, the abuse, the blasphemy of our opponents have no other purpose than to force us to declare that the raven was a dove.

107. But now examine their books and carefully consider their doctrine. Is it anything but a doctrine of works? This is good, this is honorable, they say; this you must do; the other is dishonorable and wicked, hence you must not do it. On the strength of such teaching, they believe themselves to be true theologians and doctors. But let them show us the person who either has done or will do all those things, especially if you present, not only the second table of the Law, as they do, but also the first one.

108. He who takes his stand upon this doctrine of the Law, then, is truly nothing but a hearer. He does not learn anything except its demands. Since such persons have no desire to learn anything further, it should suffice for them if they are given the poem of Cato, or given Esop, whom I consider a better teacher of morals. These two writers are profitable reading for young men. Older persons should study Cicero, who, to my astonishment, is considered by some as inferior to Aristotle in the sphere of ethics. This would be a rational course of study. So far as imparting moral precepts is concerned, the good intentions and the assiduity of the heathen must be commended. Yet they are inferior to Moses. He sets forth not only morality, but also teaches the true worship of God. Nevertheless, he who places his trust solely in Moses has nothing but the raven wandering aimlessly about outside of the ark. Of the dove and the olive branch, he has nothing.

109 The raven, then, represents not only the Law given by God, but all laws and all philosophy which are the product of human reason and wisdom. They tell us no more than what ought to be done and do not provide the strength to do it. The judgment of Christ is true: "When ye shall have done all the things that are commanded you, say, We are unprofitable servants" (Lk 17, 10).

110. True the raven is sent out. God desires the Law to be taught. He reveals it from heaven; yea, he writes it upon the hearts of all men, as Paul proves (Rom 2, 15). From this inherent knowledge originated all writings of the saner philosophers, of Esop, Aristotle, Plato, Xenophon, Cicero and Cato. And these are not unfit to set before untrained and vicious persons, that their vile tendencies may be curbed to some extent.

111. If, however, you seek for peace of conscience and for certain hope of eternal life, such philosophers are like the raven, which wanders around the ark, finding no peace outside, but not looking for it within. Paul says of the Jews, "Israel, following after a law of righteousness, did not arrive at that law" (Rom 9, 31). The reason for this is in the fact that the Law is like the raven; it is either the ministry of death and sin or it produces hypocrites.

112. Now, let those who wish, follow out this allegory by studying the nature of the raven. It is an impure bird, of somber and funereal color, with a strong beak and a harsh, shrill voice. It scents dead bodies from a great distance, and therefore men fear its voice as a certain augury of an impending death. It feeds upon carrion

and enjoys localities made foul by public executions.

113. Though I would not apply each and every one of these characteristics to the Law, yet who does not see how well they fit the servants of the Pope, the mass-priests and the monks, who were not only richly fed upon the slaughter of consciences by their false doctrines, but also used the dead bodies to obtain their livelihood, since they made a paying business out of their vigils, their anniversaries, their purifying water used in burials, and even of purgatory itself. And surely, this devotion to the dead was more profitable to them than their care of the living.

Truly, then, they are ravens, feeding on corpses and sitting upon them with wild cries. Not only may the popish priests be fitly likened to the ravens, but indeed the whole ministry of the papacy, where it is at its best, does nothing but to gash and murder consciences. It does not show the way to true righteousness, but merely makes hypocrites, as does the Law.

114. Among other crimes of false prophets, Ezekiel enumerates (ch 13, 19) the fact that, for handfuls of barley and for pieces of bread, they slay souls that should not die, and save the souls alive that should not live. This is true of these ravens, the teachers of the Law. They call those righteous who live according to the letter of the Law, and yet these are the very souls which do not live. On the other hand, they condemn those who violate their traditions, just as the Pharisees condemned the disciples when they plucked ears of corn, when they did not wash their hands and when they failed to fast. This is an outcry, fierce and dismal, reminding us of ravens which sit upon corpses.

115. When cursing a wicked person, the Greeks said, "To the ravens!" Similarly, the Germans use the expression, "May the ravens devour you." If we make this curse an element of the allegory, its serious character becomes evident. For what is more deplorably disastrous than to have teachers, the outcome of whose best teaching is death, and who ensnare the conscience with difficulties that cannot be disentangled? Though some say this allegory of the raven is inaptly applied to the priesthood, it is true nevertheless and agrees with the fundamental truth, and it is not only most apt, but very profitable for instruction.

116. On the other hand, the incident of the dove is a most delightful picture of the gospel, especially if you carefully consider the characteristics of the dove. Ten of these are usually enumerated: 1. It is without guile. 2. It does not harm with its mouth. 3. It does not harm with its claws. 4. It gathers pure grains. 5. It nourishes the young of others. 6. Its song is a sigh. 7. It abides by the waters. 8. It flies in flocks. 9. It nests in safe places. 10. Its flight is swift. These ten characteristics have been set forth in six verses, as follows:

> Free from guile is the dove; the bite of her beak does not injure;
> Wounds her claws do not strike; pure is the grain that she eats.
> Frequent and swift is her flight to shining courses of water.
> List to her voice, and lo! sighs you will hear but no song!
> Other nestlings she rears; in swarms she flies through the ether.
> Safe is the place and high where she prepares her abode.

117. The New Testament tells us the Holy Spirit appeared in the form of a dove

(Mt 3, 16). Hence, we are justified in using the dove as an allegory of the ministry of grace.

118. Moses implies that the dove did not fly aimlessly about the ark, as did the raven, but having been sent out and finding no place to rest, it returned to the ark and was seized by Noah.

119. This dove is a picture of the holy prophets sent to teach the people; but the flood, that is, the time of the Law, had not yet passed away. Thus David, Elias, Isaiah, though they did not live to see the time of the New Testament, were yet sent as messengers with the tidings that the flood would eventually be brought to an end, though that time was at a distance. Having delivered their message, they returned to the ark; that is, they were justified and saved without the Law, by faith in the blessed seed, in which they believed and for which they longed.

120. After this, another dove was sent forth, which found the earth dried, and not only the mountains, but also the trees, standing free from water. But she alighted upon an olive tree, plucked a branch, and brought it back to Noah.

121. The allegorical meaning of this incident is interpreted by the Scriptures. The olive tree is very often used as a symbol of grace, of mercy or of forgiveness of sins. The dove brings the branch in her beak, thus typifying the outward ministry, or the spoken Word. For the Holy Spirit does not teach by new revelations aside from the ministry of the Word, as the enthusiasts and Anabaptists, those truly fanatical teachers, dream. It was the will of God that a branch from a living olive tree should be carried to Noah in the mouth of the bird, to teach that in the New Testament, the time of the flood or anger being past, God desires to set his mercy before the world by the spoken Word.

122. The messengers of this Word are doves; that is, sincere men, without guile, and filled with the Holy Spirit. Isaiah 60, 8, likens ministers of the Gospel or of grace to doves which fly to their windows. And, though Christ commands them to imitate the harmlessness of doves, Mt 10, 16, meaning that they should be sincere and free from venom, yet, he admonishes them to be wise like serpents; that is, they should be wary of false and cunning people, and cautious like the serpent, which is said to shield its head with special skill in a fight.

123. The green freshness of the olive branch, also, is a type of the Word of the Gospel, which endureth forever and is never without fruit. Psalms 1, 3 likens those who study the Word to a tree, the leaves of which do not wither. We heard nothing like this above concerning the raven, which flew to and fro near the ark. This second dove which was sent forth is a type of the New Testament, where grace and the forgiveness of sins are promised openly through the sacrifice of Christ. This is why the Holy Spirit chose to appear in the form of a dove in the New Testament.

124. The third dove did not return. After the fulfilment of the promise given the whole world through the mouth of the dove, no new teaching is to be looked for, but we simply await the revelation of those things which we believe. Herein is certain testimony for us that the Gospel will endure unto the end of the world.

125. The text, furthermore, specifies the time Noah waited after he had first

sent forth a dove, namely, seven days. These seven days typify the time of the Law which, of necessity, preceded the period of the New Testament.

126. We read, likewise, that the second dove returned at dusk, carrying the olive branch. To the Gospel the last age of the world has been assigned. Nor should we look for another kind of doctrine, for it is to an evening meal that Christ compared the Gospel (Mt 22, 2; Lk 14, 16).

127. True, the doctrine of the Gospel has been in the world since the fall of our first parents, and the Lord confirmed this promise to the patriarchs by various signs. The first ages knew nothing of the rainbow, nor of circumcision, nor of other signs afterward ordained by God. But all ages have known of the blessed seed. Since it has been revealed, there remains nothing else than the revelation of that which we believe. With the third dove, we shall fly away to that other life, never to return to the life here, so wretched and so full of grief.

128. These are my thoughts concerning this allegory. I have set them forth briefly, for we must not tarry with them as we do with historical narratives and articles of faith.

129. Origen, Jerome, Augustine, and Bernard seek diligently for allegories. But this practice has one drawback. The more attention they direct to allegories, the more do they draw it away from the facts of sacred history and from faith, to the exclusion of these more important things. Allegories should be employed for the purpose of inducing and increasing, of explaining and strengthening, that faith of which all the stories treat. It is not to be wondered at, that persons who do not seek faith in the stories of the Bible, look for the region of allegorical shades as a pleasant playground in which to stroll about.

130. Just as in the popish Church false and unscriptural words are rendered in sweet music, so learned men have too often spoiled the good meaning of a Bible story, which contains a useful lesson of faith, by their childish allegories.

131. I have often spoken of the kind of theology that prevailed when I began to study. Its advocates said that the letter killeth (2 Cor 3, 6). Therefore I disliked Lyra most of all interpreters, because he followed the literal meaning so carefully. But now I prefer him, for this very reason, to all interpreters of Scripture.

132. I advise you as strongly as I can to fully appreciate the great value of the Bible history. But whenever you wish to employ allegory, take pains to follow the analogy of faith; that is, make the allegory agree with Christ, with the Church, with faith, with the ministry of the Gospel. If constructed in this manner, allegories will not go astray from faith, even though they may not be genuine in every point. This foundation shall remain firm, while the stubble perishes. But let us return to our story.

IV. NOAH AND HIS FALL.

A. NOAH.

1. Noah's character before the flood.
2. Noah's character after the flood.

3. Way Noah executed his office as bishop.

4. Way he executed his office as a civil ruler.

IV. NOAH AND HIS FALL.

A. Noah.

Vs. 20-22. *And Noah began to be a husbandman, and planted a vineyard; and he drank of the wine, and was drunken; and he was uncovered within his tent. And Ham, the father of Canaan, saw the nakedness of his father, and told his two brethren without.*

133. What manner of man Noah was during the flood, is shown sufficiently by the story of the flood itself. What manner of man he had been before the flood, is shown by Moses' declaration that he was righteous and perfect. Great as this man was, we hear nothing else about him, except that his wonderful and almost incredible continence is faintly suggested and commended by the statement that he begat his first born when five hundred years of age. This very fact shows that human nature was by far stronger in its integrity at that time, and that the Holy Spirit held more perfect sway in the holy men of the early world than He does in us who are, as it were, the dregs and the remnants of the world's production.

It surely was a commendatory record for Noah to be accorded righteous and perfect before God; that is, full of faith and of the Holy Spirit, adorned with chastity and all good works, pure in worship and religion, suffering many temptations from the devil, the world, and himself, all which he overcame triumphantly. Such was Noah before the flood.

134. Of his life after the flood, Moses tells us very little. But is it not apparent that so noble a man, living for about 350 years after the flood, could not be idle, but must have been busy with the government of the Church, which he alone established and ruled?

135. First of all, then, he performed the duties of a bishop. Beset with various temptations, his foremost endeavor was to resist the devil, to console the troubled ones, to bring back the erring to the true way, to strengthen the doubting, to cheer souls in despair, to exclude from his Church the impenitent, and to receive back with fatherly gladness the repentant. For, these are the duties a bishop must perform through the ministry of the Word.

136. Moreover, he had civil duties in establishing forms of government and in making laws, without which human passions cannot be held in check. To this was added the rule of his own household, or the care of his home.

B. NOAH'S FALL.

1. Why Moses omitted many important things about Noah and related his fall.

2. Lyra tries to excuse Noah's fall.

3. Noah's fall cannot be excused.

4. Noah's fall cannot be excused.

5. Ham scandalized himself through it.

a. Real root of this scandal.

b. Thereby Noah greatly sinned.

  * Original sin develops presumptuous people.

c. This scandal reveals Satan's bitterest enmity against God's Church.

  * Papists are Ham's disciples.

  * David's enemies rejoiced over his fall.

6. To what end should Noah's fall serve us.

* The godless are not worthy to see God's glory in believers.

* Why we should not be vexed at the infirmities of believers.

7. The conduct of Shem and Japheth in this connection.

a. They still honored their father, though they approved not his deed.

  * Origin of outward sin.

  * How to avoid offense.

  * Luther aware of his own infirmities.

  * Attitude of the opponents of the Word to true preachers.

  * Why Moses never mentioned many great events in Noah's life, and thought of his fall.

b. How the sons covered their father's shame.

c. Herein they had regard for God's will and were therefore pleasing to God.

  * Ham's scandal.

    (1) It was a wilful and grievous sin.

    (2) The lesson we may learn from it.

    (3) Reward of this scandalous deed, and why Canaan is here mentioned.

B. Noah's Fall.

137. Though reason tells us that Noah was burdened with these manifold duties after the flood, yet Moses does not mention them. It appears to him sufficient to confine his remarks to the statement that Noah began to plant a vineyard, and that he lay in his tent drunken and naked.

This, surely, is a foolish and very useless tale in comparison with the many praiseworthy acts he must have performed in the course of so many years. Other things might have been recorded for edification and for teaching righteousness of life. But this story even seems to endorse an offense, by abetting drunkards and those who sin in drunkenness.

138. The purpose of the Holy Spirit, however, is apparent from what we have said. It is to console by this record of the great sins committed by the holiest and most perfect patriarchs those righteous persons who are discouraged by the

knowledge of their own weakness and are, therefore, cast down. In them we are to find proofs of our own shortcomings, that we may come to humble confession and, at the same time, seek and hope for forgiveness. This is the real and theologically true reason why the Holy Spirit records, rather than seemingly more important matters, the great fall of this grand man.

139. Lyra states as excuse for Noah that he knew not the power of wine and was deceived into drinking a little too freely. Whether wine had been known before or whether Noah began to cultivate it by his own skill and by divine suggestion, I know not, but I believe that Noah knew the nature of this produce quite well, and that he had often made use of wine in company with his family, partly for his own person and partly also in his offerings or libations. I think that in making use of wine for his own refreshment, he partook of it too freely.

140. His action I excuse in no way. Should anyone want to do so, there would be weightier arguments than those Lyra uses. According to him this aged man, tired out by the great number of his daily duties and cares, had been overpowered by the wine although he was already used to it. For wine overcomes more easily those who are either exhausted by much work or burdened with age. Persons of mature age, on the other hand, and such of care-free mind, can drink considerable quantities of wine without greatly impairing their reason.

141. But he who makes this excuse for the patriarch, wilfully casts aside that consolation which the Holy Spirit considered needful for the Church, that even the greatest saints sometimes fall into sin.

142. Transgression like this may seem to be slight, yet it causes great offense. Not only is Ham offended, but also the other brother, possibly also their wives. And we must not imagine that Ham was a boy of seven years. Having been born when Noah was five hundred years old, he had reached an age of at least one hundred years and had one or two children of his own.

143. Hence, it was not boyish thoughtlessness which caused Ham to laugh at his father, as boys will do when surrounding a drunken rustic in the street and making sport of him. He was truly offended by his father's sin and thought himself to be more righteous, holy and religious than his father. Noah's deed was an offense not only in appearance, but in very truth, since Ham was so far tempted by the knowledge of it that he passed judgment upon Noah, and found in such sin an occasion for mirth.

144. If we wish to judge Ham's sin aright, we must take into account original sin, that is, the wickedness of the heart. This son would never have derided his father for being overcome by wine had he not first dismissed from his soul that reverence and esteem which God's commandment requires children to cherish toward their parents.

145. Noah had been considered a fool before the flood, by the majority of mankind, and had been condemned as a false teacher and despised as a man of wild ideas. Now he is laughed at by his son as a fool, and condemned as a sinner. Noah was sole governor of the Church and State, and ruled his own household with tireless care and labor. He had doubtless therein offended the proud and haughty

spirit of his son in many ways. But the depravity of his heart which now, that the father's sin had become manifest, leaped to the surface, had so far been successfully concealed.

146. When we consider the source of Ham's sin, its hideousness first appears in its true light. One never becomes an adulterer or commits murder until he has first cast out of his heart the fear of God. A pupil does not rebel against his teacher unless he has first lost due reverence for that teacher. The fourteenth Psalm, verse 2, says that Jehovah looked down from heaven upon the children of men, to see if there were any that did understand, and that did seek after God. When he saw there was none he adds there was none who did good; that they had all become worthless, sinning tongues, sinning with their hands, fearing where there was no need of fear, and the like.

147. So Ham, in his own estimation, was wise and holy. In his judgment his father had often acted unrighteously or foolishly. His attitude discloses a heart that despised, not only the parent, but also the divine commandment. Hence, nothing remains for the evil-minded son but to grasp an opportunity for obtaining evidence to betray his father's foolishness. He does not laugh at his drunken father as a boy would, nor does he call his brethren merely that they may look upon a laughable spectacle. He means that this shall be open proof that God has withdrawn from his father and has accepted himself. Therefore, he takes delight in disclosing his father's sin to others. As I said before, Ham was not a boy of seven years, but had reached the age of at least one hundred.

148. Original sin shows its depraving tendency in that it makes men arrogant, haughty and conceited. Paul admonishes in Romans 12, 3, to think of one's self soberly, "according as God hath dealt to each man a measure of faith." But, original sin does not permit Ham to occupy this lowly level; hence, he presumes to go beyond his station in passing judgment upon his father.

149. We observe the same attitude in Absalom. Before he stirs up a rebellion against David, his father, he passes unrighteous judgment upon David's government. This dissatisfaction with his father's rule was afterward followed by unconcealed contempt and open violence, with David's destruction as the object. Ham's heart being full of poison which he had gathered from his father as a spider gathers poison from the fairest rose, precisely such a result had to follow.

150. These examples serve to call our attention to the battle waged from the beginning of the world between the Church and Satan with his followers, the hypocrites, or false brethren. This deed of Ham must not be looked upon as a result of boyish love of pranks, but of Satan's most bitter enmity, wherewith he inflames his followers against the Church. Particularly does he incite them against those in the ministry, leading them to close watch at all times for material available for purposes of slander.

The Papists at present have no other business than to watch our conversation for the purpose of slander. Whenever we fall into human error (for we are truly weak and are beset by our failings), they seize upon our moral uncleanness, like famished swine, and find great delight in publishing and betraying our weaknesses, like Ham the accursed. They truly hunger and thirst after our offenses. Although by God's grace they cannot fasten adultery, murder or like errors upon us, unless by their own fabrication (this shameless class of people abhor no kind of lie), yet they gather up smaller matters, which they afterward exaggerate to the public.

151. David's experience is well known. He was surrounded on all sides by enemies who eagerly sought out every opportunity for persecution. They were envious because he had been called to the throne by God; hence, they triumphed over his horrible fall.

152. His case, however, serves for our instruction. God sometimes permits even righteous and holy men to stumble and fall into offenses, either really or apparently, and we must take heed lest we pass judgment at once, after the example of Ham, who, having secretly despised his father long before, now does so openly. He declared that his parent, being imbecile by age, had clearly been deserted by the Holy Spirit, since he was unable to guard against drunkenness, though the government of the Church, State, and household lay upon his shoulders. O wretched Ham, how happy art thou, having found at last what thou soughtest—poison in a most delightful rose!

153. Everlasting praises and blessings be given to God, whose dealings with his saints are wonderful indeed. While he permits them to be weak and to fall, to be overwhelmed with disgrace and offenses, and while the world judges and condemns them, he forgives them their weaknesses and has compassion upon them; whereas he delivers into Satan's hands those who regard themselves angels, and utterly rejects them.

The first lesson of this story is that godly persons have the needed consolation against their infirmities when they see that even the holiest men sometimes fell most disgracefully by reason of similar infirmities.

154. In the second place, the case of Ham is a fearful example of divine judgment, to teach us by Ham's experience not to condemn at once, even when we see rulers of State, Church, or household—such as our parents—fall into error and sin. Who can tell why God so permits? Such sins must not be excused, yet we see that they are of value for the consolation of the pious. They teach us that God can bear with the errors and sins of his people and that even we, when beset with sins, may trust in the mercy of God and need not lose heart.

155. But what is medicine for the righteous, is poison for the wicked. The latter do not seek to be taught and comforted by God. Their unworthiness prevents them from recognizing his glory in the saints. They see nothing but the stumbling block and the snare, with the result that they fall and are left to perish alone.

156. Let us, therefore, truly respect those in authority over us. If they fall, we must not be offended. We must remember that they are human, and that God's ways are wonderful in his saints, because it is his will that the wicked shall be offended and provoked. Thus Moses threatens the Jews: "I will provoke them to anger with a foolish nation" (Deut 32, 21). Because, during the whole period of the kingdom, they refused to hear the prophets, God gave the offense of casting away

a wise and religious people, which had the promises and was descended from the patriarchs. In its place, he chose the filth and dregs of the world, a foolish people; that is, it was without piety, without religion, without worship, without that divine wisdom which is his Word. This offense roused the Jews to insane anger.

157. This will be the lot of the papists. Some great offense shall be given them by God against which they shall find themselves helpless, and thus they shall come to grief like Ham. Renouncing the reverence due both to God and his father, in deeming himself more capable of ruling the Church than Noah, in secretly deriding or censuring his parent, he finally presents the spectacle of disclosing his wicked and irreverent attitude before others.

158. The two other brothers, Shem and Japheth, did not follow Ham's wicked example. While conscious of the scandalous fact that their father was drunk and lay in shameless nakedness like a little boy,—while recognizing that this ill became the ruler of Church and State, they remained mindful of the reverence due a parent. They gulped down the offense given; they hid the offense and gave it a worthier aspect, so to speak, by covering their father with a garment, approaching him with eyes averted. They would have been incapable of this fine outward expression of reverence for their father, had they not occupied a correct attitude toward God in their hearts and believed their father to be both priest and ruler by right divine.

159. It is a fearful example, this one of Ham. Though one of the few saved during the flood, he forgets all piety. It is profitable to carefully consider how he came to fall. Outward sins must first be committed in our minds; that is, before sins are visibly committed, the heart first departs from the Word and from the fear of God. It neither knows God nor seeks after him, as we read in Psalms 14, 2. As soon as the heart begins to set aside the Word, and to despise the ministers and prophets of God, ambition and pride follow. Those who stand in the way of our desires are overborne by hatred and slander, until finally insolent speech ends in murder.

160. Those who are to become rulers of Church or State, should daily pray earnestly to God that they may remain humble. It is the object of stories of this character to set this duty before us, for it is evident what occasioned Ham's frightful fall.

161. If, then, the saints fall into sin, let us not be offended. Much less should we rejoice over the weakness of others, haughtily esteeming ourselves braver, wiser, or holier than they. Let us rather endure and cover up, and even put a good construction upon and excuse such errors in so far as we can, remembering that perhaps tomorrow we may suffer what happened to them today. For we all constitute a unit, being born of the same flesh. Let us then heed the advice of Paul, "Let him that thinketh he standeth, take heed lest he fall" (1 Cor 10, 12). In this way the other two brothers looked upon their drunken father. Their thoughts were these: Behold, our father has fallen. But God is wonderful in his dealing with saints, whom he sometimes permits to fall for our instruction, that we may not despair when afflicted by kindred infirmity.

162. Let us imitate their wisdom! The sins of others give us no right to judge

them. Before their own master they stand or fall (Rom 14, 4). Furthermore, if the downfall of others displease us (since, in truth, many acts neither can nor ought to be excused), let us be so much the more careful lest something like it overtake ourselves. Let us not sit in proud and haughty judgment, for this is original sin in all its corruption: To lay claim to exceptional wisdom and to hunt for the moral lapses of others in order to gain the reputation of righteousness for ourselves.

163. We truly are weak sinners and must freely confess, being human, that our conversation is not always free from offense. But while we share this weakness with our enemies, we nevertheless do our duty diligently, by spreading God's Word, by teaching the churches, by bettering the evil, by urging the right, by consoling the weak, by chiding the stubborn, and, in brief, by doing whatever duty God lays upon us.

164. On the other hand since our adversaries strive after nothing but hypocrisy and an outward show of holiness, so they add to the frailty which they have in common with us, the most grievous sins, because they do not follow their calling, but concern themselves with their honors and emoluments. They neglect the churches and suffer them to miserably decay. They condemn the true doctrine and teach idolatry. In short, in public life they are wise, but in their own sphere they are utterly foolish. This is the most destructive evil in the Church.

165. This is the first part of the story, and, in the preparation of his record, Moses has confined himself to the same. It is certain that Noah was a righteous man, gifted with many heroic virtues, and that he accomplished most important things both for the Church and for the State. It is not possible either to establish political communities or to found churches except by diligent effort. Life, in both these manifestations (I will say nothing of the management of the home) is beset with many dangers; for Satan, a liar and murderer, is the most relentless enemy of Church and State.

166. But Moses passes by all these achievements, not so much as alluding to them. He records but this one circumstance—that Noah became drunk and was scoffed at by his youngest son. He intended it as a valuable example, teaching pious souls to trust in God's mercy. On the other hand, the proud, the lovers of cant, the sanctimonious, the wise-acres,—let them learn to fear God and beware of passing a reckless judgment upon others! As Manasseh the king declares, God displays in his saints both his wonders and his terrors "against wicked and sinful men." This is illustrated in the case of Ham, who did not now first come to his downfall but had cherished this hate against his father for a long time, afterward to fill the world with idolatry.

Vs. 23-27. *And Shem and Japheth took a garment, and laid it upon both their shoulders, and went backward, and covered the nakedness of their father; and their faces were backward, and they saw not their father's nakedness. And Noah awoke from his wine, and knew what his youngest son had done unto him. And he said, Cursed be Canaan; a servant of servants shall he be unto his brethren.*

167. It is truly a beautiful and memorable example of respect to a father which Moses records in this passage. The sons might without sin have approached their

father and covered him, while turning their faces toward him. What sin should it be if one, happening upon a nude person, should see what is before him without his will? Still the two sons do not do this. When they heard from their haughty and mocking brother what had happened to their father, they laid a garment upon both their shoulders, entered the tent with faces turned away (how admirable!), and lowering the garment backward, covered their father.

168. Who can fail to observe here the thoughtfulness of the will and Word of God, and reverence before the majesty of fatherhood, which God requires to be honored, not despised or mocked by children? God seems to approve this reverence and accept it as a most pleasing offering and the very noblest worship and obedience. But his utmost hatred rests upon Ham, who might have seen without sin what he saw, since it came to his view by chance, if only he had covered it up, if only he had remained silent about it, if only he had not shown himself to be pleased by the sin of his father. But he who despised God, the Word, and the order established by God, not only failed to cover his father with a garment, but even derided him and left him naked.

169. In describing the act of the two brothers Moses emphasizes the malice of Ham, who was filled with violent and satanic hatred against his father. Who of us, on finding a stranger lying by the wayside drunk and nude, would not at least cover him with his own coat to forestall disgrace? How much greater the demand in this case of a father! Ham, however, fails to do for his father, the highest ruler of the world, what common humanity teaches us to do for strangers. Moreover he publishes the circumstance joyfully, insulting his drunken father and making the sin of his father known to his brothers as if he had a piece of good news.

170. Moses, therefore, sets Ham before us as a fearful example, to be carefully taught in the churches, in order that young people may learn to respect their elders, rulers, and parents. Not on account of Noah, not on account of Ham, but on account of those to come—on our account—is this story written, and Ham, with his contempt for God and father, pictured in most repulsive colors.

171. Also the punishment of this wickedness is carefully set before us. Noah, looked upon by his son as a foolish, insane, and ridiculous old man, now steps forth in the majesty of a prophet, to announce to his son a divine revelation of future events. Truly does Paul declare that "power is made perfect in weakness" (2 Cor 12, 9); for the certainty characterizing Noah's utterance is proof that he was filled with the Holy Spirit, notwithstanding that his son had mocked and despised him as one utterly deserted by the Holy Spirit.

172. I will not attempt here to settle the question above referred to (ch 5, §95) concerning the order of the sons of Noah, as to which of them was the first-born and which the youngest. A point more worthy of our attention is the fact that the Holy Spirit is so filled with strong wrath against that disobedient and scornful son that he does not even choose to call him by his own name, but calls him Canaan after the name of his son. Some say that, because God had desired to save Ham in the ark as one under his blessing the same as the others, he had no wish to curse him, but cursed Canaan instead, a curse which, nevertheless, could not but recoil

upon Ham who had provoked it. Thus Ham's name perishes here, since the Holy Spirit hates it, whose hatred is, indeed, a serious hatred. We read in the psalm, "I hate them with perfect hatred" (Ps 139, 22). When the Holy Spirit exercises his wrath, eternal death must follow.

173. Although Ham had sinned against his father in many ways, it is remarkable that the fruit of the first sin and the devil's malice did not become manifest until the father lay drunk and bare. When, with this sin, the previous ones had attained to fullness of power and growth, the Holy Spirit condemned him, and, as a warning to others, also announced the infliction of impending, endless servitude.

V. 26. *And he said, Blessed be Jehovah, the God of Shem; and let Canaan be his servant.*

These are two sublime prophecies, worthy of close attention. They have significance in our time, though they were grossly garbled by the Jews. The Jews observe that Ham is cursed thrice; this fact they wrest to the glory of their own nation, promising themselves worldly dominion.

V. HAM CURSED; SHEM AND JAPHETH BLESSED.
A. THE CURSE PRONOUNCED UPON HAM.

1. Why Ham was thrice cursed.
* Disrespect of parents, pastors and authority signs of approaching misfortune.
2. Way Ham disregarded the curse.
3. Why Ham disregarded the curse.
4. Ham's temporal prosperity continued with his curse.
* Faith alone grasps God's threatenings and promises.
* Reason God postpones punishment and reward.
* The Papal Church is not the true Church.
* Believers have comfort in their tribulations.
* The pious have their kingdom here in faith.
5. From this curse it is clear Noah was enlightened by the Holy Spirit.
* Were all Ham's descendents cursed?.

B. BLESSING PRONOUNCED UPON SHEM.

1. This is an exceedingly great blessing.
2. Why is it clothed in praise to God.
3. This blessing proves that Noah possessed a precious light.

C. BLESSING PRONOUNCED UPON JAPHETH.

1. Why the form of Japheth's blessing differed from that of Shem's.
2. Herein lies a special secret.
3. The Jews' false interpretation of this blessing.
4. Relation of these two blessings to each other.

* The Jews' false notion about Shem's blessing.
5. The order in which these blessings are enjoyed.
* The form God's Church takes in this world.
* Divine promises and threatenings to be understood in a spiritual sense.
* Ham and Cain resemble one another in their positions and works.
* The Turk and the Pope.
    a. What strengthens them in their opposition to the true Church.
    * How a Christian should conduct himself in times of misfortunes.
    b. The power and advantages of the Turk and Pope of no avail.
    c. Attitude of Church members to their pride.
    * Why Ham's name was not mentioned when he was cursed.
6. The word dilatet the Latins use in explaining Japheth's blessing.
    a. It is not in harmony with the Hebrew.
    b. Why all Latin interpreters use it.
    c. It does not fully express the sense of the Holy Spirit.
    d. What explanation should be given here.
7. All descendents of Japheth partake of this blessing through the Gospel.
8. Translations of Latin interpreters of this blessing are to be harmonized with the original text.
* Ham's name.
    a. Its meaning and reason his parents gave it to him.
    b. The hope of his parents in this name disappointed.
9. It is ascribed to this promise that Germany in these last days received the light of the Gospel.
* Abraham had Noah as his teacher.
* The temporal prosperity of Ham's family, and their wickedness.

V. HAM CURSED; SHEM AND JAPHETH BLESSED.

A. The Curse Pronounced Upon Ham.

174. But there is another reason for this repeatedly uttered curse. God cannot forget such great irreverence toward parents, nor does he suffer it to go unpunished. He requires that parents and rulers be regarded with reverence. He requires that elders be honored, commanding that one shall rise up before a hoary head (Lev 19, 32). And, speaking of ministers of the Word, he says, "He that despiseth you, despiseth me" (Mt 10, 40; Lk 10, 16).

175. Hence disobedience of parents is a sure indication that curse and disaster are close at hand. Likewise is contempt of ministers and of rulers punished. When the people of the primitive world began to deride the patriarchs and to hold their

authority in contempt, the flood followed. When, among the people of Judah, the child began to behave himself proudly against the old man, as Isaiah has it (ch 3, 5), Jerusalem was laid waste and Judah went down. Such corruption of morals is a certain sign of impending evil. We justly fear for Germany a like fate when we look upon the prevailing disrespect for authority.

176. Let us, however, bear witness of a practice to which both Holy Writ and our experience testify. Because God delays the threatened punishment he is mocked and considered a liar. In this practice we should see the seal, as it were, to every prophecy. Ham hears that he is accursed; but inasmuch as the curse does not go into immediate effect, he securely despises and derides the same.

177. Thus did the first world hold Noah's prophecy in ridicule when he spoke of the flood. Had they believed that such a punishment was close at hand, would they have gone on in a feeling of security? Would they not rather have repented and begun a better life? If Ham had believed that to be true which he heard from his father, he would have sought refuge in mercy and, confessing his crime, craved forgiveness. But he did neither; rather did he haughtily leave his father, to go to Babylon. There, with his posterity, he gave himself up to the building of a city and of a tower, and made himself lord of all Greater Asia.

178. What is the reason for this feeling of security? It lies in the fact that divine prophecies must be believed; they cannot be perceived by our senses, or by experience. This is true both of divine promises and of divine threats. Therefore the opposite always seems to the flesh to be true.

179. Ham is cursed by his father; but he lays hold upon the greater portion of the earth and establishes vast kingdoms. On the other hand, Shem and Japheth are blessed, but in comparison with Ham, they and their posterity are beggarly.

Where then are we to seek the truth of this prophecy? I answer: This prophecy and all others, whether they be promises or threats, cannot be understood by reason, but by faith alone. God delays both punishments and rewards; hence there is need of endurance. For "He that endureth to the end, the same shall be saved," as Christ says (Mt 24, 13).

180. The life of all pious people is wholly of faith and hope. The evidence of our senses, history, and the way of the world, would teach us the opposite. Ham is cursed, yet he alone obtains dominion. Shem and Japheth are blessed, yet they alone bear reproach and affliction. Since both the promises and the threats of God reach out into the future, the issue must be awaited in faith. Habakkuk says (ch 2, 3), "It will surely come, it will not delay."

181. Great is the wrath of the Holy Spirit which here prompts him to say of Ham, "A servant of servants shall he be;" that is, the lowest and vilest of slaves. But if you let history speak, you will see Ham rule in Canaan, whereas Abraham, Isaac, and Jacob, and others who followed, and had the blessing, lived like servants among the Canaanites. The Egyptians are Ham's offspring, and how cruel was the servitude Israel suffered there!

182. How, then, was it true that Ham was cursed and Shem was blessed? In

this way: The fulfillment of the promise and of the threat was in the future. This delay is ordained in order that the wicked may fill their measure of sin and may not be able to accuse God of having given them no room for repentance. On the other hand, when the righteous suffer at the hands of the unrighteous and become the servants of servants, they undergo such trial and discipline for the purpose of increasing in faith and in love toward God; so that, trained in manifold vexations and tribulations, they may attain the promise.

When the time was fulfilled, the might of Ham's posterity was not great enough to withstand the posterity of Shem. Then, indeed, was fulfilled that curse which Ham and his posterity had so long despised and disbelieved.

183. It is much the same with us today. We have the true doctrine and the true worship. Hence we can boast that we are the true Church, having the promise of spiritual blessings in Christ. As the pope's church condemns our doctrine, we know her to be not the Church of Christ but of Satan, and truly, like Ham, a "servant of servants." And yet anyone may see that the pope rules, while we are servants and the off-scouring, as Paul says (1 Cor 4, 12).

184. What, then, shall we poor, oppressed people do? We are to comfort our souls meanwhile with our spiritual dominion. We know we have forgiveness of sins and a gracious God, through Christ, until also temporal freedom shall be vouchsafed on the last day. And we are not without traces of temporal freedom even in this life; for while tyrants stubbornly oppose the Gospel, they are cut off from the earth, root and branch.

185. So was the Roman empire destroyed after all the other world-powers perished; but God's Word and Church remain forever. Likewise, Christ weakens the Pope's power, little by little; but that he may be utterly removed and become a servant of servants with wicked Ham is a matter for faith to await. Ham is shut out from the kingdom of God and possesses the kingdoms of the world for a time, just as the pope is shut out from the Church of God and holds temporal dominion for a time. But his dominion shall vanish.

186. The divine law and order is that the righteous have dominion, but by faith, being satisfied with such spiritual blessing as a gracious God and the certain hope of the heavenly kingdom. Meanwhile, we leave possession of the kingdoms of the world to the wicked until God shall scatter also their worldly power, and, through Christ, make us heirs of all things.

187. Furthermore, we learn from this prophecy that Noah, by a special illumination of the Holy Spirit, was enabled to see, in the first place, that his posterity would remain forever, and in the second place, that the family of Ham, though they were to be rulers for a time, would perish at last and above all would lose the spiritual blessing.

188. However, the explanation given above (ch 4, §182) with reference to the descendants of Cain, applies also here. I do not entertain the opinion that the off-spring of Ham were doomed, without exception. Some found salvation by being converted to faith, but such salvation was not due to a definite promise but to uncovenanted grace, so to speak. Likewise the Gibeonites and others were saved

when the children of Israel occupied the land of Canaan. Job, Naaman the Syrian, the people of Nineveh, the widow of Zarephath, and others from the heathen were saved, not by virtue of a promise, but by uncovenanted grace.

B. Blessing Pronounced Upon Shem.

189. But why does Noah not say, "Blessed be Shem," instead of, "Blessed be Jehovah, the God of Shem"? I answer that it is because of the magnitude of the blessing. The reference here is not to a temporal blessing, but to the future blessing through the promised seed. He sees this blessing to be so great that he cannot express it; hence, he turns to thanksgiving. It seems that Zacharias was thinking of this very passage when he said, for a similar reason, "Blessed be the Lord, the God of Israel" (Lk 1, 68).

190. Noah's blessing takes the form of thanksgiving unto God. God, he says, is blessed, who is the God of Shem. In other words: It is needless for me to extend my blessing over Shem, who has been blessed before with spiritual blessing; he already is a child of God, and from him the Church will be continued, as it was continued from Seth before the flood. Full of wonderful meaning is the fact that Noah joins God with Shem, his son, and, as it were, unites them.

191. Noah's heart must have been divinely illumined since he makes such a distinction between his sons, rejecting Ham with his posterity and placing Shem in line with the saints and the Church because the spiritual blessing, given in paradise concerning the seed, would rest upon him. Therefore, this holy man blesses God and gives thanks unto him.

C. Blessing Pronounced Upon Japheth.

V. 27. *God enlarge Japheth, and let him dwell in the tents of Shem; and let Canaan be his servant.*

192. This prophecy is wonderful for the aptness of each single word. Noah did not bless Shem, but the God of Shem, by way of giving thanks to God for having embraced Shem and having adorned him with a spiritual promise, or the blessing of the woman's seed. But when he mentions Japheth he does not employ the same manner of speaking as in the case of Shem. His words are chosen for the purpose of showing the mystery of which Paul speaks (Rom 11, 11) and Christ (Jn 4, 22), that salvation is from the Jews and yet the gentiles also became partakers of this salvation. Shem alone is the true root and stem, yet the heathen are grafted upon this stem, as a foreign branch, and become partakers of the fatness and the sap which are in the chosen tree.

193. Noah, seeing this through the Holy Spirit, predicts, in dim allusions but correctly, that Christ's kingdom is to spread in the world from the root of Shem, and not from that of Japheth.

194. The Jews prate that Japheth stands for the neighboring nations around Jerusalem which were admitted to the temple and its worship. But Noah makes little ado about the temple of Jerusalem, or the tabernacle of Moses; his words refer to greater matters. He treats of the three patriarchs who are to replenish the earth.

While he affirms of Japheth that he does not belong to the root of the people of God which possesses the promise of the Christ, he declares that he shall be incorporated through the call of the Gospel into the fellowship of that people which has God and the promises.

195. Here, then, we have a picture of the Church of the Gentiles and of the Jews. Ham, being wicked, is not admitted to the spiritual blessing of the seed, except as it happens by uncovenanted grace. To Japheth, however, though he has not the promise of the seed, like Shem, the hope is nevertheless given that he will, at some future time, be taken into the fellowship of the Church. Thus we Gentiles, being sons of Japheth, have no direct promise, indeed, and yet we are included in the promise given to the Jews, since we are predestined to the fellowship of the holy people of God. These matters are here recorded, not for Shem and Japheth so much as for their posterity.

196. We learn why the Jews are so haughty and boastful. They see that Shem, their father, alone has the promise of eternal blessing, which is given through Christ. So far, so good. But when they believe that the promise pertains not to faith but rather to the carnal descent, they are in error. This subject has been splendidly treated by Paul (Rom 9, 6). There he establishes the fact that the children of Abraham are not his carnal descendants but those who have his faith (Gal 3, 7).

197. The same thought is suggested here by Moses, who says in so many words, "Blessed be Jehovah, the God of Shem." This shows that there is no blessing except by the God of Shem. Hence, no Jew will share this blessing unless he have the God of Shem; that is, unless he believes. Nor will Japheth share the blessing unless he dwells in the tents of Shem, that is, unless he associates himself with him in faith.

198. This is a grand promise, valid unto the end of the world. But just as it is limited to those who have the God of Shem, that is, who believe, so the curse also is limited to those who abide in the wickedness of Ham. Noah spoke these words, not on the strength of human authority and feeling, but by the Spirit of God. His words then refer not to a temporal, but to a spiritual and eternal curse. Nor must we understand him to speak of a curse that is a curse only in the sight of the world, but rather of one in the sight of God.

199. The same statement has been made heretofore (ch 4 §182) regarding the curse of Cain. Judged by outward appearances, Cain obtained a greater earthly blessing than Seth. God desires that his Church in this world shall apparently suffer the curse pronounced upon the wicked and that, on the other hand, the wicked shall seem to be blessed. Cain was the first man to build a city, calling it Enoch; while Seth dwelt in tents.

200. Thus did Ham build the city and tower of Babel and ruled far and wide, while Shem and Japheth were poor, living in lowly tents. The facts of history, then, teach that both the promises and the curses of God are not to be understood carnally, or of the present life, but spiritually. Although oppressed in the world, the righteous are surely heirs and sons of God, while the wicked, though flourishing for a season, shall ultimately be cut down and wither; a warning often uttered in the Psalms.

201. There is a striking similarity in the conduct and the lot of Cain and Ham. Cain killed his brother, which shows plainly enough the lack of reverence for his father in his heart. Having been put in the ban by his father, he leaves the Church of the true God and the true worship, builds the city of Enoch, giving himself up altogether to worldly things. Just so does Ham sin by dishonoring his father. When also he subsequently receives as sentence the curse whereby he is excluded from the promised seed and the Church, he parts with God and the Church without misgivings, since the curse rests not upon his person but upon that of his son, and migrates to Babylon, where he establishes a kingdom.

202. These are very illustrious examples and needed by the Church, Turk and Pope today; allow us to boast of the heavenly and everlasting promise in that we have the Gospel doctrine, and are the Church. They know, however, our judgment of them, that we consider and condemn both Pope and Turk as very Antichrist. How securely they ignore our judgment, confidently because of the wealth and power they possess, and also because of our weakness in character and numbers. The very same spirit we plainly see in Cain and Ham, in the condemned and excommunicated.

203. These truths enforce the lesson that we must not seek an abiding city or country in this bodily existence, but in its varying changes and fortunes look to the hope of eternal life, promised through Christ. This is the final haven; and we must strive for it with sail and oar, as eager and earnest sailors while the tempest rages.

204. What if the Turk should obtain sway over the whole world, which he never will? Michael, as Daniel says, will bring aid to the holy people, the Church (ch 10, 13). What matter if the Pope should gain possession of the wealth of all the world, as he has tried to do for many centuries with all the wealth at his command? Will Turk and Pope thereby escape death, or even secure permanence of temporal power? Why, then, should we be misled by the temporal blessings which they enjoy, or by our misfortunes and dangers, since we know that they are banished from the fellowship of the saints, while we enjoy everlasting blessings through the Son of God?

205. If Cain and Ham, and Pope and Turk, who are as father and son to each other, can afford to despise the judgment of the true Church on the strength of fleeting and meager successes in this life, why can not we afford in turn to despise their power and censure, on the strength of the everlasting blessings which we possess? Ham was not moved by his father's curse. Full of anger against him, and despising him as a crazy old man, he goes away and arms himself with the power of the world, esteeming this more highly than to be blessed with Shem by his father.

206. This story should give us strength for the similar experiences of today. The priests and bishops heap contempt upon us, saying, What can those poverty stricken heretics do? Priest and bishop are puffed up with their wealth and power. But let us bear this insolence of the wicked with undisturbed mind, as Noah bore that of his son. Let us take consolation in the hope and faith of the eternal benediction, of which, we know, they are deprived.

207. I said above (§172) that the Holy Spirit was so greatly angered by the sin of Ham that he could not bear even to speak his name in the curse. And it is true, as the punishment shows, that Ham sinned grievously. The other reason mentioned above as not at all unlikely, I will here repeat: Ham had been called and received into the ark by the divine Word, and had been saved with the others, and Noah wanted to spare him whom God had spared in the flood. Therefore, he transferred the curse which Ham merited, to Canaan, his son, whom Ham doubtless desired to keep with him.

208. The Jews offer a different explanation: Canaan, the son, having been the first to see his grandfather Noah lying naked, announced it to his father, who then saw for himself; hence, Canaan gave his father cause to commit the sin. Let the reader judge what value there is in this exposition.

209. But there is also a philological question which must be discussed in connection. Scholars call translators to account for the rendering, "God enlarge Japheth," when the Hebrew words do not permit it, though not only the Hebrews but also the Chaldeans, are mostly agreed that the word *jepheth* means "to enlarge." Technical discussions of this kind, however, are sometimes very useful to clear up the precise meaning of a passage.

210. Some scholars derive the name *Japheth* from the verb *jephah*, which signifies *to be beautiful*, as in Ps 45, 2: *japhjaphita mibene Adam*, "Thou art fairer than the children of men." But this may easily be shown to be an error; for the true origin of the word is the verb *phatah*, which means "to persuade," "to deceive with fair words" as in Ex 22 16: *ki jephateh isch betulah*, "If a man entice a virgin, he shall surely pay a dowry for her." And in Jer 20, 7: *pethithani jehovah va-epath*, "O Jehovah, thou hast persuaded me and I was persuaded;" Prov 1, 10: *Im-jephatukah*, "If sinners entice thee." There is no need of more examples, for the word occurs frequently, and I have no doubt that it is derived from the Greek word *peitho*, for it has the same meaning.

211. But let us turn to the question: Why have all translators made it read, "God enlarge Japheth," while it is not the word *pathach*, which means "to enlarge" or "to open", but rather the word *pathah*? I have no doubt that the translators were influenced by the harsh expression. Since this is a promise, it seemed too harsh to state that Noah had said, "God deceive Japheth." This would appear to be a word of cursing, not of blessing. Hence they chose a milder term, though it violated the rules of language. And since there is but a slight difference between *pathach*, and *pathah*, they used one for the other. They meant to preserve the important fact that this is a promise.

212. But there is no need for us to alter the text in this manner, and to violate its grammatical construction, since the word *pathah*, offers a most suitable meaning. Being a word of double meaning, as the word *suadere* in Latin, it may be accepted either in a bad or in a good sense. Hence, it is not irreverent to apply this word to God. We find it clearly so used in Hosea 2, 14, where the Lord says: "Therefore, behold, I will (*mephateha*) allure her (or, entice her by coaxing), and bring her into the wilderness, and speak comfortably unto her." I will suckle her, speak sweetly

unto her, and thus will I deceive her, as it were, so that she may agree with me, so that the Church will join herself to me, etc.

In this sense the word may here rightly be taken to mean "allure," "persuade," "coax by means of friendly words and flattery." God suckle, persuade, deceive Japheth by persuasion, so that Japheth himself, being allured, as his name signifies, may be invited in a friendly way and thus be beguiled.

213. But you say, what will be the meaning of this? or why should there be need for Japheth to be beguiled or persuaded, and that by God himself? I answer: Noah makes the names to serve his purpose in this prophecy. He gives thanks to God that he establishes them to stand like a firm root from which Christ was to spring. For the verb *sum*, signifies "to place," "to put in position," "to establish."

214. For Japheth, however, he prays that he may become a true Japheth. Since he was the oldest son, who ordinarily should have been given the right of the first-born, he prays that God would persuade him in a friendly manner, first, not to envy his brother this honor, nor to be dissatisfied that this privilege was taken from him and given to his brother. Furthermore, because this matter touches the person of Japheth only, God includes his entire offspring in the blessing. Though the promise was given to Shem alone, yet God does not shut out from it the offspring of Japheth, but speaks to them lovingly through the Gospel, that they may also become *jepheth*, being persuaded by the Word of the Gospel. This is a divine persuasion, coming from the Holy Spirit; not from the flesh, nor from the world, nor from Satan, but holy and quickening. This expression is used by Paul in Gal 1, 10, where he says, "Am I now persuading men or God?" And Gal 3, 1, "Who did bewitch you that ye should not obey the truth?"—that ye do not agree to the truth, that ye do not permit yourselves to be persuaded by that which is true?

215. Viewing the name Japheth in this case, it signifies a person of the kind which we call guileless, who believes readily, permitting himself to be easily persuaded of a matter, who does not dispute or cling to his own ideas but submits his mind to the Lord and rests upon his Word, remaining a learner, not desiring to be master over the words and works of God.

Hence it is a touching prayer which is here recorded, that God might persuade Japheth; that is, that he might speak fondly with him. Noah prays that, though God does not speak to Japheth on the basis of a promise, as he does with Shem, yet he would speak with him on the basis of grace and divine goodness.

216. This prayer of Noah foresees the spread of the Gospel throughout the whole world. Shem is the stem. From his posterity Christ was born. The Church is of the Jews, who had patriarchs, prophets, and kings. And yet God here shows Noah that also the wretched Gentiles were to dwell in the tents of Shem; that is, they were to come into that heritage of the saints which the Son of God brought into this world—forgiveness of sins, the Holy Spirit, and everlasting life. He prophesies clearly that also Japheth will hear the sweet message of the Gospel as his name suggests; so that, though he have not the same title as Shem, who was set to be the stem from which Christ was to spring, yet he should have the persuader, namely the Gospel.

217. It was Paul through whom this prophecy was fulfilled. He almost unaided taught the Gospel doctrine to the posterity of Japheth. He says: "From Jerusalem, and round about even unto Illyricum, I have fully preached the Gospel of Christ" (Rom 15, 19). Almost all of Asia, with the exception of the oriental peoples, together with Europe, belongs to the posterity of Japheth. The Gentiles, therefore, did not, as the Jews did, receive the kingdom and the priesthood from God. They had neither the law nor the promise. Yet by the mercy of God they have heard that sweet voice of the Gospel, the persuader, which is indicated by the very name of Japheth.

218. The interpreters failed to recognize this as the true meaning, and God permitted them to make this mistake. Still they did not miss the true meaning altogether. For the verb *hirchib*, which means "to enlarge," means also "to give consolation," just as conversely in Latin the word *angustiae* (narrow place) signifies also "pains," or "perils," or "disaster." Thus we read in Psalms 4, 1: "Thou hast set me at large when I was in distress." The only real enlargement, or consolation, is the Word of the Gospel.

219. Thus the several expositions are harmonized by proper interpretation. But the primary meaning of *enlarge*, which conveys the idea of *persuasion*, is the native and proper one. It sheds a bright light upon the fact that we Gentiles, although the promise was not given to us, have nevertheless been called by the providence of God to the Gospel. The promise pertains to Shem alone, but Japheth, as Paul has it in Romans 11, 17, was grafted into the olive tree, like a wild olive, and became a partaker of the original fatness, or the sap, of the olive. The older portions of the Bible agree with the newer, and what God promised in the days of Noah, he now carries out.

220. "Ham" signifies "the hot and burning one." This name was given to him by his father, I believe, because of the great things he hoped for his youngest son. To Noah the other two were cold men in comparison. Eve rejoiced greatly when Cain was born (Gen 4, 1). She believed that he would restore whatever had been wrought amiss. Yet he was the first to harm mankind in a new way, in that he killed his brother.

221. Thus God, according to his unsearchable counsel, changes the expectations even of the saints. Ham, whom his father, at his birth, had expected to be inflamed with greater zeal for the support of the Church than his brothers, was hot and burning, indeed, when he grew older, but in a different sense. He burned against his parent and his God, as his deed shows. Hence, his name was one of evil prophecy, unsuspected of Noah when he gave it.

222. This is Noah's prophecy concerning his sons, who have filled the earth with their offspring. The fact, therefore, that God has permitted the light of the Gospel to shine upon Germany, is due to the prophecy anent Japheth. We see today the fulfillment of that which Noah foretold. Though we are not of the seed of Abraham, yet we dwell in the tents of Shem and enjoy the fulfilment of the prophecies concerning Christ.

Vs. 28-29. *And Noah lived after the flood three hundred and fifty years. And all the days of Noah were nine hundred and fifty years; and he died.*

223. History shows that Noah died fifty years after the birth of Abraham. Abraham, therefore, enjoying the instruction of so able and renowned a teacher until his fiftieth year, had an opportunity to learn something of religion. And there is no doubt that Noah, being filled with the Holy Spirit, cared for this grandchild of his with special care and love, as the only heir of Shem's promises.

224. At that time the offspring of Ham flourished, spreading idolatry throughout the regions of the East. Abraham was in touch with it, and not without danger to himself. He was saved, however, by Noah, being almost alone in recognizing the greatness of a man who was the only survivor of the early world. The others, forgetful of the wrath which had raged in the flood, taunted the pious, old man; particularly Ham's progeny, puffed up by wealth and power. They heaped insults upon Father Noah, and—frenzied by success—they divided the curse of servitude pronounced upon them as a sign of his dotage. Amen.

END OF VOL. II.

Lector House believes that a society develops through a two-fold approach of continuous learning and adaptation, which is derived from the study of classic literary works spread across the historic timeline of literature records. Therefore, we aim at reviving, repairing and redeveloping all those inaccessible or damaged but historically as well as culturally important literature across subjects so that the future generations may have an opportunity to study and learn from past works to embark upon a journey of creating a better future.

This book is a result of an effort made by Lector House towards making a contribution to the preservation and repair of original ancient works which might hold historical significance to the approach of continuous learning across subjects.

HAPPY READING & LEARNING!

LECTOR HOUSE LLP
E-MAIL: lectorpublishing@gmail.com